# Science and Social Science in
# Bram Stoker's Fiction

**Recent Titles in Contributions to the
Study of Science Fiction and Fantasy**

Science Fiction, Children's Literature, and Popular Culture: Coming of Age in Fantasyland
*Gary Westfahl*

Kurt Vonnegut: Images and Representations
*Marc Leeds and Peter J. Reed, editors*

Science and Destabilization in the Modern American Gothic: Lovecraft, Matheson, and King
*David A. Oakes*

J.R.R. Tolkien and His Literary Resonances: Views of Middle-earth
*George Clark and Daniel Timmons, editors*

Rewriting the Women of Camelot: Arthurian Popular Fiction and Feminism
*Ann F. Howey*

Monsters, Mushroom Clouds, and the Cold War
*M. Keith Booker*

Science Fiction, Canonization, Marginalization, and the Academy
*Gary Westfahl and George Slusser, editors*

The Supernatural in Short Fiction of the Americas: The Other World in the New World
*Dana Del George*

The Fantastic Vampire: Studies in the Children of the Night
*James Craig Holte, editor*

Unearthly Visions: Approaches to Science Fiction and Fantasy Art
*Gary Westfahl, George Slusser, and Kathleen Church Plummer, editors*

Worlds Enough and Time: Explorations of Time in Science Fiction and Fantasy
*Gary Westfahl, George Slusser, and David Leiby, editors*

No Cure for the Future: Disease and Medicine in Science Fiction and Fantasy
*Gary Westfahl and George Slusser, editors*

# Science and Social Science in Bram Stoker's Fiction

## CAROL A. SENF

Contributions to the Study of Science Fiction and Fantasy, Number 99
*Donald Palumbo, Series Adviser*

**GREENWOOD PRESS**
Westport, Connecticut • London

**Library of Congress Cataloging-in-Publication Data**

Senf, Carol A.
  Science and social science in Bram Stoker's fiction  / Carol A. Senf.
    p. cm.—(Contributions to the study of science fiction and fantasy, ISSN 0193–6875  ;
    no. 99)
  Includes bibliographical references (p.  ) and index.
  ISBN 0–313–31203–6 (alk. paper)
    1. Stoker, Bram, 1847–1912—Criticism and interpretation.   2. Stoker, Bram,
  1847–1912—Political and social views.   3. Stoker, Bram,
  1847–1912—Knowledge—Science.   4. Science fiction, English—History and criticism.   5.
  Social problems in literature.   I. Title.  II. Series.
  PR6037.T617 Z87 2002
  823'.8—dc21      2002021624

British Library Cataloguing in Publication Data is available.

Library of Congress Catalog Card Number: 2002021624
ISBN: 0–313–31203–6
ISSN: 0193–6875

First published in 2002

Greenwood Press, 88 Post Road West, Westport, CT 06881
An imprint of Greenwood Publishing Group, Inc.
www.greenwood.com

Printed in the United States of America

∞™

The paper used in this book complies with the
Permanent Paper Standard issued by the National
Information Standards Organization (Z39.48–1984).

10  9  8  7  6  5  4  3  2  1

For my father who taught me to appreciate science and engineering
and the beauty of things that work
Harold E. Senf
April 2, 1900–December 20, 1995

# Contents

# Acknowledgments

Although this book is dedicated to my father, who was a civil engineer by profession, his influence was subtle and relatively indirect because he died before I actually started work on it.

Many people took time away from their own busy lives and jobs to answer questions or to allow me to pursue a line of thought. In fact, this book would have been impossible without the efforts of these individuals. One significant group includes all the people who have already written on Bram Stoker. Although the list of works cited provides an idea about the identities of many of these people, I owe special thanks to Stephanie Moss, Elizabeth Miller, and Katie Harse, who have become friends over the years as well as fellow scholars. Stephanie, who shares some of my interests in science and technology, turned me on to Stoker's interest in stage magic and encouraged me to think about the practical science in Stoker's life. Elizabeth, ever the scrupulous scholar, constantly reminds me that there's much about Stoker that we cannot really know. Reading *Dracula: Sense and Nonsense* provided me with a healthy dose of reality and will do the same for anyone else who is inclined to jump to conclusions. It is also an excellent source of information about what Stoker did know. Katie Harse, a graduate student at Indiana University and already an excellent scholar in her own right, worked with the librarians in the Special Collections at the Indiana University Library to help me locate a copy of *Lady Athlyene*. Because the book is now too fragile to send through the mail, I will eventually travel to Bloomington to read it once again. People at the Dracula 2000 Conference in Transylvania, Romania, asked questions and provided insights into Stoker. Above all, they encouraged me to keep working on this book.

Of course, while I especially treasure the help and support of people who have become friends, I could not have written this book without the efforts of so many other people that I appreciate mostly through the books they have written. Some of them studied archival materials; all read and studied Stoker's works; some traveled to areas of interest; and all have written on Stoker. In particular, I appreciate the work of William Hughes, who, like me, believes that Stoker is more than the writer of one work of Gothic horror, and Clive Leatherdale, whose desire to reissue everything that Stoker wrote will, I hope, enable other people to read and explore all Stoker works.

Even people who didn't necessarily share my enthusiasm for Bram Stoker were nonetheless willing to think about his works and, in the process, encouraged me to finetune my thoughts on Stoker and his world. Among the more important are the students at Georgia Tech. An exceptionally bright and curious group, they continued to ask interesting questions about *Dracula* and about Stoker. Moreover, their interest in the various branches of science and engineering helped to reinforce my appreciation for a world in which things work and, thus, provided additional insights into the mind of Bram Stoker. In addition, a number of people in my home unit, the School of Literature, Communication, and Culture (in particular Alan Rauch and Blake Leland), encouraged me to think about the distinctions in science and technology and ultimately enabled me to see that Stoker was more interested in technology than in pure science.

Finally, because I am not trained in either science or engineering beyond the general education requirements I took as an undergraduate, I had to rely frequently on people in the Georgia Tech community to answer questions about the history of technology and about the way the world works. In particular, I appreciate that the reference librarians did not bat an eye when I asked them seemingly unanswerable questions about the history of science and engineering. Included in this group of extremely knowledgeable, resourceful, and patient people are Anne Garrison, Mary-Frances Panettiere, Henry Koeppel, and Patricia A. Johnston. Not only did they pore through reference books and search the Web for information, but they also put me in contact with my colleagues in the College of Science and the College of Engineering. I would not have thought to question either Edward Thomas, Professor of Physics, or David McGill, Professor, Civil and Environmental Engineering and Aerospace Engineering. The answers I received from them encouraged me to consult my own list of experts. That group includes Dr. Ted Heath, a former student and now a physicist with the Georgia Tech Research Institute, and Bill Green, a colleague and friend in the School of Mathematics. Indeed there may be other people whom I've forgotten to identify in the footnotes. If so, I apologize.

Last but definitely not least is a small group of significant individuals without whom this book couldn't have been written—my immediate family members. My husband Jay Farlow tolerated my interest in Stoker and even answered the occasional question on physics and mechanics. Our sons Jeremy and Andy also tolerated my interest in Stoker even when they may have secretly harbored the same resentment of the dead writer that Stoker's son Noel held for his father's boss, the living actor, Henry Irving.

It has become something of a cliché to acknowledge that it takes a village to raise a child, and it is equally true that it also takes a community of supportive and knowledgeable people to write a book. No writer exists in a vacuum. Without my personal network of people, I would still be mulling over the seeming anomalies in what Stoker wrote and staring at a blank computer screen. Answering questions, providing information, and offering encouragement, that network of people kept me thinking and writing. They are not to be blamed for any errors that you may discover in this book, however. For those mistakes, I must take full responsibility.

# Introduction

The name Bram Stoker is hardly a household word—or name. Indeed, Stoker's name had been almost entirely eclipsed by the title of his best-known work, *Dracula* (1897), until Frances Ford Coppola decided to include it in the title of his film *Bram Stoker's Dracula* (Columbia, 1992). This strategy has been copied by both Jeffrey Obrow, who adapted *The Jewel of Seven Stars* in *Bram Stoker's The Mummy* (Goldbar Entertainment, 1997), which he wrote and directed, and by Jamie Dixon, who directed *Bram Stoker's Shadowbuilder* (Studio Home Entertainment, 1997). People who view the latter film are unlikely to learn much about Stoker's original work, however.

Because of the undeniable popularity of *Dracula*, most people who think of Stoker at all today think of him as the writer of this one indisputably Gothic novel. For example, the brief entry on Stoker in *The Oxford Companion to English Literature* says that he "wrote a number of novels and short stories, as well as some dramatic criticism, but is chiefly remembered for *Dracula*," [1] a conclusion that is shared by the slightly more complete entry in *Victorian Britain: An Encyclopedia*, which notes that his reputation depends on "a single Gothic novel: *Dracula*." [2] Apparently thinking of *Dracula* as well, Stephen Arata, who has written elsewhere on Stoker and should therefore know better, refers to "the Gothic tales of Robert Louis Stevenson and Bram Stoker" [3] in his entry on 1897.

Even Stoker's biographers, individuals who know more about the man than do most other people, have contributed to this oversimplification, all of them including the word Dracula in their titles: Harry Ludlam, *A Biography of Dracula: The Life Story of Bram Stoker* (1962); Daniel Farson, *The Man Who Wrote Dracula: A Biography of Bram Stoker* (1975); and Barbara Belford, *Bram Stoker: A Biography of the Author of Dracula* (1996). [4] Judging from the titles makes it seem as though the man had been subsumed by his most famous book. In fact, Farson, whose grandfather was Bram's brother Tom and who therefore had access to a number of family stories, describes his great uncle as "one of the least known authors of one of the best known books ever written" (ix). Belford, who criticizes her predecessors for ignoring unpublished archival material, nonetheless concentrates on *Dracula* as well, devoting two to three pages to each of his other works. As a result, the mystery continues.

Bram Stoker was not always such an unknown, however. During his life, Stoker was well known in both Great Britain and the United States as the business manager for Henry Irving's Lyceum Theatre (Irving, the first actor to be knighted, rubbed elbows with politicians, scientists, and businessmen as well as with writers and actors) and as a writer of seventeen books besides *Dracula*— novels, romances, and works of nonfiction—plus numerous short stories, articles, and reviews. In fact, Clive Leatherdale, who is in the process of editing and reprinting much of what Stoker wrote in the Desert Island Dracula Library series, attributes Stoker's difficulty to the fact that he experimented with so many genres but "could not settle on a genre that best suited his talents. This problem would stay with him throughout his life." [5] Oddly enough to people who know Stoker primarily through *Dracula*, many of these works reveal his interest in issues that seem antithetical to the Gothic and to its mysteries and excess. Indeed, because much of what he wrote features the science and technology of his day and even projects that science into the future, it is tempting to see Stoker as an early writer of science fiction rather than as a Gothic novelist who came too late to participate in the great period of English Gothic literature. Jessica De Mellow's introduction to *The Mystery of the Sea* makes a similar observation when she describes Stoker as "a writer of stories that combined mystery and occult themes with a fascination for scientific theories and technological innovation." [6]

Stoker's work with the popular Irving often brought him in contact with the leading figures of his day as he reveals in his two-volume retrospective, *Personal Reminiscences of Henry Irving*. In addition to providing anecdotes about Irving's life, Stoker also provides information about the people with whom he and Irving were familiar, a group that included literary figures, such as Tennyson and Walt Whitman, political figures like Liberal Prime Minister William Ewert Gladstone, the explorers Henry Morton Stanley and Sir Richard Burton, and even the powerful businessmen Sir William Pearce, head of the great Glasgow shipbuilding firm of John Elder & Co. *Reminiscences* also details Stoker's interest in practical science, especially in the science of stage "magic," a discipline that included lighting and numerous other special effects. Because Irving was interested in verisimilitude, he and Stoker and other members of The Lyceum traveled to various locations to make sure that sets, costumes, and properties were authentic. Stoker even admits to querying his brother George, who had been a surgeon during the Russo-Turkish War,[7] about the best way to carry a dead body. The grisly details that Stoker includes in *Reminiscences* suggest that he was as interested in accurate scientific information as his employer was.

Indeed, Stoker's Gothic and adventure novels often reveal his knowledge of science or technology. Both *The Snake's Pass* (1890) and *The Mystery of the Sea* (1902) reveal the potential power of science and technology over all aspects of human life and suggest that people who understand these rapidly developing fields are more likely to survive natural and man-made catastrophes than are primitive people. *Lady Athlyne* (1908) and *The Lady of the Shroud* (1909) demonstrate Stoker's fascination with recent technological developments (the automobile in the first novel and the airplane in the second) and, like *Dracula*, suggest that technology can help human beings overcome primitive forces. Finally, in *The Lair of the White Worm* (1911), Stoker's protagonist, Adam Salton, uses his knowledge of explosives to destroy a primeval monster.

A similar enthusiasm about the power of technology appears in a short piece that he wrote for a special Irish edition of *The World's Work* in 1906, "The World's Greatest Shipbuilding Yard," [8] which describes his observations on Harland and Wolff's shipbuilding yard in Belfast. Here Stoker waxes positively euphoric about "the magnitude, stability, and prosperity" (648) of the business, concluding that it "is an instance, and no mean one, of human endeavour" (650). This brief article makes it appear that there is nothing that human beings, most particularly their technological innovations, cannot achieve.

Whereas most of Stoker's novels and shorter pieces suggest the beneficial effects of science and technology, *The Jewel of Seven Stars* (1903) focuses on the dangers of science. Abel Trelawny, an Egyptologist, is consistently enthusiastic about the power of science to increase human understanding. Anticipating the resurrection of the Egyptian queen Tera, he describes the scientific knowledge that will ensue when he and his companions manage to bring her back to life: "For science, and history, and philosophy may benefit; and we may turn one old page of a wisdom unknown in this prosaic age." [9] Trelawny's prediction turns out to be absolutely wrong, however. In the first edition of *The Jewel of Seven Stars*, Tera arises only to kill the scientists who have worked to bring her back, a devastating conclusion that suggests the harmful impact of science rather than its benefits.

Recognizing that scientific experimentation frequently results in technological advancements, I have attempted to keep the two categories separate whenever possible in this study. [10] Under the heading of science, this study includes everything that falls under the systematic understanding of the world and its people based on observation and experimentation. Influenced by Thomas Kuhn's pioneering work on scientific discoveries, [11] however, I also recognize that science changes with new discoveries and is, therefore, not a synonym for absolute incontrovertible truth. When looking at the science of the past, it is even appropriate to remember that what passed for science in one generation may be discarded by subsequent generations. Nonetheless, science tends to be sure of itself because it is posited on the "assumption that the scientific community *knows* what the world is like" (5, emphasis added). (It is thus the opposite of the Gothic, which accepts that the world is a mysterious place.) Technology, on the other hand, is generally defined as "applied science" and is not necessarily as systematic as pure science. Indeed, although technology often utilizes new scientific discoveries, engineers and technicians are generally more interested in what works than in understanding why something works. (Therefore, one might expect that the Gothic and technology could coexist more comfortably than could science and the Gothic.) There is considerable overlap in science and technology, however, especially as the two words are used in ordinary discourse.

Stoker (or at least his characters) sometimes seems to confuse the two. For example, the participants in Trelawny's attempt to resurrect Tera use the word "experiment," a word usually associated with the sciences, to characterize their efforts. They also confuse the systematic scientific approach to the world with the "smoke and mirrors" associated with magic: "The experiment which is before us is to try whether or no there is any force, any reality, in the old Magic" (172). However, a true scientific experiment must be capable of being replicated under controlled circumstances, a situation that could never happen here because only one mummy had been preserved with the intention of being resurrected at some future point. In addition, once that mummy was resurrected, she could not be resurrected again. More important, however, is the fact that when Trelawny tries to reassure Malcolm Ross about their plans, he also seems to confuse science and pseudoscience, a category that Carl Sagan describes as disciplines that "purport to use the methods and findings of science, while in fact they are faithless to its nature—often because they are based on insufficient evidence or because they ignore clues that point the other way." [12] Although Ross remains apprehensive, Trelawny insists on the knowledge they will gain:

Bear in mind that in old Egypt the science of Astronomy began and was developed to an extraordinary height; and that Astrology followed Astronomy in its progress. And it is possible that in the later developments of science with regard to light rays, we may yet find that Astrology is on a scientific basis.  Our next wave of scientific thought may deal with this.  (174)

That Trelawny finally links contemporary scientific knowledge with the esoteric wisdom of the ancients raises several important issues about the subject of this book, Stoker's synthesis of science/technology with the Gothic. Trelawny comments, for example, on the science of his day: "Acoustics, for instance, an exact science with the builders of the temples of Karnak, of Luxor, of the Pyramids, is to-day a mystery to Bell, and Kelvin, and Edison, and Marconi" (175). One wonders here whether Trelawny is confusing the branch of physics that attempts to understand sound and sound waves with the practical issue of designing a room or building to determine the audibility and quality of sounds in it. Because of his experience in the theater, Stoker could have been aware of both the scientific and the practical meanings of the word "acoustics." Looking at the place of science in Western culture during the past two centuries, Sagan suggests that many people confuse a genuinely scientific approach to the world with the desire to find the answers to life's questions. He notes also that many people have adopted a scientific vocabulary without also adopting the scientific method.

   Whether Stoker himself was aware of the distinct meanings of the word "acoustics" remains in question. His character Trelawny is definitely muddled. Despite his apparent enthusiasm for science, he might even be accused of confusing science, pseudoscience, and technology. Certainly the novel demonstrates that Ross, the only character who urges caution about dabbling in ancient mysteries, is finally proven correct. In the first edition of the novel, the scientists (two archeologists and a physician) as well as Trelawny's daughter Margaret are annihilated by Queen Tera, whose mummy is successfully resurrected, because they do not know enough about her character or her motivation, not to mention the impact of being buried in a tomb for several thousand years. Ross, the single character who is apprehensive about science, is the only one to survive Tera's destructive powers. (He is also the only character who puts his life in the hands of God, a willingness to trust in a mysterious and overwhelming power that represents the positive impact of the Gothic.) Unlike *The Snake's Pass, Dracula, The Mystery of the Sea, The Lady of the Shroud,* and *The Lair of the White Worm,* which conclude with the representatives of the modern community complacently celebrating their conquest, *Jewel* ends by destroying the embodiments of the modern community.

Although the reasons behind his decision remain unknown, Stoker modified the grim conclusion in subsequent editions to make *Jewel* both less bleak and hopeless (and most modern reprints until recent years continued to print the sanitized "happy" ending in which Ross and Margaret marry and the mummy is not resurrected) and more positive about the potential of science and technology. Nonetheless, because of Ross's questioning attitude, *The Jewel of Seven Stars* is consistently more ambivalent about the power that the past exerts and less optimistic about the power of modern science.

As the rest of this study demonstrates, however, *The Jewel of Seven Stars* is an anomaly, for Stoker is generally enthusiastic about science and technology. Such enthusiasm is consistent with the period in which he lived, a period that can be identified with the rise of science and technology. Compared to all earlier historical eras, the nineteenth century witnessed unprecedented scientific discoveries and technological developments that have helped to determine the shape and nature of our own age. Because their impact on daily life—including transportation, communication, medicine, and industry—was so dramatic and so immediate, no one living during Stoker's lifetime could have failed to be aware of the power of science and technology. The entry on "1848" that Antony H. Harrison prepared for *A Companion to Victorian Literature and Culture* provides a succinct summary of both the enthusiasm that people felt at the time and some of the reasons for that enthusiasm:

New scientific theories and discoveries, along with the breathtaking velocity of technological advance, appeared to many observers evidence of an increasing cultural emphasis on secular matters that threatened traditional religious belief. The expanding dominion of scientific inquiry was demonstrated by the opening of honours schools in natural science at Cambridge in 1848 and at Oxford four years later, while the marvels of new technology were both exhibited and embodied in the "Great Exhibition of the Works of Industry of All Nations." The Crystal Palace, Joseph Paxton's architectural masterpiece of prefabricated iron and glass, remained open for six months in 1851. Britain and its colonies dominated the 13,000 exhibits of raw materials, machinery, fine arts, and manufactures which included huge marine engines, locomotives, hydraulic presses, newly designed reapers, and a telegraph connected with Edinburgh and Manchester. (26)

The real question was (and *is* even today) whether the impact of science and technology was entirely positive, or even predominantly positive. Because Stoker's attitudes anticipate some of our own concerns about the power of science and technology over human life, coming to terms with these themes in his novels is of more than merely academic interest.

In addition to the practical impact that the proliferation of scientific discoveries and technological developments had on people's lives, science and technology also changed both the way people thought about themselves *and* the way they thought about thought. As Josephine Guy observes in her introduction to the "Science and religion" section of *The Victorian Age: An Anthology of Sources and Documents*, science in the nineteenth century came to be equated with knowledge: "It is only the undeniable efficacy and utility of Victorian science which can explain the intellectual normalizing of what we would now loosely term a scientific epistemology: that is, the belief that scientific knowledge, to all intents and purposes, *is* knowledge." [13] Confident in their conquest of both nature and the indigenous peoples that representatives of the Empire encountered around the globe, the typical nineteenth-century Englishman often came to believe that there was no problem that science could not solve.

Living in a period that celebrated technological progress and scientific knowledge, Stoker may have had more compelling reasons than many of his contemporaries to be interested in science and technology. Stoker graduated from Trinity College, Dublin, in 1871. Like so much in Stoker's life, the precise nature of his education remains ambiguous. Stoker himself describes his education in *Personal Reminiscences of Henry Irving*: [14] "In my College days I had been Auditor of the Historical Society . . . and had got medals, or certificates, for History, Composition and Oratory. I had been President of the Philosophical Society; had got Honours in pure Mathematics." (I, 32) Belford states authoritatively that Stoker graduated in 1871 with "a degree in science and stayed on for a master's," (34), but William Hughes argues there is little evidence to support Stoker's claim of receiving honors. In *Beyond Dracula: Bram Stoker's Fiction and its Cultural Context*. [15] Hughes also stipulates that Stoker's degree was not in science, observing that Stoker graduated with a Bachelor in Arts on March 1, 1870, and received a Master in Arts "as was customary at Trinity . . . without further study" on February 9, 1875 (5). Hughes also asserts that he gained access to information on Stoker from the "Muniment Records and catalogue of Graduates of the University of Dublin" (182).

Although there is some question about Stoker's educational experiences, if he was trained in science, that training would connect him to many other writers of science fiction. Indeed, Connie Willis explores the backgrounds of many science fiction writers: [16]

Many science fiction writers are scientists themselves—Isaac Asimov was a biochemist, Arthur C. Clarke is a physicist and mathematician, David Brin is an astrophysicist, and Philip Latham is an astronomer. Many others are noted for their careful research and attention to scientific detail. (21–22)

He was also trained in law (he was called to the bar in 1890). Though he never practiced law and never worked as a scientist, he seems to have remained interested in both fields throughout his life. Leslie Shepard, who studied the printed catalogue of Sotheby, Wilkinson, and Hodge in 1913 that disposed of much of Stoker's library, reveals the extent of Stoker's reading.[17] Shepard observes that the catalogue "indicates the wide range of Stoker's interests and associations" (412). He notes in particular the following: H. Ward, *Five Years with the Congo Cannibals* (1891 . . . J.C. Lavater, *Essays on Physiognomy* (5 vols., 1789) . . . J.W. Powell, *First and Second Annual Reports of the Bureau of Ethnology, 1880–81* (413).

Furthermore, Stoker came from a family that valued science and the rational inquiry associated with it as well as one that understood the importance of careful empirical research and of testing evidence rather than accepting faith or intuition. Three brothers, an uncle, and a brother-in-law were physicians, his brothers well known in the medical community throughout the United Kingdom. Thornley served as president of the Royal College of Surgeons in Ireland and was knighted by Queen Victoria. George settled in London after serving as a physician with the Turkish Army. At the time *Dracula* was published, he was director of The Oxygen Home, which later became the Fitzroy Clinic, as well as the inventor of a new process for the treatment of wounds. According to Haining and Tremayne, the opening of the clinic was accompanied by the publication of another book by George on *The Oxygen Treatment for Wounds, Ulcers & etc.*, published by Messrs. Baillière of London (20). Chapter 2 includes more specific information on Stoker's education and family.

Seemingly at odds with the rigors of science is the Gothic, a field that emphasizes mystery, excess, and frequently horror rather than rational inquiry and careful discipline. If science focuses on what is known (or at least on fields of endeavor that *can* reasonably be known), then Gothic delights in all those things that are unknown and that will never be thoroughly understood. As Fred Botting summarizes in his overview of the Gothic, Gothic figures "shadow the progress of modernity with counter-narrative displaying the underside of enlightenment and humanist values" and focus on whatever threatens these values. Botting lists a number of the threats featured in the Gothic: "supernatural and natural forces, imaginative excesses and delusions, religious and human evil, social transgression, mental disintegration and spiritual corruption" and concludes that although the Gothic is "not a purely negative term, Gothic writing remains fascinated by objects and practices that are constructed as negative, irrational, immoral and fantastic." [18] Seemingly, then, Gothic is the polar opposite of science. Fearful where science is hopeful and awestruck rather than confident, the Gothic explores a world that remains mysterious, overwhelming, and beyond human control.

Stoker's interest in Gothic is as understandable as his interest in science and may have been acquired within the bosom of his family at an even earlier age. An invalid for the first seven years of his life, Stoker had the opportunity to listen to his mother's stories while his brothers and sisters were involved in less sedentary play. Though it is impossible to trace the influence of Charlotte Stoker's stories on her son, one tale in *Under the Sunset*, "The Invisible Giant," is often said to be influenced by her experiences during the cholera epidemic when she was a young girl in Sligo. Instead of treating his mother's story from a scientific perspective, however, Stoker turns it into Gothic horror by featuring the disease as a giant, unseen to all but a few of the characters.

Stoker's earliest works of fiction are full of Gothic horrors. His first short novel, *The Primrose Path* (1875), which was not reprinted until 1999, features the Gothic horror of a common disease, alcoholism, and is clearly "a superior version to the notorious 'penny dreadfuls' of the early and mid-nineteenth century" as Richard Dalby's introduction reveals:

Recently established at 33 Lower Abbey Street, Dublin, *The Shamrock* had quickly become a very popular magazine for the masses, with its self-publicised hype running as follows: "Four Original Serial Stories and a Piece of Original Music now form the chief Attractions of the Shamrock, for which the charge is but One Penny weekly—a fact quite unprecedented in the History of Cheap Literature." (8)

*The Primrose Path* relates the story of a carpenter, Jerry O'Sullivan, and his family who leave Ireland to seek their fortune in London. Instead of gaining prosperity, however, O'Sullivan falls into the clutches of the unscrupulous barkeeper Grinnell and ends up first as an alcoholic and ultimately as a murderer. Dalby's introduction describes *The Primrose Path* as a "moral tract on the degradation and evils of alcoholism" (9) but also notes that the "grisly climax to this tragic horror story comes as no surprise. As with the original climax of *The Jewel of Seven Stars* . . . Stoker preferred the true-to-life realistic denouement, rather than a false happy ending" (9). Despite several references to *Faust*, however, and the fact that Grinnell is described as having "a face so drawn and twisted, with nose and lips so eaten away with some strange canker, that it resembled more the ghastly front of a skull than the face of a living man," (52) most of the horrors of *The Primrose Path* remain within a world that the reader can readily recognize. Indeed, the horrors in the novel include poverty, wife abuse, and disease rather than supernatural horrors.

A second short work, *Buried Treasure*, which also appeared in 1875, includes mystery but not horror. Foreshadowing Stoker's interest in storms and treasure, though not in either scientific or technological methods of protecting oneself from nature or locating lost treasure, it also includes a heroic rescue that takes place because Tom Harrison suspects that his friend is in trouble. Though not quite as mysterious as the voice that summons Jane Eyre back to Rochester, the summons cannot be entirely explained away by any scientific means. Several days earlier Tom had said to Robert: "Never fear, old boy. Nothing short of death shall keep me away; but if I should happen not to turn up do not wait for me. I will be with you in spirit if I cannot be in the flesh" (123). Instead of appearing as a spirit, however, he sends a message to Robert's fiancée:

Poor fellow, when hurrying home to Robert, he had been knocked down by a car and had his leg broken. As soon as he could he had sent word to Ellen, for he feared for Robert being out alone at the wreck, knowing how chilled he had been on the previous night, and he thought that if any one would send him aid Ellen would. (127)

Of course, *Buried Treasure* is a kind of Christmas story, with the miraculous rescue taking place on Christmas Eve, a day when wondrous events can be expected. *The Primrose Path* and *Buried Treasure* are slight works, neither of them offering much more than the merest glimmer of the power that would come in *Dracula* and in many of Stoker's other works.

As the rest of the current study demonstrates, Stoker's novels and short stories often include both science *and* Gothic material. In fact, I originally began this study to attempt to make sense of the enigmatic Stoker and particularly to come to terms with the particular juxtaposition of seemingly contradictory things that I often discerned in what he wrote. Much of what he wrote appears to be a rather uncritical celebration of science and technology. Other works, including *Dracula*, seem to recognize that the world is an infinitely more complex place, one that demonstrates Hamlet's caution to Horatio, that there are "more things in heaven and earth" than are "dreamt of in your philosophy." And, of course, looming constantly in the background as a reminder of that complexity was the specter of *Dracula*, that novel so rich and complex that it has become practically synonymous with the ambiguity of the modern human condition.

Chapter 1 looks at *Dracula* in greater detail, for it seemed only sensible to begin at the point where most people encounter Stoker. In fact, because so many of Stoker's other works are difficult or impossible to locate except in rare book collections and research libraries, many readers know of Stoker only through *Dracula*. Moreover, one of my reasons for undertaking this study in the first place was to place *Dracula* both within the context of Stoker's other works and within the context of other late nineteenth-century works, paying special attention to Stoker's unusual juxtaposition of science/technology and the Gothic. Thus, it is important to consider exactly what part science plays in that work. Does the Crew of Light defeat Dracula because its members understand contemporary science and technology as some commentators have suggested? Or alternatively are they simply deluded by their own complacency and thus duped into believing that they have conquered an ancient evil who, in fact, remains unscathed by their modern weapons? Or is something entirely different going on? Answering these questions became even more challenging when I discovered in Belford's biography of Stoker that his original conclusion to *Dracula* was much more dramatic than the one that was finally printed:

The startling change from manuscript to novel . . . is the ending. Stoker destroyed the castle after Dracula's death, obliterating all vampiric traces. But someone, at the last moment, deleted 195 words including . . . "From where we stood it seemed as though the one fierce volcano burst had satisfied the need of nature and that the castle and the structure of the hill had sunk again into the void." (267–68)

Thus, the explosion at the end of *Dracula* seems to stem from nature, "one fierce volcano burst." It is definitely *not* something created by the group that tracks and destroys Dracula even if they do use science and technology to trap him before he can return to his castle. Furthermore, the present conclusion is not nearly as total as what Stoker originally contemplated.

An even more interesting postscript on the evolution of *Dracula* can be found by reading "Bram Stoker's Preface to the Icelandic Edition of *Dracula*" (1901), which was recently reprinted in the *Journal of Dracula Studies*, No. 2 (2000) (46). If anything, this short preface emphasizes the science and realism of the novel to an even greater extent. For example, Stoker says, "The events here described really took place" and suggests that the novel is really a Roman à Clef: "All the people who have willingly—or unwillingly—played a part in this remarkable story are known generally and well respected." Indeed, Stoker mentions that the name of at least one character is a household word: "the highly respected *scientist*, who appears here under a pseudonym, will also be too famous all over the educated world for his real name, which I have not desired to specify" (emphasis added). Perhaps most important in terms of this study is the attention that Stoker devotes to science as he suggests that science will one day be able to explain events that are now "incomprehensible, although continuing research in *psychology* and *natural sciences* may, in years to come, give logical explanations of such strange happenings which, at present, neither *scientists* nor the secret police can understand" (emphasis added). If this preface is any indication of Stoker's thoughts on the fictional world that he had created in *Dracula*, he continued to mull over the science that he had included in his most famous novel for years after it was published.

Chapter 2 looks carefully at the known facts of Stoker's life, including his family, his education, his professional experiences, and his numerous works of nonfiction. As the business manager for Henry Irving's Lyceum Theatre, Stoker was a man of the world who rubbed shoulders with political figures, artists, and other public figures. Despite his public posture, however, Stoker remains personally enigmatic, so elusive that many scholars simply bemoan their ability to know him. Because many of his nonfiction works comment directly on his experiences, they are useful indices of his attitudes.

Chapter 3 looks at Stoker's most anomalous work, *The Jewel of Seven Stars*. Whereas most of what Stoker wrote seems generally either positive or neutral about science and technology, this book pointedly demonstrates scientific hubris and reveals what happens when science oversteps its bounds. A version of this chapter has already been published—"*Dracula, The Jewel of Seven Stars*, and Stoker's 'Burden of the Past'", in *Bram Stoker's Dracula: Sucking through the Century, 1897–1997*, which was edited by Carol Margaret Davison.

Whereas Chapter 3 focuses on Stoker's apprehensions about science, Chapter 4 examines his positive treatment of both science and technology. In addition, because *The Snake's Pass* (1890) is Stoker's first novel and *The Lair of the White Worm* (1911) Stoker's last, the chapter covers almost the entirety of Stoker's efforts in fiction and suggests that he continued to think about the impact of science and technology on his world. In addition, it is interesting to note that these works touch on almost every branch of the science and social science of his day, including civil engineering, anthropology, physics, chemistry, and archeology. There is apparently no field of science about which he did not think. Chapter 4 will, I hope, provide a transitional chapter because it reveals the different ways in which Stoker viewed science. Both *The Snake's Pass* and *The Mystery of the Sea*, although they include characters who are reminiscent of various Gothic villains, feature the science/technology of Stoker's day. *The Lady of the Shroud* also features the science of the day although on such a grand scale that it might be regarded as utopian, perhaps even apocalyptic. In his final novel, *The Lair of the White Worm*, Stoker returns to a bona fide supernatural monster, though Stoker demonstrates that it is one that can easily be controlled by science.

Finally, Chapter 5 examines the interplay of Gothic mystery and scientific knowledge in Stoker's works and goes on to argue that many of his works are arguably closer to science fiction, as it is defined by Lynn Hamilton, rather than to Gothic literature. Hamilton notes that science fiction, speculative fiction that is based in "plausible, if untested, scientific theory" appeared at the same time that important advances were being made in science and industry during the nineteenth century. Victorian science fiction reveals its creators' "fascination with the possibilities inherent in new scientific discoveries" while it simultaneously reflects a concern over "the potentially destructive results of such investigation" as well as a despair that is demonstrated by three concerns of early science fiction: time travel and space travel; world cataclysm; and scientific breakthroughs that produce "transformations or adaptations of the human physique and psyche." [19] Indeed, though Stoker shows no interest in either time travel or in outer space, much of what he wrote is interested in world cataclysm (or the near escape from world cataclysm) and in the transformation or adaptation of the human being.

Although the designation itself is perhaps unimportant to everyone except genre specialists, what is significant is the fact that seeing Stoker as a writer of science fiction places him as a man of his time, a time that began in a nineteenth century that still valued traditional ways of doing things but that spanned into a definitely modern period. Furthermore, Stoker seems genuinely torn between acceptance of the promises that science and technology seemed to offer human beings and reservations that the world was simply more inscrutable than the scientists and social scientists believed. Writing in the midst of a culture that was both hopeful and apprehensive about the place of science and social science in their lives, Stoker mirrored this ambivalence in his fiction even though he is generally scrupulous about the science that he includes.

Moreover, Stoker is a particularly important figure for study. Friends with adventurers, such as Henry M. Stanley and Sir Richard Burton; political leaders, such as Liberal Prime Minister William Ewert Gladstone; and with most of the important artistic figures of his day, he often incorporated his thoughts about science, politics, and art into his own writings. Thus he is an important touchstone for various fin de siècle values and beliefs. Not only do his works reveal much about the times in which he wrote and provide insights about the people whom he knew, but they also touch on subjects that are important to us today, such as the role that science and technology play in our lives.

This study began when I first read *Dracula* almost thirty years ago. The novel raised more questions than it answered, and it continues to intrigue me. Although *Dracula* concludes with the English characters returning to the site of their victory over the vampire and thus seems to point to the fact that modern science and technology can overcome primitive forces, I thought that Stoker included some rather surprising information about his Western European characters, especially his scientific characters, Dr. Seward and Dr. Van Helsing. Though they seem to have many answers to the problems that they confront, they also seem to embody many of the traits that they condemn in Dracula, including violence and deceptive behavior. Horrified by the sadism with which they dispatched their friend Lucy Westenra (and I remain horrified by that scene, which still seems more like a gang rape and mutilation than like the destruction of a social threat) and with their treatment of Mina Harker, I was initially most concerned with Stoker's treatment of his women characters.

Several years later, when I saw John Badham's *Dracula* (Universal, 1979), I started thinking about some of these issues once again. Although Badham's interpretation of Stoker's novel is not precisely the same as mine, it is nonetheless an interpretation that focuses on science and technology, most dramatically on the lunatic asylum and the automobile. Furthermore Badham's *Dracula* criticizes the world of science and law in the persons of Dr. Seward, Dr. Van Helsing, and Jonathan Harker and suggests that the scientific and technological progress with which they are associated do not necessarily help people who are outside the power structure, a group that includes women, members of the working class, [20] and the mentally ill. Badham's interpretation also raises a possibility that I had not considered when I first read the novel— that Dracula may well survive the onslaught of his professional opponents. Thrust into the sun by his enemies, Dracula seems to dissolve. The last scene of the film focuses on Dracula's cape fluttering off into the horizon. At the very last moment, however, the cape seems to be transformed into a bat, a transformation that suggests life rather than death.

Over the years I remained fascinated by Bram Stoker, initially by the gender issues that I saw there, which I explored in several articles, and later by the fact that so much of what he wrote combines scientific material with Gothic excess. My work on *The Critical Response to Bram Stoker* (Greenwood Press, 1994) gave me the opportunity to read practically everything that Stoker wrote and once again pointed me to the many facets of Bram Stoker. By that time the academic unit at the Georgia Institute of Technology (with which I am affiliated) had established a major that combined science studies with cultural studies. As a result, I often teach classes in which my students and I have to confront the role that science and technology play in our lives. Reading and rereading Stoker, I became acutely aware of how frequently the conclusions to his novels, even his so-called Gothic novels, depend on science or technology.

Most recently I confronted *Dracula* once again for Twayne's Masterwork Studies series. Thinking particularly of a way to introduce Stoker's most famous novel to nonspecialists, I thought of my own students and the issues that interest them, including questions about gender and the place of science in their world. As a result, *Dracula: Between Tradition and Modernism* (1998) includes one chapter that looks at science in the novel and another that looks at technology. Moreover, looking closely at *Dracula* once again convinced me that Stoker was caught between his wish that science and technology could provide the answers to age-old problems and his fear that the mysterious forces associated with the Gothic would once again prove overwhelming.

An exploration of Stoker's works, this study looks at the rather peculiar relationship between the mysteriousness of the Gothic (the recognition that certain things are beyond human comprehension) and the science/social science of the nineteenth century (fields of study that suggest that everything is ultimately knowable). That these issues concerned Stoker is clear, for he continues to explore the relationship between science and a numinous world in practically everything he wrote. That he never arrived at a definite conclusion is also clear. Practically everything he wrote continues to combine scientific certainty with Gothic mystery, and confidence in technology with apprehensions about the future. This combination of interests is entirely consistent with the origins of science fiction as they are defined by Thomas D. Clareson in "The Emergence of Science Fiction: The Beginnings Through 1915." [21] Clareson points out that science fiction is less concerned with scientific discovery or with technology than with examining the impact of science and technology on individuals  and on society as a whole. He adds that recent attempts to distinguish between science fiction and fantasy have muddled the fact that both science fiction and fantasy borrow from the tradition of social realism and literary naturalism and that the most obvious examples of works that explore the impact of science and technology on individuals "occur in that fiction dealing with horror—from the gothic novel, at least, to the contemporary best-seller; from Mary Shelley and Edgar Allan Poe to the film *Aliens*" (4). Stoker, though concerned with the impact on the individual, is nonetheless also more interested in what Clareson characterizes as the "nuts and bolts of technology" than are many of his contemporaries, and he weaves those details into the framework of his novels.

After studying Bram Stoker for almost thirty years, I confess to a continued fascination with the man and his works. Unlike Leatherdale, who believes that Stoker's problem was his inability to "settle on a genre that best suited his talents," I find that his willingness to experiment with various genres and his willingness to bend the conventional limits of genres are part of what continues to fascinate me. Even when I find myself irritated by his tendency to reduce his characters to gender stereotypes—"good brave men" and "sweet, sweet, good, good women" [22]— or frustrated by his inconsistencies, I find that practically everything he wrote is worthy of more critical attention than it has previously received. Stoker may have spent more time on *Dracula* than he did on many of his other works and also succeeded in producing this one time a masterpiece that has succeeded in eclipsing everything else that he wrote. It's hard to argue with Kenneth W. Fair, Jr., who observes that Stoker's other novels do not equal "*Dracula* in their imaginative force." [23] Nonetheless, many of his other works— including *The Snake's Pass*, *The Jewel of Seven Stars*, *The Mystery of the Sea*, and *Famous Impostors*—show the evidence of careful factual research. Even more important, practically everything that he wrote reveals him thinking about issues that continue to plague us today: questions about political intervention in the developing world, [24] anxieties about race and gender, questions of human identity during a period when the traditional sources of identity had been relinquished, and, of course, the subject of this study—the place of science and technology in our world. Recognizing Stoker's concerns in these disparate fields means that readers need to take Stoker more seriously than has generally been the case and to recognize that his works are not merely wish fulfillment and dream but serious considerations of the world in which he lived, a world that resembles our own.

## NOTES

1. *Oxford Companion to English Literature*, 5th ed, edited by Margaret Drabble. Oxford: Oxford University Press, 1985, 940.

2. Bette B. Roberts, "Stoker, Bram" (1847–1914) in *Victorian Britain: An Encyclopedia.*, edited by Sally Mitchell. pp. 760–61. New York: Garland.

3. Stephen Arata, "1897," in *A Companion to Victorian Literature and Culture*, edited by Herbert F. Tucker. pp. 51–65. Malden, MA: Blackwell Publishers, 1999. The precise reference occurs on page 52.

4. Harry Ludlam, *A Biography of Dracula: The Life Story of Bram Stoker*. London: Foulsham, 1962; Daniel Farson, *The Man Who Wrote Dracula: A Biography of Bram Stoker*. New York: St. Martin's, 1975; Barbara Belford, *Bram Stoker: A Biography of the Author of Dracula*. New York: Alfred A. Knopf, 1996.

5. Clive Leatherdale, "Series Editor's Note," *The Primrose Path*. p. 13. Westcliff-on-Sea, Essex: Desert Island Books, 1999.

6. Jessica De Mellow, introduction to *The Mystery of the Sea*, p. ix Gloucestershire: Sutton, 1997.

7. Peter Haining and Peter Tremayne, in *The Un-Dead: The Legend of Bram Stoker and Dracula* (London: Constable, 1997) remind readers of George Stoker's background:

George had served as a surgeon in the Imperial Ottoman Army during the Russo-Turkish War of 1877-78 and had been Chief of Ambulance of the Red Crescent. He had even received a medal from the Turks for his services when in charge of transporting the Turkish wounded to safety...The Turks had then lost 4,000 killed and wounded and 36,000 prisoners. George had written a memoir of the war, *With 'The Unspeakables', or two years campaigning in European and Asiatic Turkey*, published in Dublin in 1878. (16)

8. Bram Stoker, "The World's Greatest Ship-Building Yard," *The World's Work* 9 (special Irish edition, May 1907), 647-50. The same volume includes another article by Stoker that also celebrates technological developments in Ireland.

9. Bram Stoker. *The Jewel of Seven Stars*, annotated and edited by Clive Leatherdale. Westcliff-on-Sea, Essex: Desert Island Books, 1996, 170. (Future references will be to this edition and will be included in the text.)

10. Frank M. Turner, in "Practicing Science: An Introduction," which is included in *Victorian Science in Context*, edited by Bernard Lightman (Chicago: University of Chicago Press, 1997, 283–289), describes the distinction between these two categories as a frontier and observes that it is a border "across which most historians have been very uncomfortable passing" (287).

11. Thomas S. Kuhn. *The Structure of Scientific Revolutions*. 3rd edition. Chicago: University of Chicago Press, 1996.

12. Carl Sagan, "The Most Precious Thing," in *The Demon-Haunted World: Science as a Candle in the Dark*, p. 13. New York: Random House.

13. Josephine M. Guy, *The Victorian Age: An Anthology of Sources and Documents*. London: Routledge, 1998, 200–201.

14. Bram Stoker. *Personal Reminiscences of Henry Irving*. New York: Macmillan, 1906.

15. William Hughes. *Beyond Dracula: Bram Stoker's Fiction and Its Cultural Context*. New York: St. Martin's, 2000.

16. Connie Willis, "Science in Science Fiction: A Writer's Perspective," in *Chemistry and Science Fiction*, edited by Jack H. Stocker, pp. 21–32. Washington, DC: American Chemical Society, 1998.

17. "The Library of Bram Stoker/ A Note on the Death Certificate of Bram Stoker," in *Bram Stoker's Dracula: Sucking through the Century, 1897–1997*. edited by Carol Margaret Davison, pp. 411–415. Toronto: Dundurn Press, 1997.

18. Fred Botting, *Gothic*. New York: Routledge, 1996, 1–2.

19. Lynn Hamilton, "Science Fiction," *Victorian Britain: An Encyclopedia*, 696–97. This quotation appears on page 696.

20. Although Stoker's novel definitely presents Renfield as a gentleman, Badham characterizes him as a carter who helps Dracula move into his new home. Thus Badham's interpretation brings workingclass characters to the foreground. In Stoker's novel, these working characters mostly appear as comic relief.

21. Clareson's essay is included in *Anatomy of Wonder 4: A Critical Guide to Science Fiction*, edited by Neil Barron. New Providence, NJ: R.R. Bowker, 1995, 3–61.

22. I took these characterizations from two of the chapter titles in Clive Leatherdale's study, *Dracula: The Novel and the Legend* (Wellingborough,

Northamptonshire: The Aquarian Press, 1985). They actually are adaptations of characterizations in *Dracula*.

23. Kenneth W. Fair, "About Bram," *The Romantist*, 4-5 (1980–1981): 39.

24. Reading *The Balkans: Nationalism, War and the Great Powers, 1804–1999* by Misha Glenny (New York: Viking, 2000), I was surprised to encounter the following reference to Stoker:

"Kosovo," the British Prime Minister, Tony Blair, informed his public in early April 1999, "is on the doorstep of Europe." Yet no geographer would consider Kosovo and its neighbours part of Asia. If neither in Europe nor in Asia, where does the Balkan peninsula lie? Perhaps Mr Blair had been influenced by Bram Stoker's Dracula in which the Balkans occupied "the centre of some sort of imaginative whirlpool", where "every known superstition in the world is gathered." For many decades, Westerners gazed on these lands as if on an ill-charter zone separating Europe's well-ordered civilization from the chaos of the Orient. (xxi)

Because Glenny is writing about historical matters, has visited the Balkans—as Stoker had not—and has written two books on the subject, I found the reference especially interesting. Nonetheless, both nineteenth-century novelist and contemporary historian are wrestling with questions about the relevance of this region to the rest of the world.

# Chapter 1
# Gothic Monster versus Modern Science in
# *Dracula*

Film versions of *Dracula* tend to emphasize its folkloric origins and its Gothic sense of mystery and suggest that vampires tend to cringe from various religious artifacts, Stoker's best-known novel suggests that modern science and technology are perhaps equally important in the fight against ancient evil. [1] *Dracula* opens with an important scene that immediately confronts a practitioner of modern science and technology with the very embodiment of Gothic mystery. Thus *Dracula* is an important place to begin this study of the juxtaposition of science with the Gothic. Moreover, although *Dracula* is not the first work that Stoker wrote, it is both the work with which readers are likely to be most familiar as well as one of the works in which the conflict of science with the Gothic is most direct and revelatory. According to all accounts, it is also the work on which Stoker lavished a great deal of attention. Belford observes that he spent seven years working on it. She observes that Stoker made his first notes on *Dracula* on March 8, 1890, and that the last recorded date was March 17, 1895, after publication of *The Watter's Mou'* and *The Shoulder of Shasta*. She adds that he had sketched out a plot by February 1892 and put the events of the novel in the year 1893 (260–61).

As a result of this care, readers would be wise to pay particular attention to the way that Stoker handles both Gothic materials and science. The contrast is evident on the very first page when a mildly irritated Jonathan Harker complains about the primitive conditions that he discovers on his way to Dracula's castle. In fact, almost the first thing he observes is that the "train was an hour late." [2] Although Harker is an attorney (he had recently received notification that he is now a "full-blown solicitor" [48]) as was Stoker himself rather than a scientist or technician, he is enthusiastic about all new ways of doing things. For example, he keeps his journal in shorthand (which he describes as "nineteenth century up-to-date with a vengeance" [77]), memorizes train schedules so that he can travel quickly from place to place, takes pictures of Dracula's English property with his Kodak camera, [3] and is highly critical of those who do not share his enthusiasm for all things modern. Although he does occasionally recognize that "the old centuries had, and have, powers of their own which mere 'modernity' cannot kill" (77), he and the other individuals who battle against Dracula do so with all the weapons of modern science and technology. That enthusiasm for science and technology is characteristic of turn-of-the-century England and probably stems from Stoker's personal interests in both, a topic that is handled in greater detail in Chapter 2.

It is tempting to say that Dracula and the other vampires are Gothic while their opponents are scientific/technological (and the simplification does work to an extent), but Stoker's rendering of the conflict is much more complex and interesting and therefore worthy of our attention. The Crew of Light [4] consists of all those who oppose Dracula: Jonathan and Mina Harker; Lucy Westenra (Mina's friend and Dracula's first English victim, who quickly becomes allied with him); the madman Renfield (also allied with Dracula at various times); Dr. Seward and his friends Arthur Holmwood (later Lord Godalming) and Quincey Morris; and Dr. Van Helsing, Seward's mentor and finally the leader of the Crew of Light. All these individuals might be described—at least some of the time in Harker's words—as "nineteenth century up-to-date with a vengeance" (77).

Pitted against these individuals are Lucy in her vampiric state and the three vampire-women in Dracula's castle, Renfield, and, of course, Dracula. Their tastes for blood or living flesh and their allegiance with various forces of nature as well as their unfamiliarity with science and technology identify them as primitive. Furthermore, their failure to adhere to the most basic of social codes identifies them as Gothic and inscrutable.

Although Chapter 5 providesa more thorough summary of Stoker's synthesis of science and the Gothic throughout his works, an overview of Gothic conventions may be useful here. For example, most critics of the Gothic note that it originated in 1765 with Horace Walpole's *The Castle of Otranto* and that Gothic works before *Dracula* subscribe to a set of conventions that includes the presence of supernatural events, a medieval setting, and the presence of a persecuted maiden and a sexually depraved villain. Moreover, Gothic works characterize the world as infinitely complex and ambiguous rather than simple and easy to describe and/or categorize. In fact, *The Harper Handbook to Literature* explains that the Gothic novel responds to the scientific rationality of its time and provides an alternative view of the world:

Walpole wanted "to blend the two kinds of romance, the ancient and the modern," having wearied of the "strict adherence to common life" in Samuel Richardson and Henry Fielding . . . He wanted to revive the mysterious and supernatural from the huge seventeenth-century French romances while cutting them down to modern form . . . Ann Radcliffe's five Gothic thrillers . . . rejected Walpole's supernatural and rationalized the mysteries, as her English girls . . . encounter spooky French or Italian castles and ruined abbeys. . . . Indeed, all mystery stories derive from the Gothic, and those that evoke terror . . . are frequently called Gothic. [5]

Although many critics dismiss the Gothic as a short-lived genre at the turn of the nineteenth century, others recognize that Gothic tendencies remain in art and literature even today. Bette B. Roberts looks especially at the period during which Stoker wrote and notes that the Gothic of the fin de siècle responded to the unique anxieties of that period:

Fear of the present and future rather than the past also distinguishes the most significant Gothics of the period: Robert Louis Stevenson's *Dr. Jekyll and Mr. Hyde* (1886), Oscar Wilde's *The Picture of Dorian Gray* (1891), H.G. Wells's *The Island of Dr. Moreau* (1896) and Bram Stoker's *Dracula* (1897). Analyzed in view of late Victorian cultural phenomena—sexual repression, loss of religious faith and moral absolutes, scientific and psychological research, and imperialism—these novels demonstrate . . . the shifting anxieties of readers coping with the changes, uncertainties, and dangers of both Victorian and modern worlds. [6]

Finally, Avril Horner and Sue Zlosnik in "Comic Gothic," [7] reinforce the degree to which Gothic literature (and, in the twentieth and twenty-first centuries, film as well) attempts to address various social and cultural anxieties:

Gothic writing manifests a deep anxiety about the permeability of such boundaries and their instabilities, whether between the quick/the dead, eros/thanatos, pain/pleasure, 'real'/'unreal', 'natural'/'supernatural', material/transcendent, man/machine, human/vampire or 'masculine'/ 'feminine'. Serious Gothic writing manifests a deep anxiety about the permeability of such boundaries. The serious gothic writer deliberately exploits the fear of the 'Other' encroaching upon the apparent safety of the post-Enlightenment world and the stability of the post-Enlightenment subject. In serious Gothic texts, then, lines of confrontation are invariably drawn early in the plot, and satisfactory resolution depends upon the clear reestablishment of such boundaries. However, the threat of their being breached again always remains. (243)

*Dracula* is thus especially interesting because it emphasizes the conflict between people who believe that the world is systematic and subject to both reason and human control and individuals whose very existence embodies mystery and the total lack of human control over a powerful and overwhelming universe.

As was mentioned earlier, Jonathan Harker goes to Transylvania secure in the belief that the world is an orderly and rational place. As a solicitor, he is understandably proud of the fact that English law has attempted to codify various forms of behavior, and he is equally methodical in other areas. For example, he bemoans the fact that there are "no maps of this country as yet to compare with our own Ordnance survey maps" (29), and he clearly expects the people he encounters to behave in certain predictable ways. As a result, he is troubled by Dracula's behavior from the very beginning even before he begins to suspect that Dracula is not human. Furthermore, he is troubled by the three women in Dracula's castle because they appear to be "ladies by their dress and manner" (79), but they behave in an aggressive manner more appropriate to common prostitutes. Later, when they gratefully accept Dracula's gift of a "half-smothered child" (83), he begins to believe that they are not women at all but are "devils of the Pit!" (102). Terrified about the potential loss of his life, his sanity, and his manhood, Harker eventually escapes from Dracula's castle and returns to England, where he joins up with others who oppose Dracula. Indeed, it is his hand that ultimately dispatches Dracula, [8] and his rather self-assured commentary concludes the novel:

Seven years ago we all went through the flames; and the happiness of some of us since then is . . . well worth the pain we endured . . . .In the summer of this year we made a journey to Transylvania, and went over the old ground which was, and is, to us so full of vivid and terrible memories. It was almost impossible to believe that the things which we had seen with our own eyes and heard with our own ears were living truths. (511–12)

At least in Harker's mind, the world is once more an orderly and predictable place. Evil has been eradicated and good rewarded, though the careful reader of *Dracula* is never quite as confident about this fact as Stoker's characters.

His wife Mina, nee Murray, is equally orderly. More religious than her husband, Mina is inclined to see the world in terms of good and evil. Confronted with the monster who had almost destroyed her husband's sanity and who had destroyed the life of her childhood friend, Mina determines to understand their opponent, a task that she undertakes in a systematic manner that is reminiscent of the methodical nature of the best scientific inquiry: "In this matter dates are everything, and I think that if we get all our material ready, and have every item put in chronological order, we shall have done much" (319). Thus, it is Mina who organizes and compiles the mass of material with which they are confronted: journal entries, newspaper clippings, telegrams, indeed the entire flotsam and jetsam of everyday life. In addition, Stoker reinforces exactly how modern Mina is by having her learn shorthand and use a typewriter, [9] as well as travel great distances both alone and accompanied by various men. For example, upon learning of Jonathan's illness, she takes a boat trip to Hamburg and then a train to Bued-Pesth, and she later travels from Exeter to London to meet with Van Helsing. Despite her objections to the New Women writers for their sexual license, [10] Mina in many ways resembles the independent New Woman. Not only has she worked for a living as a young woman, but she continues to use the skills that she had acquired as a young professional woman. More important, she continues to be an independent thinker.

Mina's friend Lucy is far more traditional. Even while attempting to emulate Mina's habit of keeping a journal and even Mina's independent thinking, Lucy never seems to understand what is happening to her. Indeed, Stoker happens fortuitously on Lucy's sleepwalking behavior, indicating that many of the important events in her life take place while she is either unconscious or asleep. Even her succumbing to Dracula and her subsequent fall into vampirism are presented as being largely unconscious rather than the result of conscious choice, a characteristic that Van Helsing explains to Seward:

She was bitten by the vampire when she was in a trance, sleep-walking. . . . In trance she died, and in trance she is Un-Dead, too. So it is that she differ from all other. Usually when the Un-Dead sleep at home . . . their face show what they are, but this so sweet that-was when she not Un-Dead she go back to the nothings of the common dead. (292)

In addition to her general lack of awareness, Lucy is also unlike Mina who wishes to understand and use all the modern technology at her disposal. Indeed she seems to have very little contact with the modern world. Although she seems to come from an affluent family and would, therefore, have access to the most recent scientific and technological developments, she appears not to be especially interested in these developments. Seward mentions that Lucy also has a phonograph, but there is no evidence that she actually uses it. The reference seems to be more of a plot device to enable Seward to complete his diary without needing to transport the bulky machines of the 1890s from his office to the Westenra home. [11] Perhaps Lucy is the equivalent of the people at the turn of the twenty-first century who are unable to program their VCR.

Lucy's three suitors, who are old hunting buddies, seem somewhat more comfortable with the use of contemporary technology, Dr. Seward most of all. Seward, who is in charge of a large lunatic asylum, is also presented as being up to date in terms of scientific matters. For example, he keeps his diary on a phonograph and complains late in the novel when he has to revert to keeping his journal with a pen. More important, however, is his commitment to science and his desire to advance its practice:

Why not advance science in its most difficult and vital aspect—the knowledge of the brain? Had I even the secret of one such mind . . . I might advance my own branch of science to a pitch compared with which Burdon-Sanderson's physiology or Ferrier's brain-knowledge would be as nothing. (127)

Indeed, because Seward is the most scientific and rational of all the characters, it takes him the longest to accept the presence of what is Gothic and mysterious. Furthermore, like Jonathan and Mina Harker, Seward is presented as a compulsive collector of data, material that he believes will enable him to understand and control the world and may bring him fame as well.

Even the madman Renfield has been influenced by the scientific discoveries of the nineteenth century. He is, for example, a compulsive taker of notes, and Seward observes that "he keeps a little note-book in which he is always jotting down something. Whole pages of it are filled with masses of figures" (124). Of course, before falling under Dracula's sway, Renfield had apparently been a well-educated gentleman, a circumstance that no film version has depicted. He recognizes Van Helsing's name and mentions his familiarity with the professor's work; he observes that he knew Arthur Holmwood's father; he speaks intelligently of international politics; and he eventually tries to protect Mina from Dracula's advances. Renfield is thus a character who embodies the belief in the power of science though his very existence confirms that much of life is beyond the control of science.

Van Helsing, because of his age and experience, is the leader of the group that battles against Dracula, and Stoker goes to great lengths to present him as an expert in a variety of fields. For example, his professional letterhead identifies him as "Abraham Van Helsing, M.D. D.Ph, D. Lit., Etc." (185) and thus establishes him as an acknowledged expert in medicine and the humanities. Furthermore, he reminds Seward that he is a "lawyer as well as a doctor" (248). Despite his degrees in other fields, however, Stoker emphasizes his skills in medicine. Seward, for example, mentions Van Helsing's bag, which he describes as holding the "ghastly paraphernalia of our beneficial trade" (193). Indeed, Van Helsing is most important in terms of the four blood transfusions that he performs on Lucy Westenra to protect her from Dracula. One recent work, Teresa Mangum, "Growing Old: Age," [12] looks at *Dracula* in terms of nineteenth-century developments in medical technology:

The sunny periodical essays that continued to advise moderation of diet, pleasures, and sex form a curious foil for what is perhaps the most famous of all prolongation narratives, Bram Stoker's *Dracula* (1897). Dracula's erotic appetite for life-sustaining young blood was a motif in vampire-manqué tales as well. The title character of Mary Elizabeth Braddon's "Good Lady Ducayne" (*The Strand*, 1896) hires a doctor to use the new and dangerous technology of blood transfusion to milk the veins of young women. These writers . . . were merely exaggerating experimental medical practices of the day, such as injections of crushed animal testicles, which promised to rejuvenate youth, vitality, and sexual performance, or the still extremely dangerous transfusion of blood. (107)

Braddon and Stoker were acquaintances, and Braddon wrote to compliment Stoker when *Dracula* came out: "I have done my humdrum little story of transfusion, in the *Good Lady Ducayne*—but your 'bloofer' lady" (cited by Belford, 275).

It is clear from *Dracula* that Stoker has done his own medical homework—most critics believe that he questioned his brothers Thornley and George on medical practice. Even though transfusions were rarely practiced until 1909 when the Austrian-American immunologist Karl Landsteiner discovered different blood groups and made the practice safer, knowledge of transfusions had been available to physicians for over a century and had been attempted as a last desperate measure to save the lives of patients.

Certainly Van Helsing frequently alludes to the wonders of modern science, saying that "there are things done to-day in electrical science which would have been deemed unholy by the very men who discovered electricity—who would themselves not so long before have been burned as wizards" (280). Thus, Van Helsing seems to take pride in the advances on modern science and, in fact, frequently suggests that their victory over the vampire will stem from their understanding of science: "We have on our side power of combination—a power denied to the vampire kind; we have resources of science" (334).

On the other hand, Van Helsing seems less familiar with some of the technological tools at his disposal than do many of the other members of the Crew of Light. Because he, Dracula, Quincey, and Arthur do not keep journals or diaries, they do not study the data available to them and can, therefore, be accused of impulsive behavior, a most unscientific trait. Nor do they take advantage of the various communication technologies at their disposal. Furthermore, there is at least one situation where Van Helsing's lack of familiarity with contemporary communication technology causes great harm. Van Helsing errs in sending a telegram to Dr. Seward. Because of his mistake, the telegram is therefore delivered a day later. It is an error that may cost Lucy her life, for neither physician is watching the house on the evening when Dracula has Bersicker break into the Westenra home. The terrified Mrs. Westenra, already suffering from a weak heart, dies of a heart attack, and Dracula visits Lucy for a final and fatal time. Perhaps if Van Helsing had been more familiar with the technology, the telegram would have arrived in time.

In addition to being uncomfortable with various technologies, Van Helsing also seems to recognize that science is not always the answer because there are "always mysteries in life" (280). Among the many insurmountable mysteries that he cites to which contemporary science has no answers is the aging process. Thus, Van Helsing is one of the few characters in *Dracula* who reminds readers of the limitations of contemporary science:

But there are things old and new which must not be contemplate by men's eyes, because they know—or think they know—some things which other men have told them. Ah, it is the fault of our science that it wants to explain all; and if it explain not, then it says there is nothing to explain. But yet we see around us every day the growth of new beliefs, which think themselves new; and which are yet but the old, which pretend to be young. (279)

As a result, Van Helsing maintains a foot in both camps: A practitioner of modern science, he also recognizes that the science of his day cannot yet explain everything that needs explanation. When it comes to a powerful supernatural force like Dracula, Van Helsing recognizes that their arsenal must include folkloric weapons, such as garlic, the wild rose, and wooden stakes, as well as religious artifacts, and modern science. Indeed he comes close to arguing that science may even be the enemy here because it encourages modern people NOT to believe in things they can not see or quantify.

If Van Helsing takes advantage of contemporary science while at the same time maintaining a healthy skepticism about its efficacy, Dracula and the other vampiric characters are almost entirely creatures of tradition who are incapable either of understanding or of adapting to modern life. Even though he has filled his library with contemporary works, including *Bradshaw's Guide* and other reference works such as the "London Directory, the 'Red' and 'Blue' books, Whitaker's Almanack, the Army and Navy Lists, and . . . the Law List" (54) and apparently has read them so that he can understand the England to which he hopes to emigrate, he tends to be uncomfortable with what is modern. He tells Harker that he cannot live in a new house, and he generally chooses traditional forms of transportation; both coming to England and retreating from it, he chooses sailing vessels instead of steamships.

Dracula and his fellow vampires also meet the essential characteristics of Gothic figures. Not only are they supernatural beings who reside in a medieval setting and who also adhere to the conventions of that medieval world in which they first drew breath, but they also convey the basic plotline of the earliest Gothic novels by featuring several persecuted maidens and a sexually depraved villain. Stoker "ups the ante," however, by showing that Jonathan Harker can be a persecuted gentleman at the hands of sexually depraved villainesses when he encounters the three vampire brides at their castle.

In addition to being supernatural beings, Dracula and his fellow vampires are also linked with the natural world, though Van Helsing also notes Dracula's unscientific control over Nature: "he can, within his range, direct the elements: the storm, the fog, the thunder; he can command all the meaner things: the rat, and the owl, and the bat—the moth, and the fox, and the wolf" (333). He is also immensely physically strong, as so many characters observe. On the other hand, Stoker presents vampires as both prisoners of their own nature and unable to use science to escape from that nature. [13] While films often suggest that vampires MUST return to their coffins during the daytime, Stoker allows Dracula to travel during the daytime, the victim merely of reduced physical capacity.

Besides being allied with the natural world rather than with those scientists and technologists who desire to harness natural power for their own purposes, Dracula also reveals that he remains a medieval being rather than a modern. Jonathan Harker notes, for example, that Dracula looks back with pride to the old days, "stirring times, when the Austrian and the Hungarian came up in hordes, and the patriots went out to meet them" (57). Acutely aware of past glory, Dracula is evidently unwilling to share that power with others, a trait that distinguishes him from the novel's other aristocrat, Arthur Holmwood, later Lord Godalming. Contemptuous of his followers, Dracula asks, "What good are peasants without a leader?" (69) and notes that he is unwilling to share his power with anyone: "Here I am noble; I am boyar; the common people know me, and I am master" (55). Indeed, he taunts Mina with his power, noting that he had "commanded nations, and intrigued for them, and fought for them" (396). Because of these antidemocratic attitudes, Dracula has no qualms about using human beings as a source of nourishment and of discarding them when they are no longer of use to him. In fact, he taunts his European opponents by telling them that they are important only as a food supply:

You think to baffle me, you—with your pale faces all in a row, like sheep in a butcher's. You shall be sorry yet, each one of you! You think you have left me without a place to rest; but I have more. My revenge is just begun! I spread it over centuries, and time is on my side. Your girls that you all love are mine already; and through them you and others shall yet be mine—my creatures, to do my bidding and to be my jackals when I want to feed. (421)

Thus, Dracula persists in thinking like a warlord, ignoring the fact that much of the western world has come to recognize the need to take advantage of the abilities of all people. He is, at least for the time being, trapped in a medieval way of thinking.

There is untapped potential in Dracula's character, though, and Stoker suggests that Dracula is a formidable threat because he seems capable of learning new ways. He may for the moment have only a "child-brain" (414), but he is learning. Moreover, he is sufficiently aware of the values of the period to have his boxes of earth labeled "for experimental purposes" (321). (One wonders how the customs officials would have responded to boxes labeled "cemetery soil" or even "Transylvanian native earth.") Furthermore, even Van Helsing praises his opponent for "experimenting, and doing it well" (414). A Dracula who was comfortable with both alchemy and late-nineteenth-century science and technology would have been a virtually unbeatable opponent. He is beaten primarily because he remains mired in the middle ages.

Before discussing the significance of the conflict between the modern, scientific world and a Gothic and mysterious one, it is appropriate to discuss two characters who, though generally included among the Crew of Light, seem to have their feet in the opposing camp, Arthur and Quincey Morris. For example, Leatherdale suggests in a footnote that Arthur and Quincey are excluded from many of the strategy sessions after September 30: "With hindsight, these appear to be the last written documents Arthur and Quincey ever see, and the process of their exclusion gathers pace" (p. 332, note 30).

Of the two, Arthur is less complex. Though the pun included in his name, Lord Godalming (Lord God), suggests that Stoker at one point may have thought of him as a suitable opponent for Dracula, who assumes the equally pun-filled pseudonym, Count de Ville (devil), nothing in Arthur's behavior suggests the power of the deity except for the brief period when he is pictured in the Westenra tomb looking "like a figure of Thor as his untrembling arm rose and fell, driving deeper and deeper the mercy-bearing stake" (310). Aside from this scene, however, Arthur is generally presented as a remnant of a rather moribund feudal structure rather than as an omnipotent force. Indeed he seems more than a bit out of touch with the modern world and generally as a rather dim bulb. For instance, when Dracula's opponents are trying to locate his various lairs so that they can prevent his reentry, Arthur volunteers to wire his staff "to have horses and carriages where they will be most convenient" (404). Even Quincey, who is generally presented as another dim bulb, recognizes that the presence of such official transport is not a great idea: "don't you think that one of your snappy carriages with its heraldic adornments . . . would attract too much attention?" (404). By the end of the novel, Arthur is reduced to providing financial support for the expedition and to driving a steam launch up the Sereth and Bistritza Rivers to ambush the count. Later, he and Seward cover the gypsies with their Winchester rifles while Jonathan Harker and Quincey Morris dispatch Dracula. To his credit, Arthur shows himself perfectly willing to accept the direction that the modern world is taking, and, unlike Dracula, he is willing to share his wealth and his power with representatives of the middle class.

Quincey Morris is more problematic, especially because Stoker's notes suggest that he had initially planned for the sole American character to have a different and more important role. The notes refer to a Brutus M. Moris, an inventor from Texas, an occupation that would ally Quincey more completely with the scientists and technologists. In fact, making Morris an inventor seems to suggest an intelligence and creativity that is absent in the character who appears in the finished novel. As it is, Quincey seems placed in the story only to provide another member to the Crew of Light and finally to become a noble sacrifice at the conclusion. In the novel as it was finally published, he is definitely a follower rather than a leader, confessing, "I don't quite see the drift of it; but you people are all so good and kind, and have been working so earnestly and so energetically, that all I can do is to accept your ideas blindfold and try to help you" (324). Quincey is important primarily because he provides the group with Winchester repeating rifles and because he is associated with the careless use of firearms. Patrolling the grounds of Seward's mental institution, he notices a large bat sitting on the window and, instead of waiting for a better opportunity, fires at the creature. Such impulsive behavior puts the other members of the Crew of Light in danger of ricocheting bullets and other debris. Indeed, Stoker often seems to think of Americans in terms of their impulsive behavior. Not only is Quincey guilty of rash actions, but so is Colonel Ogilvie in *Lady Athylene*. Suspecting that his daughter's honor has been compromised, the Kentucky Colonel threatens to shoot first and ask questions later.

Because of Quincey's inscrutable and sometimes dangerous behavior, several critics link him with the Count, among them Franco Moretti, who characterizes Quincey in the following manner:

What places? What adventures? Where does all his money come from? What does Mr Morris do? Where does he live? Nobody knows any of this. But nobody suspects. Nobody suspects even when Lucy dies—and then turns into a vampire—immediately after receiving a blood transfusion from Morris. . . . Nobody, finally, suspects when, in the course of the meeting to plan the vampire hunt, Morris leaves the room to take a shot . . . at the big bat. . . . or when, after Dracula bursts into the household, Morris hides among the trees, the only effect of which is that he loses sight of Dracula and invites the others to call off the hunt for the night. . . . He would be a totally superfluous character if, unlike the others, he were not characterized by this mysterious connivance with the world of the vampires. So long as things go well for Dracula, Morris acts like an accomplice. As soon as there is a reversal of fortunes, he turns into his staunchest enemy. [14]

Moretti is wrong about at least one thing: Lucy never receives Quincey's blood. His other observations are more legitimate, and Leatherdale, after examining Stoker's notes for the novel, provides several additional connections between Dracula and Morris:

His Texan . . . was forever turning up, then disappearing. Once, Seward was intended to receive two visitors: the Count and the Texan together. Significantly, chapters three and four of Book Three were supposed to have the Texan journey to Transylvania alone and at his own request. Although this was later scrapped from the finished novel, the question remains: what did Stoker intend should happen to him there? [15]

There is one more similarity that neither Moretti nor Leatherdale mentions, the fact that both Dracula and Morris are described as hunters, a primitive occupation that is more relevant to medieval Transylvania or frontier America than to nineteenth-century England. Dracula, for example, explains to Jonathan Harker that modern human beings have lost their instinct for hunting: "You dwellers in the city cannot enter into the feelings of the hunter" (52). When Quincey offers to provide Winchester rifles for the journey, Van Helsing exclaims: "Quincey's head is level at all times, but most so when there is to hunt" (442).

Of course, there is one area in which Dracula and Quincey are distinctly different: Dracula prides himself at being a member of an old family and comments frequently on the heroic past of both his family and his nation. Quincey, on the other hand, is an American and thus a representative of a new way of doing things, and Stoker, who traveled widely throughout the United States, is generally enthusiastic about America and Americans. *A Glimpse of America*, which Stoker initially delivered as a lecture in London and later published, is positively euphoric about the future of the New World. Indeed, he praises the United States both for its lack of class-consciousness and for its technological expertise:

A traveller, going through the country in the ordinary way, by railways, steamboats, stages, and road-cars, could not possibly distinguish classes as at home, except when they are of very marked difference, or, of course, in the case of tramps, and other excretions of civilization. [16]

Among the technological marvels that Stoker praises are American plumbing and masonry. He is particularly enamored, however, of American fire-fighting technology, mentioning both the speed with which fire brigades respond to fires and the American method of delivering water to a fire:

In New York and some other places a system of steam-pipes has been laid through some streets, so that participants can take in, as we do our gas, whatever amount of pressure as may be required, and regulate it accordingly, a practice which minimises danger of fire. (18-19)

Summarizing everything that he had seen in the United States, Stoker concludes the lecture by expressing "joy that England's first-born child has arrived at so noble a stature" (47) and by summarizing America's strengths:

We have not, all the world through, so strong an ally, so close a friend. America has got over her childhood. The day of petty jealousy has gone by. Columbia is strong enough in her knowledge of her own power and beauty to sail, unruffled and unawed, into the salon of old Time amidst the queens of the world. There is every reason we can think of why the English on both sides of the Atlantic should hold together as one. Our history is their history—our fame is their pride—their progress is our glory. They are bound to us, and we to them, by every tie of love and sympathy; on our side, by the bright hopes of parents who send their children to seek fortune in the Sunset Land; on theirs, by the old remembrances of home and common kin, and by the memories of their buried dead. We are bound each to each by the instinct of a common race, which makes brotherhood and the love of brothers a natural law; a law which existed at the first, and which, after the lapse of a century, still exists—whose tenets were never broken, even by the shocks of war, and whose keen perception was never dimmed in the wilderness of stormy sea between. (47–48)

Of course, Stoker, who consistently praises Americans for both their technological sophistication and for their lack of class distinctions, is also aware of their occasional cruelty and boorishness. Quincey Morris, for example, provides a "mixed bag." Honored for his heroism and his gallant death, he is also portrayed as somewhat of a buffoon. One wonders whether Stoker disposes of both Quincey and Dracula because there is simply no place in the modern world for such primitive individuals. Certainly the group that remains at the conclusion of the novel is so homogenous that Jonathan Harker can speak for all of them:

Seven years ago we all went through the flames; and the happiness of some of us since then is, we think, well worth the pain we endured. It is an added joy to Mina and to me that our boy's birthday is the same day as that on which Quincey Morris died. His mother holds, I know, the secret belief that some of our brave friend's spirit has passed into him. His bundle of names links all our little band of men together; but we call him Quincey. (510)

Stoker had linked all the characters through the exchange of blood, either blood drained by vampiric ingestion or blood given by transfusion. Lucy had received the blood of Arthur, Seward, and Van Helsing and therefore feels married to all of them. Dracula drinks blood from Lucy and thus shares in the blood of everyone but Quincey. Later, when Dracula drinks from Mina, he also forces her to drink from him. One wonders whether Stoker has forgotten that Quincey is one of the few characters whose blood does not flow in the veins of Mina's son. This technicality does not diminish the fact that the group can stand together nor that young Quincey Harker is the embodiment of a new scientific and technological world.

At this point, it is important to return to the central question with which this chapter, indeed this entire book, is concerned, the relationship of the Gothic to science/technology. On the surface at least *Dracula* is Gothic, for it includes supernatural events, a medieval setting (at least in the opening and closing scenes), and the presence of a persecuted maiden and a sexually depraved villain. Moreover, as the previous discussion of characters should indicate, *Dracula* presents the world as infinitely complex and ambiguous rather than simple and easy to describe and/or categorize. Doublings and parallels exist throughout the novel, and it is difficult to come to terms with the novel because boundaries are so completely unstable. It is even difficult to suggest an answer to the question of whether Stoker believes that the world is a complex and inscrutable place or whether he hopes that the world will yield its secrets to the probing of science. *Dracula* seems to conclude happily for the practitioners of modern science and technology. However, can readers trust their judgment of events? Does Dracula succumb to the collective power of modern science and technology? Or does he disappear? Having time on his side, he could simply decide to return at some future date.

However readers answer those questions, they must recognize a tension that can be rather simplistically stated as the tension between modern science and the Gothic, between a perspective that believes that the world can be quantified, categorized, and ultimately explained and a perspective that accepts that the world is ultimately mysterious, a place either of awe or terror or a combination of both. Over a century after the publication of *Dracula*, readers continue to confront these and similar questions.

The Gothic nature of *Dracula* was recognized from the beginning, with both Charlotte Stoker and the review in the *Athenaeum* praising its supernatural terrors. Indeed, Charlotte, who had shared her own horrific tales with her son, gushed, "No book since Mrs. Shelley's 'Frankenstein' . . . has come near yours in originality, or terror—Poe is nowhere" (cited by Belford, 274). The *Athenaeum* also compares it favorably to other Gothic works:

Stories and novels appear just now in plenty stamped with a more or less genuine air of belief in the visibility of supernatural agency. The strengthening of a bygone faith in the fantastic and magical view of things in lieu of the purely material is a feature of the hour, a reaction—artificial, perhaps, rather than natural—against late tendencies in thought. Mr. Stoker is the purveyor of so many strange wares that 'Dracula' reads like a determined effort to go, as it were, "one better" than others in the same field. [17]

A review in the *Spectator* also compares *Dracula* to other Gothic works:

Mr. Bram Stoker gives us the impression . . . of having deliberately laid himself out in *Dracula* to eclipse all previous efforts in the domain of the horrible,—to "go one better" than Wilkie Collins (whose method of narration he has closely followed), Sheridan Le Fanu, and all the other professors of the flesh-creeping school.[18]

Furthermore, the *Spectator* reviewer even comments on the unique blend of Gothic mystery and contemporary technology in the novel though the reviewer finds that blend a flaw rather than a strategy that would enable readers to think about the problems of the modern world:

Mr. Stoker has shown considerable ability in the use that he has made of all the available traditions of vampirology, but we think his story would have been all the more effective if he had chosen an earlier period. The up-to-dateness of the book— the phonograph diaries, typewriters, and so on—hardly fits in with the mediaeval methods which ultimately secure the victory for Count Dracula's foes. (151)

It is a clear vote on the side of magic and mystery, a decision that has been followed by most film adaptations.[19]

Although most commentary on *Dracula* has tended to focus on the novel's Gothic elements, some recent critics examine Stoker's interests in science and technology. Among them are Stephen D. Arata, Troy Boone, Ernest Fontana, Regenia Gagnier, John Greenway, Rosemary Jann, and Jennifer Wicke. [20]

Of this group, Gagnier is perhaps the most confident about the place of science in the novel. Indeed, she comments on the fact that information, science, and technology triumph in *Dracula*:

The operation of stopping the vampire enlists the aid of scientists, scholars and clerks, and exploits an international information industry, drawing upon institutional collaboration across public and private lines in business, family, law, government and modern technology. (147)

She also notes that this triumph resembles the efforts of the British during the period in which the novel appeared:

In the battle between Transylvania's genealogy and history and the mobilised British State, as we know, the British win. They have the 'powers of combination' . . . (or networks of power), science, technology and daylight, or longer work hours. As we have shown, this theme is consistent with the rise of 'research', the social sciences and professionalism in Britain. It is also consistent with British entre-preneurial activity in Romania. (152)

Whereas Gagnier's essay focuses on the positive impact of science and technology, Greenway suggests that *Dracula* is critical of science:

The bland, asexual tableau at the end, when the characters return to Transylvania for old times' sake, officially announces the triumph of the Victorian conventions of rationality and progress. At first glance, the Victorian view of history as a conquest of barbarity and superstition seems affirmed in the happy ending. The men, emblems of the establishment as scientist, solicitor, and aristocrat, have become husbands and providers while Mina, who has the best mind of the lot, has become Jonathan's secretary. . . . The irony in this tableau, however, suggests that these conventions, just as Seward's science, are merely forms of structured ignorance. The novel grows from this irony: not just from the ignorance of the heroes of a world they cannot understand, but the larger irony that the "other" world is more real than their own. (83–84)

Boone has a similar view, suggesting that Stoker recognizes both the power of science and the fact that science is unlikely to be able to solve all the world's mysteries:

Harker the solicitor realizes the impotence, in this foreign context, of his society's most valued institutions, even the law: "It makes me rage to think that this can go on, and whilst I am shut up here, a veritable prisoner, but without that protection of the law which is even a criminal's right and consolation." . . . His age's technology is similarly useless: "I fear that no weapon wrought alone by man's hand would have any effect on him.".. Even symbols of modern efficiency, like the post office, fail to help the vampire-hunters, as a wonderfully ironic document heading demonstrates: "Telegram, Van Helsing, Antwerp, to Seward, Carfax (Sent to Carfax, Sussex, as no county given' delivered late by twenty-two hours)." (80)

In fact, Boone observes that Van Helsing's response to the vampire is to use "a science that validates reason but does not deprivilege the supernatural" (81). Thus, Boone suggests that Stoker's novel recognizes both the power of modern science and technology and the power of an older, more mysterious worldview. Jann, too, recognizes that Stoker's view is more complex than is usually recognized. She notes that "*Dracula* clearly has a place among popular late Victorian reactions against materialist science." She adds, however, "Stoker's narrative is also heavily invested in valorizing the rationalistic authority conventionally associated with scientific thought."

Stoker's narrative proclaims the power of belief, faith, and imagination, but the plot makes these dependent on logic, deduction, and proof for their ultimate success. The novel thus speaks in two voices: one that urges the superior reality of the supernatural, and a second—and, I think, ultimately the more authoritative one— that affirms the status quo of scientific reasoning and aligns it firmly with the conventional bases of cultural power at the time. (273)

No matter whether these critics argue that science/technology comes out ahead in the novel or that Gothic mystery comes out a winner, almost all recent commentary focuses on the fact that Stoker is far more interested in his own world than in attempting to re-create or comment on a medieval one.

Though it may be a moot point, *Dracula*—indeed every Stoker novel—seems more interested in technology (practical, applied science) than in pure science. Thus, Van Helsing is perfectly willing to blend folklore with medicine so long as the procedure works. Indeed none of Stoker's characters is driven by ideology. Harker is perfectly willing to bend the law to his own use; Seward and Van Helsing bend medical protocol by avoiding inquests of the mysterious deaths of Lucy, her mother, and Renfield. Countless other examples exist, all of them pointing to the highly practical nature of their quest. Their lives and their souls in danger, the Crew of Light is willing to do whatever it takes to destroy their opponent.

The pragmatism of the Crew of Light can be linked to larger cultural concerns as Arata demonstrates:

Early in his stay at Castle Dracula, Harker to his great surprise finds his host stretched upon the library sofa reading . . . an English *Bradshaw's Guide*. . . . We probably share Harker's puzzlement at the Count's choice of reading material, though like Harker we are apt to forget this brief interlude amid ensuing horrors. Why is Dracula interested in English train schedules? The Count's absorption in *Bradshaw's* echoes Harker's own obsessive interest in trains. . . . An obsession with trains—or, as in Harker's case, an obsession with trains running on time— characterizes Victorian narratives of travel in Eastern Europe. . . . Harker immediately invokes a second convention of the travel genre when, having crossed the Danube at Buda-Pesth, he invests the river with symbolic significance. . . . In crossing the Danube, Harker maintains, he leaves "Europe" behind, geographically and imaginatively, and approaches the first outpost of the ' Orient.'" (93)

Arata reminds readers of the important contrast between the technologically sophisticated Harker and the technologically naïve Dracula, a contrast that remains central to the novel. Moreover, Arata, whose essay includes excerpts from various Victorian travel narratives, demonstrates the extent to which Stoker's enthusiasm for technological developments is a common characteristic of the age. Of course, not everyone demonizes primitive peoples in quite the way that Stoker does in *Dracula*. The contrast nonetheless is a familiar one at the end of the nineteenth century.

There were, of course, reasons for these feelings of smug superiority about technological progress. Josephine Guy alludes to "the enormous leaps made in Victorian technology" and mentions the following specifically:

. . . the perfection of steam-powered locomotion, the extensive use of iron and steel (particularly in naval and civil engineering), the development of electric lighting, photography, the telegraph, the use of anaesthetics and antiseptics and, at the very end of the century, the internal combustion engine and early cinematography—it becomes clear that one of the outstanding features of Victorian science and technology was their immediate, large-scale and irreversible impact on everyday life. (200)

It is interesting to think of how many of these technological developments feature prominently in Stoker's works. Indeed, one of the most frequent is, of course, reliable transportation by rail, a mode in which England held the lead during the period in which Stoker wrote. Although there were fewer railways in Ireland when Stoker was growing up, [21] transportation by train was already well established in the United Kingdom before Stoker's birth. Construction of the first railway in the world designed for steam locomotives began in 1821 and was completed in 1825. This event was followed by a burst of railway construction during the 1830s and a veritable "railway mania" during the 1840s. The following account of travel by John Ranlett demonstrates just how important trains were to Stoker's contemporaries:

From the mid-Victorian period, travel in England was normally railway travel, road services being used only to reach the nearest railway station, of which there came to be some 9,000. Frequency of passenger service was notable; in 1888 there were twenty-nine express trains daily between London and Manchester and fifty-seven between Liverpool and Manchester, while intervals of only two or three minutes separated trains on some sections of the London underground railway system, which had first offered service in 1863. Even most rural lines carried four or five trains daily. Passengers, choosing between first- and third-class accommodation . . . numbered 540.7 million in 1880 and 992.4 million in 1900. [22]

It is thus little wonder that Stoker, accustomed to these kinds of wonders, thought of progress in terms of technological sophistication. Stoker was born into a world in which extremes in travel were still evident though the most modern modes still seemed almost magical.

Whereas Arata reinforces the extent to which *Dracula* fits a familiar paradigm, Belford points to more personal reasons for Stoker's enthusiasm for technology. Her biography reminds readers that Stoker made all the travel arrangements when the Lyceum went on provincial tour either in the United States or the United Kingdom and also that Stoker had loved trains since his childhood. She also comments on the number of problems that the company encountered during these provincial tours and observes that Stoker enjoyed being a problem solver, a characteristic that he shares with a number of his characters both in *Dracula* and elsewhere.

The knowledge of trains and train schedules (and also of boats and their schedules in the case of international travel) was definitely an important part of his job with the Lyceum. Getting the company from town to town quickly was not the life-and-death matter that it was in *Dracula*, but it could mean the difference between having well-rested actors and crew or a tired and grumpy staff. In fact, because both Mina and Jonathan Harker share Stoker's predilection for memorizing train schedules, they manage to keep one or more steps ahead of their adversary and ultimately prevent his arriving at the safety of his castle. Their familiarity with various forms of travel and with various forms of communication technology is one reason that the Crew of Light is ultimately so effective against Dracula.

Although the interest in the transportation of goods and people pervades Stoker's other works, none of them uses this still relatively new technology as effectively as does *Dracula* where the ability to travel quickly is a matter of life and death. Nor do these other works use that interest to emphasize the contrast between a scientific and technological present and the mysterious past as effectively as *Dracula* does. Looking at several of the works that Stoker wrote while he was working on *Dracula* serves to reinforce the message that comes across in *Dracula*, that the magic, mystery, and terror do exist but that scientific reasoning can be used to keep those terrors under control.

### THE SHOULDER OF SHASTA

*The Shoulder of Shasta* (1895) is especially important because Stoker published it while he continued to work on *Dracula*. Thus, readers might expect to find various parallels. In fact, both open with references to train travel. *The*

*Shoulder of Shasta* opens with a description of a railway journey from San Francisco to the mountains around Mount Shasta that was based on a journey that Stoker himself took on September 17, 1893. [23] Not surprisingly, because Stoker was working on *Dracula* at the same time that he was writing *Shasta*, the two have a number of additional similarities. Not only is Grizzly Dick, a trapper and guide in *Shasta*, a less sophisticated forerunner of Dracula's Quincey Morris, but the two novels rely on the conflict between primitive people and more sophisticated individuals. In *Shasta*, however, the conflict is resolved in an almost entirely comic way. Furthermore, although Stoker implies that both Dick and the Shoshonies are capable of shedding blood, the novel ends with no human blood spilled and with no one having their feelings seriously wounded either.

In this little-known novel, the young heroine Esse Elstree (a character who in many ways resembles *Dracula*'s Lucy Westenra) has been advised by her physician to "spend the coming summer high up on some mountain side" and "have iron and other natural tonics suitable to her anaemic condition" (23). Trying to do the best for Esse, her mother locates a suitable summer home near Mount Shasta. Here in the American wilderness, the Estrees, along with Esse's governess and her mother's male factotum, encounter Native Americans in their natural element, and both Esse and her governess become infatuated with their guide. The mountain man Grizzly Dick is loosely modeled on Colonel W.F. "Buffalo Bill" Cody, an individual Stoker had met and admired. [24] Similarities in *Dracula* and *Shasta* are most evident, however, in the contrast between the civilized English tourists and the primitive people they encounter in the California wilderness.

Initially as fascinated by Native Americans as Jonathan Harker is by Slovaks, Esse quickly becomes as disgusted as Harker, and Stoker even suggests that primitive people are not even members of the same species as civilized human beings. "In fact, she went with them through somewhat of those phases with which one comes to regard a monkey before its place in the scale of creation is put in true perspective" (52). The English tourist might be expected to be horrified by the behavior of people who collect the scalps of their adversaries, but Stoker reveals that even the rough-and-tumble mountain man is horrified at their cruelty:

There's times when the cruelty of that lot of ours makes me so mad, I want to wipe them all out; but I know all the same that there isn't one of them, man, woman, or child, that wouldn't stand between me and death. Ay, or between any of you and death either. Guess, you're about beginnin' to size up the noble red man without his frills! (52)

This speech serves to contrast the unsophisticated Dick with the even more primitive native Americans. This sense of Caucasian (or even Anglo-Saxon) superiority is evident in much that Stoker wrote, including *The Mystery of the Sea*, *The Lair of the White Worm*, and *Dracula*.

Although *Dracula* reveals the erotic power of the primitive even at the end of the nineteenth century, the conflict in *Shasta* is less complex, for Esse is never in danger of falling in love with any Native American men. She does, however, become briefly infatuated with Dick  and eventually invites him to visit her family in San Francisco, an invitation that she will later come to regret.

Once back among civilized people, however, it doesn't take long for Esse to lose her infatuation with Dick, especially when she meets the young painter Reginald Hampden and falls in love with him:

Esse had already begun to appreciate the refinements of life sufficiently well to make it impossible for her to even contemplate an isolated life in the woods or on the mountains. . . . Such life, without relief, would never suit her as an unvarying constancy. (108)

Unfortunately, however, Dick has not forgotten her invitation, and the following scenes reveal, albeit in a comic manner, how unsuited Dick and Esse are for one another: "Dick had opened his conversation with a piece of complimentary pleasantry such as he would have used to a barmaid in a dancing saloon, nothing coarse, nothing unpleasant, but altogether familiar and out of place in a conventional assembly" (119). Dick's brash behavior produces little more than a moment's embarrassment for Esse and her mother, however, for, unlike Dracula, Dick is no real threat to the *status quo* because, unlike Dracula,  he knows his place and is willing to return there:

Let me get back to the b'ars an' the Injuns. I'm more to home with them than I am here. Be easy, Little Missy, an' ye too, all ye ladies and gentlemen; it'll be no pleasant thinkin' for me up yonder, away among the mountings, that when I kem down to 'Frisco, meanin' to do honour to a young lady that I'd give the best drop of my blood for . . . I couldn't keep my blasted hands off my weppins in the midst of a crowd of women! Durn the thing! I ain't fit to go heeled inter decent kempany. (124)

Thus, *Shasta* ends with the promise of Esse's marriage to Reginald and with Dick's return to the mountains. Unlike *Dracula*, there seems no need to eradicate primitive people.  In fact, *Shasta* ends with the friendship of the principal characters:

"Never mind, Dick," said Reginald heartily; "we are all friends of yours here! If there are any who are not so, then they are no friend of our hostess or of me either; and I'll stand back to back, if you'll let me, when we slice up the last of them!" (127)

There is obviously no need either to chase Dick back to his mountains or to attempt to destroy him.

Alan Johnson's introductory notes to the recent reprint of *The Shoulder of Shasta* put Reginald's resolution into the perspective of Stoker's political views and also contrast it with *Dracula*:

The concept of internationalism, a harmony between nations, is suggested at the end of *The Shoulder of Shasta* by the harmony achieved by Reginald, Esse, and Dick. Like the idea of a scheme of nature, the concept of internationalism has a root in Stoker's own past experience and, as it is dramatized in *The Shoulder of Shasta*, it sheds interesting light on the ending of *Dracula* with its final tableau. . . . Stoker advocated what he explicitly called 'internationalism' as early as November 13, 1872, in a speech to the University of Dublin's College Historical Society. (19)

Thus, *The Shoulder of Shasta* suggests that the modern world can accept, even celebrate, its primitive origins. In *Dracula*, however, there is no place for the primitive, for Dracula and his three brides and even Quincey Morris have been killed off.

Johnson further explains the contrast by referring to Ronald Hyam's *Britain's Imperial Century, 1815–1914*, which explains that the kind of internationalism imagined by Stoker was a "Liberal alternative to an Imperial federation, the device favoured by Conservatives for governing Britain's widely dispersed colonies and for preserving Britain's power against other nations":

> The Liberal solution to the problem of governing the colonies was to grant them responsible self-government while retaining them . . . in a loose union such as a Commonwealth. According to Hyam, although Liberals 'had no wish to work with colonials, of whom they were frequently contemptuous,' and although Liberals generally 'liked the empire,' their 'major loyalty was to the international community.' . . . Hyam adds that the idea of Home Rule for Ireland . . . was an application of the 'internationalism' concept. In *Personal Reminiscences of Henry Irving* . . . Stoker describes himself as having been 'a philosophical Home-Ruler' during the controversy over Gladstone's Home Rule bills in the 1880s and early 1890s. The conclusion of *The Shoulder of Shasta* shows the wide scope of Stoker's internationalism and its definitely political character by giving Reginald a friendly relationship with a European emperor as well as with the American Dick. Stoker shows the British bias . . . by making Reginald the saviour of the emperor's life . . . during their boar hunt and . . . by making Reginald the suitor who wins Esse. *The Shoulder of Shasta* . . . is a piece of light reading which reveals important foundations of Stoker's thought and of its expression in *Dracula*. (20) [25]

*The Shoulder of Shasta* also reveals Stoker's preference for the technologically sophisticated rather than for the primitive. Here, however, rail transportation and sophisticated weaponry are at the disposal of Native American, white mountain man, English painter, and German emperor. There is thus a contrast between various types of people in *Shasta* but not the life-and-death conflict presented in *Dracula*.

## "THE SQUAW"

"The Squaw," a short story, that Stoker wrote during the period he was working on *Dracula*, also addresses the American temperament and the importance of technology. "The Squaw" was published in "the special Christmas 1893 number of *The Illustrated Sporting and Dramatic News*." [26] Though there are no supernatural occurrences in the story, it is nonetheless one of Stoker's most horrifying. In addition, it reveals the ambiguities about boundaries that are so frequently found in Gothic works.

The story, which has only five characters, is told by a man who has come to Nuremberg with his young bride, Amelia, for their honeymoon. Meeting Elias P. Hutcheson, who hails from "Isthmian City, Bleeding Gulch, Maple Tree County, Neb." (86), they decide to join forces to tour the city. The other characters are the custodian of the torture tower and a black cat whose kitten Hutcheson accidentally kills.

Hutcheson, as it turns out, is a much crueler version of Grizzly Dick. While looking over the wall of the moat, the three are admiring a mother cat and her kitten when Hutcheson—despite Amelia's protests—decides to drop a stone from the top of the wall so that the cat and kitten will "both wonder where it came from" (88). A pleasant summer day then turns horrifying as the stone "fell with a sickening thud that came up to us through the hot air, right on the kitten's head, and shattered out its little brains then and there" (88). The mother cat's response is equally horrifying:

With a muffled cry, such as a human being might give, she bent over the kitten, licking its wound and moaning. Suddenly she seemed to realize that it was dead, and again threw her eyes up at us. I shall never forget the sight, for she looked the perfect incarnation of hate. Her green eyes blazed with lurid fire, and the white, sharp teeth seemed to almost shine through the blood which dabbled her mouth and whiskers. (88)

If this episode were not grisly enough, Hutcheson observes to Amelia and her husband that it reminds him of an experience he had on the frontier. In fact, he compares the grief-stricken mother cat to a grief-stricken Native American mother:

Wall, I guess that [the mother of the kitten] air the savagest beast I ever see—'cept once when an Apache squaw had an edge on a half-breed . . . 'cos of the way he fixed up her papoose which he stole on a raid just to show that he appreciated the way they had given his mother the fire torture. . . . She got that kinder look so set on her face that it jest seemed to grow there. She followed Splinters more'n three year til at last the braves got him and handed him over to her. They did say that no man . . . had ever been so long a-dying under the tortures of the Apaches. The only time I ever see her smile was when I wiped her out. (88–89)

While Hutcheson focuses on the savagery of mother cat, half-breed, and Apache squaw, Stoker's story reveals that Hutcheson himself has succumbed to the same savagery. Indeed, Hutcheson confesses—almost as an afterthought—that he continues to carry the pocketbook that he had made from Splinters' skin. Like Conrad's Kurtz, Hutcheson has, in the presence of savages, become savage himself.

Once again it is possible to see several parallels with *Dracula*. Not only does "The Squaw" emphasize the savagery of primitive people and suggest that America is still a primitive place, but the description of the mother cat closely resembles Stoker's description of the vampiric Lucy. Note the similarities. The cat's "green eyes blazed with lurid fire, and the white, sharp teeth seemed to almost shine through the blood which dabbled her mouth and whiskers." In the following passage, Dr. Seward describes Lucy Westenra and focuses on *her* blazing eyes and blood stained mouth:

Van Helsing raised his lantern and drew the slide. . . . we could see that the lips were crimson with fresh blood, and that the stream had trickled over her chin. . . . When Lucy . . . saw us she drew back with an angry snarl, such as a cat gives when taken unawares. . . . As she looked, her eyes blazed with unholy light, and the face became wreathed with a voluptuous smile. (304)

Both Lucy and the mother cat are presented as monstrous and demonic even though it is arguable that the mother cat is more victim than monster.

Very little criticism exists on "The Squaw," but one recent article looks at Stoker's characterization of America and Americans. In "Virgin Territory and the Iron Virgin: Engendering the Empire in Bram Stoker's 'The Squaw,'" [27] Lillian Nayder suggests that Stoker was thinking specifically about the fact that the United States was gaining economic and political power at the same time that Britain's power was diminishing:

Despite the focus on Hutcheson and his native American enemies, Stoker is primarily concerned in 'The Squaw' with Britain's declining imperial status, although his anxieties about this decline are both obscured and displaced. While Stoker registers the threat posed to the British empire by an American that has come of age, he assuages his imperial anxieties by sexualizing them. Situating his characters among the relics of fallen imperial powers, in a European city originally defended against the Huns, Stoker transforms his narrator's American rival into an emasculated brother. He does so by identifying wives and mothers as the real enemies of his male characters, American and English alike, and by suggesting that the primary threat posed to the British empire lies at home. (78)

Because Quincey Morris and Grizzley Dick share many of Hutcheson's traits, it is possible to apply Nayder's observations to them as well. The major difference is that Dick is willing to return to his mountains, whereas Morris and Hutcheson, like Dracula, can be described as invaders of another culture.

As is evident from the previous quotation and the anthology in which her essay appears, Nayder is most concerned with Stoker's treatment of gender, certainly a valid interest. Indeed, she focuses on the fact that the torture device in which Hutcheson dies is a representation of a female, the Iron Virgin. When the doors close unexpectedly upon him, Hutcheson "is impaled by the spikes that line them." Nayder adds that "the pleasures of sexual conquest give way to the agonies of castration, and the delight of empire-building to the terror of colonial dispossession" and notes Stoker's depiction of female power. Even though this female had been penetrated by previous explorers, these earlier explorers had met with Hutcheson's fate. "Stoker thus suggests that the Iron Virgin is virginal not because she is 'new-found', but because her deadly internal design ensures that no man will ever appropriate or possess her" (76). Nayder concludes her discussion of female imagery by noting that Stoker's "account of Hutcheson's end reads like a sinister childbirth scene; 'bound' with rope like an infant tangled in an umbilical cord, the bones of his skull crushed, the 'embrionic' American seems to have been killed in the process of delivery" (92).

Although Nayder's interesting and insightful reading of "The Squaw" directs readers to a number of interesting parallels between it and *Dracula* (and I would encourage readers to consider parallels to *The Shoulder of Shasta* as well and to the other novels that feature monstrous women, including *The Jewel of Seven Stars* and *Lair of the White Worm*), the present study is concerned with Stoker's presentation of science and technology. Therefore, I would like to focus on the instrument of torture as an example of technology. In fact, Stoker, who had visited Nuremberg with Irving to research the Lyceum's production of *Faust*, describes the technology of the various torture instruments in almost painful detail:

In racks, and leaning in disorder against the walls, were a number of headsmen's swords, great double-handed weapons with broad blade and keen edge. . . . Round the chamber, placed in all sorts of irregular ways, were many implements of torture which made one's heart ache to see—chairs full of spikes which gave instant and excruciating pain; chairs and couches with dull knobs whose torture was seemingly less. . . . racks, belts, boots, gloves, collars, all made for compressing at will; steel baskets in which the head could be slowly crushed into a pulp if necessary. (92)

While the narrator catalogues the various torture instruments, Hutcheson is particularly interested in the Iron Virgin, which he contemplates taking back to the United States to show Native Americans the superiority of European technology. In a dramatic attempt to demonstrate his own bravery, Hutcheson gets into the instrument again over Amelia's protest. Once he is inside, with the heavy door held open by the custodian, the mother cat springs at the custodian who drops the rope. The door springs shut, impaling Hutcheson on the spikes with which the Virgin was lined, and the story concludes with the narrator destroying the cat.

Like so many of Stoker's villains and demivillains, Hutcheson winds up a victim of his own cruelty and his own hubris. Is it too much to add, however, that he is also destroyed because he fails to understand either technology or the power of technology? Enamored of his own power as a civilized American, Hutcheson has come from the New World to "see the most all-fired Methuselah of a town in Yurrup" (86) and discovers while he is there that he has a lot to learn about the art and technology of torture. Indeed, he falls victim to a creature even more primitive than he, the mother cat who extracts her vengeance at the cost of her own life. Like Dracula and Quincey Morris, he is trapped by a primitive worldview. In a world that has consigned the instruments of torture to a museum and resettled Native Americans onto reservations, there is no place for individuals like Elias P. Hutcheson. Although it is never a good idea to attempt to guess at a writer's intentions, I wonder how many readers wind up sympathizing with either the Native American woman whose child was murdered or with the mother cat. As with many Gothic tales, "The Squaw" blurs the boundaries between the animal and the human world just as it blurs the distinctions between male and female, rational and irrational. Furthermore, the mere fact that its horrifying conclusion is the result of an unpredictable accident makes it Gothic without being the least supernatural.

One of the main subjects with which the present work is concerned, however, is Stoker's use of science and/or technology. So far, it appears that Stoker uses science/technology in a variety of ways. *Dracula* suggests that individuals who understand technology are better equipped to overcome existing evils than are primitive people and that science and technology will ultimately produce a better world; *The Shoulder of Shasta* focuses on technology that links different groups of people though it also recognizes that certain people may adapt that technology to cruel ends; and "The Squaw" suggests that understanding technology may well be essential to human survival. Even though both "The

Squaw" and *The Shoulder of Shasta* are less sophisticated than *Dracula*, they are important for the mere fact that Stoker wrote them at the same time he was working on *Dracula*. If *Dracula* wrestles with the place of science and technology in the modern world and asks whether these new discoveries can solve ancient problems, the other works provide important supporting materials.

## SNOWBOUND

Several short stories in *Snowbound* (1908) also examine the place of science and/or technology in the world. Rarely memorable in themselves, they are interesting because of their particular slant on this topic. Moreover, they are frequently worth examining because some of them may have been written while Stoker was working on *Dracula*. [28]

Indeed, the basic plot that connects the fifteen short stories in *Snowbound* suggests a failure of modern technology or at least the fact that technology is helpless in the face of natural forces: A theatrical touring company is stuck in the snow somewhere between Aberdeen and the next stop on the tour. As the members of the company wait for a snowplow to clear the tracks, they tell stories that, as Bruce Wightman observes in his introduction to the recent edition, "are assuredly semi-factual. There is little doubt that they are based on the Irving days and are therefore disguised portraits of those theatricals the author worked and toured with" (9). Wightman also notes that the frame tale was probably based on an episode in January 1904 when the "company's train became 'snowbound' in the Adirondack Mountains in upstate New York" (9), an episode that Stoker describes in *Personal Reminiscences* (II, 286–88).

The frame tale may be based on Stoker's own experience, and his brief preface encourages the reader to think of the truthfulness of the stories: "The Truth—or rather Accuracy—of these Stories may be accepted or not as the Reader pleases. They are given as Fiction" (6). Indeed, the tales in *Snowbound* reveal more about the theatrical world and about the individuals who tell the stories than they do about Stoker's views on science and technology. Furthermore, there is no supernatural mystery in *Snowbound*, only the mysterious and overwhelming power of the natural world and the mystery of when the tracks will be cleared and the company allowed to proceed to its next stop.

On the other hand, several stories reinforce Stoker's interest in science and technology and in those individuals with the understanding to control those new fields. A few of the individuals featured in *Snowbound*, including the business manager and the engineer of "Mick the Devil," are heroic precisely because they understand technology and are thus able to effect solutions to the problems with which they are confronted.

Faced with the discomfort and possible danger of remaining on the stranded train while they wait for rescue, the Manager organizes members of the company to build a fire to keep them warm even though the representatives of the railway expressly forbid their doing so. His solution, which adapts theatrical special effects for a more practical purpose, turns out to be both safe and ingenious:

You'll see it will be all right. Just wait a while, and you will be satisfied; and then we shan't have to knock you on the head or tie you up. Now, Hempitch, you get out the thunder and lay it here on the floor. . . . the iron sheet will protect the floor. You, Ruggles, get a good lump of modelling clay. . . . and make a rim all round to keep in the ashes. Then, Hempitch, have half-a-dozen iron braces and lay them on billets or a couple of stage boxes. On this platform put down one of the fireplaces. . . . Then, Ruggles, you will put a Louis XI chimney over it, with a fire backing behind, and make an asbestos fire-cloth into a chimney leading out of the window; you can seal it up with clay. The Engine-Driver here will bring us some live coals from his engine, and one of the carpenters can take his saw and cut down a piece of the fence that I saw outside. . . . The railway servants were intelligent men, and recognised the safety and comfort of the plan. (16–17)

As a result of their technological know-how, the saloon that had been "deathly cold" (17) and therefore even dangerous for the inhabitants of the stalled train becomes safe and comfortable, and the members of the company decide to use the time to swap stories.

I am indebted to Stephanie Moss for reminding me of Stoker's familiarity with theatrical special effects and the fact that these special effects often relied on at least a rudimentary knowledge of science. [29] Entire chapters of *Personal Reminiscences* are devoted to theatrical special effects and to the pleasure Stoker took in stage magic. The following discussion of electricity is typical:

Twenty years ago electric energy, in its playful aspect, was in its infancy; and the way in which the electricity was carried so as to produce the full effects without the possibility of danger to the combatants was then considered very ingenious. Two iron plates were screwed upon the stage at a given distance so that at the time of fighting each of the swordsmen would have his right boot on one of the plates, which represented an end of the interrupted current. A wire was passed up the clothing of each from the shoe to the outside of the indiarubber glove, in the palm of which was a piece of steel. Thus when each held his sword a flash came whenever the swords crossed.

Stoker emphasizes the playfulness and safety of the stage magic and also the degree to which human beings are in total control of it:

The arrangement of the fire which burst from the table and from the ground at command of Mephistopheles required very careful arrangement so as to ensure accuracy at each repetition and be at the same time free from the possibility of danger. . . . The stage and the methods of producing flame of such rapidity of growth and exhaustion as to render it safe to use are well known to property masters. By powdered resin, properly and carefully used, or by lycopodium great effects can be achieved. (I, 176–77)

The reader can see evidence of Stoker himself in *Snowbound*'s Manager.

Whereas the Manager and his helpers pretty much epitomize the practical aspects of technology, the railway engineer of "Mick the Devil" epitomizes the heroic nature of technology. The story, which is related by the Prompter, tells of a journey from New Orleans to Memphis during a flood. Because of the high water, the engineer must confront the mysterious power of the natural world, as it is explained by the Sectional Engineer:

You see, I am afraid of Bayou Pierre. There's a spongy gap a couple of miles wide, with a trestle bridge across it over which you have to pass. At the best of times I am anxious about that trestle, for the ground is so bad that anything might happen at any time. But now, with a fortnight's rain and the Mississippi up the levees and the bottoms flooded all over the country, that blessed place will be like an estuary of the sea. The bridge isn't built for weather like this, and the flood is sure to be well over it. A train running on it will have to take chance whether it is there at all; and if any of it is gone . . . well, God help the train! (64)

Faced with this natural disaster, the Prompter, who tells the story, also reveals some knowledge of the science of physics when he contrasts the response of the Sectional Engineer with the response of Mick Devlin, the Engineer:

The Sectional Engineer is a permanent-way man, and he looks on his work from the standpoint of statical force. But . . . Mick's special province is dynamics. He knows all the dangers . . . and he takes his chances on them blindfold. (66)

Thus, Mick's strategy is to outrun the danger of collapse:

A pier can't fall all in a second; it takes time to break up anything that it has taken time to put together, even if it has to be hoisted with dynamite. Now, our pressure is great, but it doesn't last long. The quicker we go, the shorter it lasts; so that when things are real bad—so near a collapse that it only wants a finishing touch—we can be up and over before the crash comes. (68)

It is a strategy that ultimately proves to be successful:

It was with glad hearts that we felt the solid ground under us and heard the old roar of the wheels again. The squealing of the brakes was like music as we drew up on the track a little later on. (69)

Indeed Mick's knowledge of dynamics proves more than merely heroic or practical, for it is ultimately responsible for saving the lives of all the people on the train. [30]

Whether Mick's success is the result of good science or good luck remains something of a mystery, however, even though I have consulted with several experts in various fields associated with the questions raised by the story. After all, I thought that I was ideally placed to get an answer to this question because Georgia Tech abounds with physicists, engineers, and other kinds of "rocket scientists." Their answers were inconclusive and—to me—disappointing. Edward Thomas, Professor of Physics, writes that Stoker's conclusion would be possible if the train were travelling at enough speed, [31] a probability that both William Green, Professor of Mathematics, and Ted Heath, Ph.D. in physics, doubted. In fact, both Green and Heath believe that the conclusion depends more on luck than on science. [32] Perhaps my own frustration with the extremely hesitant answers that I received betrays my own sense that science should have definite answers.

Certainly Stoker's own account of the Bayou Pierre episode in *Personal Reminiscences* is far tamer than his fictional account. Although a "short and hurried conference between our train master and the local engineer" results in the decision to "'take the chances,'" (II, 280) the train on which the Lyceum Company is traveling goes slowly rather than racing across the bridge. Furthermore, they learn the following day that part of the bridge had collapsed: "Ours by the way was the last train that crossed the bayou till the flood was over. We heard next day that one section of the bridge close to the bank had gone down ten minutes after we had crossed" (II, 281). Stoker concludes this adventure by observing that the "only really bad result to us was that we arrived in Memphis too late to get anything to eat" (II, 281). The change in the story is evidence that, although the stories in *Snowbound* may be based on fact, Stoker also knew how to create an entertaining story as well.

The stories in *Snowbound* are relatively slight pieces, based as Belford suggests on the casual notes that Stoker kept "on the company's touring misfortunes" (191), but they nonetheless reveal Stoker's ambivalent attitudes to science and technology. Both the frame tale and "Mick the Devil" suggest the extent to which science and technology can be used to protect—even preserve— human life. Indeed *Snowbound* concludes with a glorious technological rescue:

Presently there was a loud knock at the side door of the saloon, and the door was dragged open, to the accompaniment of drifting snow and piercingly cold wind. Two railway men came in, shutting with difficulty the door behind them. One of them shouted out:
'It's a' richt! A snow-ploo wi' twa engines has been sent on frae Dundee. A rotary that has bored a road through the drifts. (159)

The conclusion reminds readers once more of the real danger with which the company had been faced and of the technological know-how necessary to bring about the rescue.

Looking at the frame tale and at "Mick the Devil" encourages me to argue that *Snowbound* presents technology as a positive force. On the other hand, "A Star Trap" provides a powerful reminder that both science and technology can also be used for evil purposes. Rather than being used either to gain understanding or to benefit human beings, a character in "A Star Trap" uses technology to wreak a grisly vengeance on the man who had cuckolded him.

"A Star Trap" is told by the Master Machinist and refers to a particular piece of stage equipment that Wightman's note explains:

A star trap is an opening in the stage which propels an actor upwards through the floor at great speed. Each segment is triangular, the points of the star meeting in the middle. The wedges are hinged to the circumference, which enables them to fly upwards as the body is catapulted through the trap. The wedges fall back in place so quickly that the audience cannot see what has happened, the actor materialising as if by magic. The star trap was so dangerous it was eventually banned. If the pieces of the star failed to open and close properly, a performer could jump short and be impaled around the waist. (138)

Indeed, the resolution to Stoker's story depends on the precise danger that Wightman mentions. Relating something that happened when he was a mere boy, apprenticed to John Haliday, the Master Machinist tells of a lovers' triangle involving his boss; Loo, Haliday's young and attractive wife; and Henry Mortimer, a handsome Harlequin.

The affair of Mortimer and Loo Haliday becomes a source of gossip for other members of the company though Haliday himself seems not to pay any attention to them. During a performance, however, the trap fails to open, and the results are horrifying, as the Master Machinist remembers:

The trap didn't work smooth, and open at once as the harlequin's head touched it. There was a shock and a tearing sound, and the pieces of the star seemed torn about, and some of them were thrown about the stage. And in the middle of them came the coloured and spangled figure that we knew. (140)

The apprentice does not suspect sabotage even when he discovers among the wreckage "a queer-looking piece of flat steel with some bent points on it" (141). Knowing that it was not part of the trap, the boy puts the piece into his pocket. Later, however, he awakes in the middle of the night with the certain knowledge that his boss had used his technological knowledge to murder his rival.

It was Mr Haliday who made that star and put it over the star trap where the points joined! That was what Jack Haliday was filing at when I saw him at his bench; and he had done it because Mortimer and his wife had been making love to each other. . . . Of course, the steel points had prevented the trap opening, and when Mortimer was driven up against it his neck was broken. (143–44)

Compounding the crime, the apprentice throws away the evidence. Because the police investigators, apparently less familiar with the technology of theatrical special effects, never suspect Haliday of foul play, Mortimer's death remains a mystery to everyone except for the technologically sophisticated.

"The Star Trap" is a chilling story of murder, revenge, and guile as well as a tale of the use one can make of technological expertise. Although frequently anthologized—perhaps because of its relative compactness—it is in my opinion a comparatively slight story. In the context of the present study, however, it does suggest that technology—perhaps science itself—is a neutral field that can be used for both fair means and foul. As disciplines, however, they are unlikely to usher in a new age because they will be used by human beings with the same kinds of agendas that human beings have always had. Thus Stoker suggests that, depending on the motivations of its practitioners, scientific knowledge can be used to preserve and enhance human life or to destroy it. The lesson communicated in Stoker's works continues to confront human beings at the dawning of the twenty-first century. Finding ourselves somewhat closer to understanding certain elements of the world in which we live, we are nonetheless also faced with seemingly unsolvable mysteries about climate, aging, and human—perhaps cosmic—evil.

## NOTES

1. My approach thus differs significantly from well-known science fiction author Brian W. Aldiss. In *Trillion Year Spree: The History of Science Fiction* (New York: Atheneum, 1986), Aldiss is adamant that Stoker's novel is "clearly not SF" (145). In fact, Aldiss explains his own theory that "Dracula is only metaphorically and euphemistically about vampirism. Its real subject is that obsession of the fin de

siècle, syphilis" (144). Aldiss's explanation is far too reductive, however, and cannot begin to explain the tremendous popularity of Stoker's novel.

  2. *Bram Stoker's Dracula Unearthed*, annotated and edited by Clive Leatherdale. Westcliff-on-Sea, Essex: Desert Island Books, 1998, 27. Future references will be to this edition and will be included parenthetically in the text.

  3. A number of people have commented on the technological modernity of *Dracula*. One of these is Geoffrey Winthrop-Young. "Undead Networks: Information Processing and Media Boundary Conflicts in *Dracula*," in *Literature and Science*, edited by Donald Bruce and Anthony Purdy, 107-129, Atlanta, GA: Rodopi, 1994. He notes:

The new electric world came to the public in the shape of new media. There are few other novels that acknowledge this arrival as promptly as *Dracula* with its array of post-print technologies such as telegraphs, phonographs, Kodak cameras and what must be one of the first cameo appearances of a telephone in a novel. (111)

In addition, Leatherdale's footnote on this passage reminds us of exactly how modern Harker's camera is:

In the 1880s George Eastman developed the roll film, which supplanted heavy plates and the need for professional photographers. Harker took pictures of Carfax himself. It is a pity that he did not bring his camera with him and try to snap Dracula. Stoker's notes say that photos of Dracula would come out black or like a skeleton. (59)

Stoker's own notes suggest that he was thinking about various modern technologies as he was working on the novel.

  4. I am indebted to Christopher Craft for coming up with this phrase, which is so much more efficient and elegant than referring to them as Dracula's opponents or Van Helsing's pupils. Craft explains his choice in a footnote to his essay ["Gender and Inversion in *Dracula*," in *Dracula: The Vampire and the Critics*, edited by Margaret L. Carter, pp. 167-194, Ann Arbor, MI: UMI Research Press, 1988.] Craft's footnote explains, "This group of crusaders includes Van Helsing himself, Dr. John Seward, Arthur Holmwood, Quincey Morris, and later Jonathan Harker; the title Crew of Light is mine, but I have taken my cue from Stoker: Lucy, *lux*, light" (190). I have taken the liberty with Craft's terminology to include Lucy and Renfield when they are trying to resist Dracula as well as Mina Harker.

  5. *The Harper Handbook to Literature*, edited by Northrop Frye, Sheridan Baker, George Perkins, and Barbara M. Perkins, 2nd Ed. New York: Longman, 1997, 224-25. C. Hugh Holman and William Harmon point to "a novel in which magic, mystery, and chivalry are the chief characteristics" in *A Handbook to Literature*, 6th Ed. New York: Macmillan, 1992, p. 217. Holman and Harmon add that the "term is today often applied to works, such as Daphne du Maurier's Rebecca that lack the Gothic setting or the medieval atmosphere but that attempt to create the same atmosphere of brooding and unknown terror" (218).

  6. Bette B. Roberts, "Gothic Fiction," in *Victorian Britain: An Encyclopedia*, edited by Sally Mitchell, p. 334, New York: Garland, 1988.

  7. Avril Horner and Sue Zlosnik. "Comic Gothic," in *A Companion to the Gothic*, edited by David Punter, pp. 242-54. Malden, MA: Blackwell Publishers Inc., 2000.

  8. That is, if Dracula is truly destroyed by the Crew of Light. Readers must consider that nowhere is the Kukri knife mentioned as an acceptable way to destroy a vampire. Despite the enthusiasm of the Crew of Light, is it possible that Dracula escaped? Indeed his escape is the basis for a series of novels by Fred Saberhagen. His escape is also suggested in the 1979 film *Dracula* (Universal, 1979), directed by John

Badham. In this film, Dracula (played by Frank Langella) appears to fly off into the distance while Lucy smiles enigmatically.

9. Leatherdale's footnote reminds readers that "typewriters were something of a novelty" in 1893. Further evidence of Stoker's interest in technological gadgetry is the fact that he himself used a typewriter.

10. This is a subject that has already been discussed at length in the following articles as well as others: Stephanie Demetrakopoulos, "Feminism, Sex Role Exchanges, and Other Subliminal Fantasies in Bram Stoker's *Dracula*." *Frontiers* (1977), 104-13; Gail B. Griffin, "'Your Girls That You All Love Are Mine': *Dracula* and the Victorian Male Sexual Imagination," *International Journal of Women's Studies* 3 (1980): 454-65; Carol A. Senf, "*Dracula*: Stoker's Response to the New Woman," *Victorian Studies* 26 (1982): 33-49.

11. Once again Leatherdale's footnote is useful. While the phonograph was invented by Edison in 1877, it was used "in clinical note-taking in 1890." Leatherdale cites an essay in *Science*, Vol. 15, January 17, 1890. Belford also notes that Stoker was himself familiar with the phonograph, having heard his friend Alfred Lord Tennyson read "The Charge of the Heavy Brigade" on a recorded cylinder (232). In *Personal Reminiscences*, Stoker relates the experience:

It was strange to hear the mechanical repetition whilst the sound of the real voice, which we had so lately heard, was still ringing in our hears. It was hard to believe that we were not listening to the poet once again. The poem of Scarlett's charge is one of special excellence for both phonographic recital and as an illustration of Tennyson's remarkable sense of time. One seems to hear the rhythmic thunder of the horses' hoofs as they ride to the attack. (I, 220)

It is interesting that Stoker, like Mina Harker, comments on the authentic sound of the early phonograph recording.

12. Teresa Mangum, "Growing Old: Age," in *A Companion to Victorian Literature and Culture*, 97-109.

13. Coppola has a compelling "take" on the vampire's use of technology, however, when he has Dracula walking through London streets in the daytime wearing dark glasses.

14. Franco Moretti, *Signs Taken for Wonders: Essays in the Sociology of Literary Forms*. London: New Left Books/Verso, 1983, 94-96.

15. Clive Leatherdale. *Dracula: The Novel and the Legend*, Wellingborough, Northamptonshire: The Aquarian Press, 1985, 131.

16. *A Glimpse of America: A Lecture Given at the London Institution, 29th December, 1885*. London: Sampson Low, Marston & Co., 1886, 14.

17. "Review of *Dracula*," *Athenaeum* 109 (June 26, 1897), 835.

18. "Review of *Dracula*," *Spectator* 79 (July 31, 1897), 150.

19. There are a few notable exceptions. Badham in *Dracula* (Universal, 1979) contrasts the automobile-driving Jonathan Harker with the carriage-driving Dracula. Coppola also focuses on the movement of trains and on the ghastly equipment with which Van Helsing performs his transfusions. By making Dracula a romantic figure, both side with the mysterious Dracula rather than with his scientific opponents.

20. Stephen D. Arata, "The Occidental Tourist: *Dracula* and the Anxiety of Reverse Colonization," *Victorian Studies* 33 (Summer 1990): 621–45; Troy Boone, "'He Is English and Therefore Adventurous': Politics, Decadence, and *Dracula*," *Studies in the Novel*, 25 (Spring 1993), 76–91; Ernest Fontana, "Lombroso's Criminal Man and Stoker's *Dracula*," *Victorian Newsletter* 42 (1972): 20–22; Regenia Gagnier, "Evolution and Information, or Eroticism and Everyday Life, in *Dracula* and Late Victorian Aestheticism," in *Sex and Death in Victorian Literature*, edited by Regina

Barreca. Bloomington: Indiana University Press, 1990, 140–157; John Greenway, "Seward's Folly: *Dracula* as a Critique of 'Normal Science'," *Stanford Literature Review* 3 (1986): 213–30; Rosemary Jann, "Saved by Science? The Mixed Messages of Stoker's *Dracula*," *Texas Studies in Literature and Language* 31 (Summer 1989): 273–87; and Jennifer Wicke, "Vampiric Typewriting: *Dracula* and Its Media," *ELH* 59 (1992), 467–493.

21. The first railway in Ireland, the Dublin and Kingstown Railway, opened to the public on December 17, 1834. However, construction in Ireland was slow compared to the veritable boom in railway construction in Ireland's neighbors, England, Scotland, and Wales (Mike's Railway History [accessed May 19, 2000] http://mikes.railhistory.railfan.net/r051.html).

22. This account appears in *Victorian Britain: An Encyclopedia*, edited by Sally Mitchell. pp. 663–65, New York: Garland, 1988.

23. Many details on *The Shoulder of Shasta* are taken from the recent edition of that novel annotated and introduced by Alan Johnson (Westcliff-on-Sea, Essex: Desert Island Books, 2000). In fact, Johnson notes that photographs "from the 1890s or shortly thereafter reveal that the scenic railroad journey was just as Bram Stoker describes it" (7). Future references will be to this edition and will be included within the text.

24. Johnson's note on Cody describes The Wild West Show, which began with a parade of native Americans, Mexican vaqueros, frontiersmen and cowboys, along with buffaloes and other animals. The show itself included demonstrations of marksmanship, riding, lassoing, Indian dancing, along with dramatizations of Indian attacks of a stagecoach or settler's cabin. He also mentions several notes from Cody to Stoker and suggests that Stoker met and admired the American entertainer (100).

25. Johnson cites Hyam, *Britain's Imperial Century, 1815–1914* 2nd ed. Latham MD: Barnes and Noble, 1993, 250–51.

26. Bram Stoker. "The Squaw," in *Midnight Tales*, edited by Peter Haining. London: Peter Owen, 1995. The material on publication history appears on page 86. Future references to this edition are included in the text.

27. Lillian Nayder, "Virgin Territory and the Iron Virgin: Engendering the Empire in Bram Stoker's 'The Squaw,'" in *Maternal Instincts: Visions of Motherhood and Sexuality in Britain, 1875–1925*, pp. 75–98, edited by Claudia Nelson and Ann Sumner Holme. London: MacMillan, 1997.

28. *Snowbound* is something of a bibliographical mystery as suggested by Richard Dalby's "Bibliographical Note" to the recent reprint: *Snowbound: The Record of a Theatrical Touring Party*, annotated and edited by Bruce Wightman (Westcliff-on-Sea, Essex: Desert Island Books, 2000). Dalby notes that the "verso of the title page gives two copyright dates of '1899' and '1908,'" a circumstance that implies that the stories had "been serialised in a magazine during 1899." However, Dalby notes there is "no evidence" for this (8). Assuming that 1899 is a legitimate date, however, would give weight to the assumption that Stoker wrote some or all of the stories while he was working on *Dracula*.). Wightman notes that "Mick the Devil" surely "owes its origins to floodwaters engulfing the touring company's train at Bayou Pierre, en route from New Orleans to Memphis in February 1896" (10). Future references will be to this edition and will be included in the text.

29. Moss examines some of these special effects in "Bram Stoker and the London Stage," *Journal of the Fantastic in the Arts* 10 (1999): 124–132.

30. Ray State, archivist for "Danger Ahead—Historic Railway Disasters" (http://danger-ahead.railfan.net/search.html), a site maintained by David Fry), responded to my query about possible sources for this incident (July 22, 2000) and noted that such behavior would have been rare at the time Stoker wrote. State

observed that the history of railroads in the United States is replete with examples of trestles that collapsed after being weakened by floodwater. One bridge, the Gayandotte Bridge in West Virginia on the C&O, collapsed in 1880, 1889, and 1913. In the 1913 case, the engineer had been warned that the bridge was unsafe. State also notes that the railroad company would have been more likely to discipline the engineer than to treat him as a hero. The public, on the other hand, might encourage an engineer to attempt a risky crossing. Such encouragement ceased, however, when 88 passengers died in "the Eden Colorado wreck" on August 7, 1904 "when the trestle collapsed under the locomotive" and took "the first three cars with it," a tragedy that caused the interest in "taking risks" to wane.

31. In all fairness to Professor Thomas, I am including the entirety of his response (July 11, 2000) to Patricia A. Johnston, the reference librarian whom I queried initially:

Trains on collapsing bridges?? I certainly do not know of a formula or law related to this. But I can give some common sense ideas.

If the bridge is collapsing then inevitably the road bed is distorting but this is probably happening slowly. Let us suppose that the train can still proceed if the road bed has depressed by a meter at the center of the bridge (assuming of course that the rails are not broken) and that the bridge is say 200 meters long and the train is say 200 meters long. If it takes say ten seconds for the collapse of one meter to occur at the center then the train will make it provided it goes 400 meters (the whole 200 meters of the train over the whole 200 meters of the bridge) in ten seconds. That would be a speed of 144 km/hr which is quite feasible (even for a good steam train). I would think this all to be a realistic scenario for a case where the foundations are being washed away.

The real/practical question here is whether the collapse occurs as slowly as 1 meter depression at the center in ten seconds. If the bridge was to be in free fall (as in the case of your army friends having blown up the supports) then the depression of 1 meter would occur in about 0.45 seconds and the train would need to go 400 meters in those 0.45 seconds which would be a speed of about 3600 km per hour which is about the speed of a Concord airliner at full throttle. Unrealistic.

If your contact just wanted to confirm a scenario for a novel then I think he/she could take the first scenario, assume collapse (to 1 meter depression -about 3 feet) occurred in 10 seconds then the train would get across at a speed of 140 km/hr (or a bit under 100 mph).

I suspect that there is some elegant way of looking at this to calculate the rate of collapse on the basis of strength of materials and elastic limits (breaking points). I am not smart enough to do this in a few minutes and suggest if you need a better answer you contact somebody who teaches the first statics course in ME.

32. Almost ready to give up in despair, I received the following message (July 13, 2000) from Patricia A. Johnston, who had discussed the question with David McGill, Professor, Civil and Environmental Engineering and Aerospace Engineering, "our campus dynamics expert (ME). He says that without more data (length of train, length of trestle, speed, weight etc.) there would be no way to say yay or nay."

# Chapter 2
## Stoker's Life: The Facts behind the Fiction in *The Duties of Clerks of Petty Sessions in Ireland, A Glimpse of America, Personal Reminiscences of Henry Irving,* and *Famous Impostors*

Although the present study is primarily interested in examining Stoker as a creator of fictional works that intertwine the Gothic emphasis on mystery with the hope that science and technology will be able to solve some of society's problems, it is entirely relevant to examine the known facts of his life, including his family, his education, his work, and his numerous works of nonfiction. Much of this material helps readers to understand the public persona that Stoker chose to present to the world.

As I suggested in the introduction, however, there is far more to Stoker than meets the eye. In fact, because many of the known pieces of his life seem not to fit together, Stoker has gained a reputation as an enigma among those who have studied his life and works. Leonard Wolf, for example, observes in *A Dream of Dracula*, one of the first critical studies to examine Stoker and his best-known work, that Stoker eludes him even though he had read "his biography and nearly all of his books" and could not find a man he "could clearly recognize or confidently describe. In Harry Ludlam's account of Stoker's life, the public facts are detailed, but the man himself remains shadowy." [1] Clive Leatherdale, who is perhaps even more familiar with Stoker and his works, agrees with Wolf about the difficulty of knowing Stoker. In *Dracula: The Novel and the Legend*, Leatherdale comments on the inscrutable Stoker:

Close acquaintance with Bram Stoker is regrettably not possible. His immortal creation lives on but the author remains elusive. Even with the arrival of a number of biographies, nothing but the basics of Stoker's life have been revealed. It is known what he did, but not who he was. (56)

Even Belford, who was able to take advantage of unpublished archival material in both England and the United States unknown to previous biographers, confesses that Stoker "took many secrets with him" (xv).

Though I am not a biographer and have not studied the archival materials, I found it necessary to revisit some of the material that has been covered before and to reexamine it in the context of everything that Stoker wrote. In particular, much of the commentary on Stoker attempts to psychoanalyze him, but I am more interested in considering how Stoker wrestled with the ideas of his day and how he translated his thoughts into literary works.

Focusing on the public man, the writer who wrote confidently about his experiences, this chapter looks at the decidedly unmysterious aspects of Stoker's life and establishes his positive attitudes regarding the rise of science and technology as well as his fascination with mysteries and with questions that could not be explained scientifically. There are numerous reasons for both his confidence in science and technology *and* for his continued interest in what is mysterious and overwhelming. Indeed, the experiences of his life could have caused him to look in both directions. As the business manager for Henry Irving's Lyceum Theatre, Stoker was a man of the world who rubbed shoulders with political figures, artists, and other public figures. It was a full and interesting life, and a number of his nonfiction works comment directly on the experiences that he ultimately turned into fiction. Moreover, like many other writers—perhaps most writers—Stoker wove aspects of his own character into the fictional characters that he created. Although it is dangerous to do so, it is extremely tempting to read Stoker by the characters that he created because the links are often so obvious.

## STOKER'S FAMILY INFLUENCES

Stoker's interest in both science and the Gothic may have been fostered by his family. Although his father was a civil servant rather than a scientist, the Stoker family included a number of physicians. In *The Un-dead*, Haining and Tremayne observe that his grandfather, William Stoker, writer of *Treatise on Fever* in 1815, was affiliated with the Dublin House of Recovery and later the Cork Street Fever Hospital in Dublin (42) and that his uncle Edward Alexander Stoker was a surgeon and one of the chief examiners at the Royal College of Surgeons, Ireland (47). Another uncle, William, who was affiliated with Dublin's Fever Hospital and House of Recovery, treated Bram during the first seven years of his life when he was an invalid. Although Stoker grew up to be a robust and athletic youth and adult, Belford speculates that Stoker might have been scarred by the treatment he received. Standard treatment at the time would have involved bleeding the child, either by opening the temporal artery or by applying leeches, a supposedly scientific procedure rendered horrifying.

Much of the biographical material on Stoker also suggests that it was during this period that the young Stoker gained his first experience of Gothic material through his mother's stories. [2] Daniel Farson, as Stoker's grandnephew, had access to a number of family stories, including one that his grandmother had related about Charlotte's experiences during the 1832 cholera epidemic: On "one of the last, desperate days, Charlotte saw a hand reaching through the skylight. Seizing an ax, she cut it off with one tremendous blow" (15). Farson questions whether the story could be true and whether Charlotte shared this and similar stories with her young son. Certainly it is difficult to document the exact nature of Charlotte's influence on Bram. It is clear, however, that Charlotte Stoker was one of the first people to recognize the Gothic power of *Dracula*. Haining and Tremayne quote from two letters that she sent to him after its publication. The first letter describes *Dracula* as "splendid, a thousand miles beyond anything you have written before" and as a work that "will place you very high in the writers of the day" (175). The second reveals Charlotte's own knowledge of the Gothic:

No book since Mrs Shelley's *Frankenstein* or indeed any other at all has come near yours in originality, or terror—Poe is nowhere. I have read much but I never met a book like it at all. In its terrible excitement it should make a widespread reputation and much money for you. (175)

The letter suggests that Charlotte remained close to Bram and may have continued to influence her adult son. Thinking back to Stoker's early childhood, however, tempts me to examine scenes in which various characters lie helpless at the hands of a more powerful being as well as to contemplate Stoker's treatment of scientific and medical professionals. The truth may be much less romantic, however, for Stoker may simply have been aware of the Gothic conventions that emphasize the protagonist's fear and helplessness. His own adult commentary suggests that he was rarely afraid and also that he was unlikely to remain passive in the face of adversity though he definitely remembered his childhood weakness: "I was a very strong man. It is true that I had known weakness. In my babyhood I used, I understand, to be often at the point of death. Certainly till I was about seven years old I never knew what it was to stand upright" (I, 31). Though there may be a certain amount of posturing here, the emphasis here is on obstacles overcome rather than on overwhelming fears.

Interest in medicine continued in Bram's generation as well, with three of his four brothers (Thornley, Richard, and George) and a brother-in-law (Margaret's husband, William Thomson) choosing medicine as a career. Thornley joined the City of Dublin Hospital as a surgeon, served as president of the Royal College of Surgeons in Ireland, and was knighted for his services to medicine in 1895. Richard was affiliated with the Royal College of Surgeons, Ireland, and the King's and Queen's College of Physicians, Ireland. He later joined the Indian Army as a surgeon and retired in 1897. George served as a surgeon with the Turkish army and later as Chef de L'Ambulance du Croissant Rouge, the Turkish version of the Red Cross, during the Russo-Turkish war of 1876-1878, and Bram supposedly helped him prepare his memoir of the war, *With 'The Unspeakables', or Two Years Campaigning in European and Asiatic Turkey*, which was published in Dublin in 1878 just before Bram left Ireland for good. George later settled in London near Bram. A specialist in diseases of the throat, he also served as director of The Oxygen Home and published a book on the use of oxygen to treat wounds. George also served as consulting physician to the Lyceum and as the Honorary Medical Officer of the actors benevolent fund. Margaret's husband William Thomson also achieved honors for his work in medicine, being knighted in 1897. Haining and Tremayne speculate that Thomson's research might have appealed to Bram, especially "those on the workings of the arteries and blood supply! Among other works, Thomson edited the third edition of *Power's Surgical Anatomy of the Arteries* (1881)" (94).

## EDUCATION AND TRINITY COLLEGE

Unlike his grandfather, uncle, and brothers, Bram Stoker was apparently more interested in theoretical science, for he graduated from Trinity College, Dublin, in 1871 during a period when Trinity was expanding its offerings in scientific fields. In *Trinity College Dublin: The First 400 Years*, J.V. Luce describes the curriculum in science at Trinity during the mid-nineteenth century:

Up to 1855 foundation scholarships were awarded only in classics, but from then on students also could compete in 'science', defined as philosophy, mathematics and physics. In 1858, the scope of the moderatorship in experimental physics (instituted in 1849) was widened to include some geology, palaeontology, botany, and zoology. The name of the moderatorship was altered to experimental and natural sciences, and, by a natural progression, separate moderatorships in each branch were instituted in 1871. [3]

According to the history of Trinity prepared by R.B. McDowell and D.A. Webb, these separate moderatorships included Experimental Science (Physics, Chemistry, and Mineralogy) and Natural Science (Zoology, Comparative Anatomy, Botany, and Geology). [4] McDowell and Webb also describe the 1860s, the very period when stoker was enrolled at Trinity, as "years of rapid advance in almost all departments of natural science" and thus an "exciting time to be involved in the sciences" (273). Even if Stoker did not graduate with a degree in science, he would have been aware of these developments. As the present study demonstrates, Stoker frequently wove his appreciation for science and technology into literature. There are surprisingly few references to mathematics, with the exception of the early "How 7 Went Mad," which was included in *Under the Sunset*, and an extremely grim Gothic tale, "The Judge's House," that combines mathematics with Gothic terror. In this story, a young Cambridge mathematician is plagued by rats as he tries to study. At the end of the story, one giant rat transforms into the former tenant of the house, a hanging judge, who uses the bell-pull to hang the unfortunate mathematician.

Ever since I started to consider the strange combination of science/technology and the Gothic in so much of what Stoker wrote, I've wondered about both his education and his subsequent choice of occupation. Given his obvious enthusiasm for both literature and technology, why didn't he pursue an education in one of them? One answer may stem from the curriculum at Trinity. During Stoker's years at Trinity, modern languages and literature were still considered extras rather than essential fields of study. Once again, McDowell and Webb provide useful historical information about Trinity during Stoker's tenure there:

It was in 1870, nearly a century after the establishment of the Professorships of modern languages, that the first move was made to introduce these subjects into academic courses instead of maintaining them as 'fancy' embellishments which could be studied on an extracurricular basis by those who had a taste for such things. In January of that year Ingram [John Kells] proposed that the comprehensive . . . Moderatorship in History, Jurisprudence, Economics and English Literature should be broken up. . . . he Board accepted . . . and English Literature was detached from the complex and set up as one half of a new Moderatorship in Modern Literature, of which the other half could consist of either French or German. (271)

If Trinity was expanding its offerings in languages, it was also offering more in the way of professional training. However, though McDowell and Webb note that the number of students enrolled in both medicine and engineering increased dramatically during this period, engineering was still considered something of a second class degree:

It was set up . . . 'with a view of combining, as far as is practicable, the theoretical and practical instruction necessary for the Profession of Civil Engineering, and of imparting to the members of that Profession the other advantages of academical education. With these objects in view it has been deemed advisable that a Student preparing for the Profession of Civil Engineering should be a member of the College and subject to its general discipline.' The students of the new school, however, were to be in the College, but in a sense not of it. In 1841 the idea of conferring a degree in anything but arts or one of the old-established faculties was unheard of, and in any case the course as originally planned was of only two years' duration. Students of engineering were, therefore, to work for a diploma, and their position was to be something like that of the medical students who were working for a diploma but not a degree. . . . After two years' experience it was agreed that two years was insufficient to provide the professional training required, and the course was lengthened to three. (182)

Luce is more positive about engineering, though one can understand why Stoker's professional family might have discouraged him from pursuing a career in it:

In thus recognising engineering as an academic discipline, Trinity followed hard on the heels of Durham, Glasgow and London, and is the proud possessor of one of the oldest Engineering Schools in the world.

In the first two decades of its existence, students . . . read for a diploma and not a degree, degrees in Engineering being as yet unheard of. But . . . the Board was keen to integrate them as much as possible into academic life, and stipulated that they must matriculate and pass the Junior Freshman [equivalent to the U.S. freshman] year in Arts, with its strong emphasis on mathematics. Being members of the College, most of them decided to continue with Arts along with their professional studies, emerging in due course with a BA, as well as their engineering diploma. (88)

Reading W.E. Coe's study, *The Engineering Industry of the North of Ireland*, provides an additional reason for its second-class status during this period, one based on class relationships rather than academic policy:

The upper classes in Ireland were . . . contemptuous of trade and industry; at the end of the eighteenth century, according to Arthur Young, the country gentlemen 'might be poor until doomsday but they were too proud to enter trade or manufacture, and Trinity College, Dublin, swarmed with lads who ought to be educated to the loom or the counting house'. Even in 1896 the Recess Committee felt that to the middle and upper classes in Ireland there were still only three professions—the law, medicine, and the church. In Belfast it was recognised by the middle of the nineteenth century that 'men were wanted in the more lucrative and perhaps equally learned employments concerned with the working of iron, the management of railways and kindred businesses' for which the town tended to import labour; in the foundries 'the best situations were frequently held by Scotch and English people'. Up to 1900, however, little progress was made in evolving formal courses to supplement practical training on the job. [5]

Though he apparently hoped not to follow in the footsteps of his ancestors, Stoker may not have felt a strong enough commitment to science to enter a field that was still so closely identified with trade.

Equally important, Stoker remained committed to literature and the arts as well as to physical development. His own memories of his college days include remarkably little about either science or mathematics:

When I was in my twentieth year I was Athletic Champion of Dublin University. . . . In my College days I had been Auditor of the Historical Society—a post which corresponds to the Presidency of the Union in Oxford or Cambridge—and had got medals, or certificates, for History, Composition and Oratory. I had been President of the Philosophical Society; had got Honours [6] in pure Mathematics. I had won numerous silver cups for races of various kinds. I had played foryears in the University football team, where I had received the honour of a "cap!" In fact I feel justified in saying I represented in my own person something of that aim of university education *mens sana in corpore sano*. (I, 32)

Luce's only mention of Stoker is as an athlete:

A Trinity man later recorded his memory of cycling and long distance walking (races of four and seven miles) as leading features of the Races [an annual event], mentioning the 'exceptionally tall' undergraduate Bram Stoker, the future author of *Dracula*, as an outstanding champion in the walking events [N.J.D. White, *Some Recollections of Trinity College, Dublin*, 8]. (108)

A kind of Renaissance man, Stoker was evidently interested in a number of seemingly disparate fields, and Alison Milbank, in "'Powers Old and New': Stoker's Alliances with Anglo-Irish Gothic" comments on this diversity. [7] She observes that his career at Trinity is "noteworthy in two ways relevant to his future writing career." He achieved "the unique honour of holding top positions in both the rival Historical and Philosophical Societies," an achievement that demonstrates the "inclination to unite groups of men that would characterize his fiction to the extent . . . of mediating between Catholic and Protestant conceptions of Christianity in *Dracula*" (12). Despite (or perhaps because of) his diverse interests, Bram left Trinity with no clear sense of direction.

That lack of direction is a trait that he incorporates into many of his male characters. Arthur Severn (*The Snake's Pass*), Archie Hunter (*The Mystery of the Sea*), Harold An Wolf (*The Man*), and Rupert St. Leger (*The Lady of the Shroud*) share Stoker's lack of clear professional direction and are finally fortunate to be pulled by circumstances into one vocation or another just as Stoker was fortunate to be drawn into Henry Irving's circle. Unlike the others, Harold leaves England only when he has been rebuffed by the woman he loves and almost immediately makes a fortune in the Alaskan gold fields. Another character who shares Stoker's diverse interests though not his lack of direction is, of course, Dracula's chief foe, Abraham Van Helsing. Van Helsing, who shares Stoker's name, hair coloring, and physiognomy,  is a veritable Renaissance man with advanced degrees in a variety of fields, including law, philosophy, literature, and medicine.

Furthermore, many of Stoker's heroes share his physical strength and athletic ability, often using their physical prowess to rescue those weaker than themselves. In fact, Stoker received a bronze medal from the Royal Humane Society for rescuing an attempted suicide. Rafe Otwell (the hero of *Miss Betty*), Archie Hunter, and Harold An Wolf all rescue people from drowning. His heroic characters are all more fortunate in their rescues than was Stoker himself. The man he attempted to rescue subsequently died.

## PROFESSIONAL LIFE

Apparently for lack of anything better, Stoker decided to join his father in the Anglo-Irish civil service at Dublin Castle. His brief references to that period in *Personal Reminiscences of Henry Irving* reveal a certain ambivalence about the work. For example, he observes that his father's fifty years of loyal service to four monarchs—George III, George IV, William IV, and Victoria—had produced very little in the way of financial rewards and adds that his own prospects were no better: "In those days, as now the home Civil Service was not a very money-making business, and it was just as well that he preferred the pit. I believed then that I preferred it also; for I too was then in the Civil Service!" (I, 20). Unlike his father, though, Bram manages to turn his love of the theater into a vocation:

I asked the proprietor of one of the Dublin newspapers . . . to allow  me to write on the subject in the *Mail*. He told me frankly that the paper could not afford to pay for such special work, as it was in accordance with the local custom of the time done by the regular staff who wrote on all subjects as required. I replied that I would gladly do it without fee or reward. This he allowed me to carry out. (I, 13)

At the same time Stoker continued to submit short stories to various periodicals as well as to write "a dry-as-dust book on *The Duties of Clerks of Petty Sessions*." [8]

Although the experiences may not have been entirely absorbing, he confesses that they did allow him to work on the craft of writing:

In those five years I think I learned a good deal. As Bacon says, "Writing maketh an exact man," and as I have always held that in matters critical the critic's personal honour is involved in every word he writes I could always feel that the duty I had undertaken was a grave one. I did not shirk work in any way; indeed, I helped largely to effect a needed reform as to the time when criticism should appear. In those days of single printings from slow presses "copy" had to be handed in very early. The paper went to press not long after midnight, and there were few men who could see a play and write the criticism in time for the morning's issue. It thus happened that the critical article was usually a full day behind its time. (I, 13)

Although he spent thirteen years as a civil servant, Stoker reveals his lack of enthusiasm for the field by the speed with which he abandons it when Irving offers him employment:

He asked me if I would give up the Civil Service and join him; I to take charge of his business as Acting Manager. I accepted at once. I had then had some thirteen years in the public service, a term entitling me to pension in case of retirement from ill-health (as distinguished from "gratuity" which is the rule for shorter period of service); but I was content to throw in my lot with his. In the morning I sent in my resignation. (I, 60–61)

Indeed Stoker credits his employer with giving him the opportunity to get to London, where he could gain exposure as a writer:

I may here give an instance of his thoughtful kindness. Since our first meeting the year before, he had known of my wish to get to London where as a writer I should have a larger scope and better chance of success than at home. (I, 44)

Ironically, much of that writing was handling Irving's voluminous correspondence:

I had taken over all the correspondence and the letters were endless. It was the beginning of a vast experience of correspondence, for from that on till the day of his death I seldom wrote, in working times, less than fifty letters a day. (I, 61–62)

For the next twenty-seven years, until Irving's death in 1905, Bram served his employer and was able to concentrate full attention on his writing only during his brief vacations.

Given the conditions of his employment, it is remarkable to think that he managed to produce eleven books during this period: *Under the Sunset* (1882), *A Glimpse of America* (1886), *The Snake's Pass* (1889), *The Watter's Mou'* (1894), *The Shoulder of Shasta* (1895), *Dracula* (1897), *Miss Betty* (1898), *Snowbound: The Record of a Theatrical Touring Party* (1899), *The Mystery of the Sea* (1902), *The Jewel of Seven Stars* (1903), and *The Man* (1905). It would have been an impressive achievement for someone who was able to write full-time. On the other hand, his experiences with Irving gave him the opportunity to rub shoulders with the leading people of his day. and to combine his love of literature with his practical training in mathematics. Although Stoker was able to pass on his enthusiasm for mathematics to his son Noel, who became a chartered accountant, he did not manage to pass on his enthusiasm for Henry Irving. Christened Irving Noel Thornley Stoker, he dropped his first name when he grew up because he resented Irving's impact on his father's life. Farson observes that Noel's "will stated that he was 'commonly called Noel Thornley'. 'He seemed to dislike Irving,' says his daughter, 'both the man and name. He thought that Irving had worn Bram out'" (215–16).

### PERSONAL REMINISCENCES OF HENRY IRVING

Stoker was a notably private person, but his two-volume book on Irving, *Personal Reminiscences of Henry Irving*, does provide readers with a few insights into the public Stoker as well as a few details about some of the material that he would ultimately weave into what he wrote. Whereas there is evidence of his interest in both science and technology as well as in other topical subjects, including the British desire to conquer the globe, *Personal Reminiscences* includes no information on Stoker's use of Gothic materials.

The desire for privacy that continues to cause problems for students of his works was undoubtedly a desirable characteristic in an employee:

Thus I can say that all through Irving's management from the time of my joining him in 1878 till the time of my handing over such matters as were in my care to his executors—by their own desire, after his will had been found, and before his funeral—no one, except Irving himself, myself, and the chartered accountants (who made audit and whose profession is one sworn to individual secrecy) knew Irving's affairs. (II, 306)

*Personal Reminiscences* suggests that Stoker did not always agree with his employer about financial management or even about certain social issues, including Home Rule for Ireland. However, Stoker clearly prided himself on being circumspect.

As a reader who is interested primarily in his attitudes to science and technology, I hoped to gain information on these subjects from reading *Personal Reminiscences*. Many of his novels reveal a definite interest in scientific issues, as do a number of his short, nonfiction pieces. Because *Personal Reminiscences* is largely about Irving's attitudes and beliefs, it does not provide much information on Stoker. On the other hand, several episodes are suggestive. One, included in the previous chapter, expresses Stoker's enthusiasm about the use of electricity to produce special effects in the theater. Of course, theatrical magic presents science that is definitely under the control of human beings, safe science. Personally aware of what happened when the science involved in stage magic did not work, Stoker frequently comments on the dangers of fire in the theatrical profession throughout *Personal Reminiscences*. The most important of those fires was the destruction of the Lyceum Storage, a disaster that resulted in the demise of the Lyceum Company and may have hastened Irving's death. Though Stoker writes passionately about this fire in *Personal Reminiscences*, there is little evidence that it influenced Stoker's other works, however.

Several other episodes reveal his interest in applied science. Because Stoker was responsible for getting the members of the Lyceum Touring Company and their property to various locations in Britain and the United States by rail or ship, he was greatly concerned with speedy and efficient rail transportation, a trait shared by his character Jonathan Harker. The previous chapter explores Stoker's enthusiasm for travel by rail. A short story in *Snowbound* even points fun at a character who, like Stoker, is obsessed with efficiency. "A Lesson in Pets" warns about what happens when members of the company bring too many pets on tour. Told by the company's manager, the story includes a darkly comic denouement when the manager brings along his "pets," a crate of boa constrictors. "Mick the Devil" is a suspense tale of a flood and a train going over a bridge. In addition, in *The Man*, the narrator describes the advantages of this relatively new means of transportation: "Thirty miles is not a great distance for railway travel; but it is a long drive. The days had not come, nor were they ever likely to come, for the making of a railway between the two places" (27). *The Man* is interesting, however, because it is one of the few Stoker works to hint at the dangers of technology, for the narrator notes that Harold's mother had been killed in a railway accident.

Stoker is equally enthusiastic about efficient travel by ship, and he comments on one particularly memorable trip:

Irving was across the Atlantic eighteen times. . . . There were many times when there was bad weather; but on one crossing in 1899 we encountered a terrific storm. The waves were greater by far than any I had ever seen when I crossed in the *Germanic* in the February of the same year during the week of the worst weather ever recorded. . . . As we went on the seas got bigger and bigger till at last they were mountainous. When we were down in the trough the waves seemed to stand up higher than our masts. The wind was blowing furiously something like a hundred miles an hour, but there was no rain. (II, 289)

Stoker never admits to being frightened by rough waters, and many novels—including *The Mystery of the Sea*, *Lady Athlyne*, and *The Man*—have scenes that take place on board ship. Harold An Wolf, in *The Man*, participates in two rescues, one of the drowning Pearl, the second of an entire ship full of people. Stoker's description of the ride bears the ring of someone who had personal experience of such rough seas:

After some days the fine weather changed; howling winds and growing seas were the environment. The great ship, which usually rested even-keeled on two waves, and whose bilge keels under normal conditions rendered rolling impossible, began to pitch and roll like a leviathan at play. At times the screws would race dangerously when the whole stern would stick out starkly as some great wave fell away below her. So persistent did this racing become that often the engines would have to be slowed down, and now and again stopped altogether; then the great ship would roll drunkenly in the trough of mountainous waves. Much damage was done to the ship and to the machinery. The decks, swept by gigantic seas, were injured wherever was anything to injure. Bulwarks were torn away as though they had been compact of paper. More than once the double doors at the head of the companion stairs had been driven in. . . . Nearly all the boats had been wrecked, broken or torn from their cranes as the great ship rolled heavily in the trough, or giant waves had struck her till she quivered like a frightened horse. (356)

This description of his discomfort as well as some of his anecdotes in *Personal Reminiscences* about travel reveal why he would have been so enthusiastic about improved rail and ocean transportation. In addition to knowing firsthand the advantages of more sophisticated oceanic travel, Stoker was also enthusiastic about smaller sailing vessels. *Personal Reminiscences* praises Sir William Pearce, one of Irving's close friends and "head of the great Glasgow shipbuilding firm of John Elder & Co."

To him it is that we owe the great speed of ocean-going ships. For years all the great racers were built at his works on the Clyde. He also built many superb yachts, notably the *Lady Torfrida* and the *Lady Torfrida the Second*. (II, 43)

Such praise is honest because Stoker knew firsthand the dangers of sailing on less sophisticated vessels. *Personal Reminiscences* relates a hair-raising experience in which he and other members of the Lyceum Company travel on a small boat to the *Lady Torfrida*, which was berthed in the estuary of the Clyde off Greenock:

By this time matters were getting really serious. Some one had to keep baling all the time, and on the weather side we had to sit shoulder to shoulder as close as we could so that the waves might break on our backs and not over the gunwale. It was just about as unpleasant an experience as one could have. I drew the lad [Ellen Terry's son] next to me as close as I could partly to comfort him and more particularly lest he should get frightened. . . . Ellen Terry with the strong motherhood in her all awake . . . was making cheery remarks and pointing out to her boy the many natural beauties with which we were surrounded. . . . The place seemed to become beautiful in the glow of her maternity. (II, 45–46)

The passage suggests that much of Stoker's enthusiasm for manly men and womanly women, in addition to his enthusiasm for technological developments, comes from his own personal experience.

Another experience reveals that Stoker's interest in naval battles, evident in *The Mystery of the Sea* and *The Lady of the Shroud*, comes from an adventure that he and Irving had in August 1880. Tired of the adulation of people who recognized Irving, they rented a boat from a very deaf sailor. Because they had been followed by fans, they thought very little about the fact that the people who followed them were "gesticulating and calling out."

We could not distinguish what they said; but we were both so accustomed to hear people shouting at Irving that we took it that the present was but another instance of clamorous goodwill.

We had got away from shore about half a mile when suddenly there was a terrific sound close to us, and the boat was thrown about just as a rat is shaken by a dog. A column of water rose some thirty yards from us and for quite half a minute the sea round us seemed to boil. (II, 266–67)

It turns out that the boat had sailed right into the middle of military maneuvers, "an attack on Fort Monckton—the low-lying fort which guards the mouth of the harbour of Portsmouth—by the *Glatton*, then the most up-to-date of our *scientifically equipped ships*. We appeared to have come right over the mine-bed" (II, 268, emphasis added). Realizing their mistake, they decide to sit back and watch the remainder of the maneuvers as well as the mock attack later that night:

I think, however, that we both enjoyed the attack more that night when the actual sham battle was fought. In those days search-lights were new and rare. Both the *Glatton* and Fort Monckton were well equipped with them, and during the attack the whole sea and sky and shore were perpetually swept with the powerful rays. It was in its way a noble fight, and as then most people were ignorant of the practical working of *the new scientific appliances of war*, it was instructive as well as fascinating. We, who had been out in the middle of it during the day, could perhaps appreciate its possibilities better than ordinary civil folk unused to the forces and horrors of war! (II, 269, emphasis added)

Stoker, who had no military training, is able to translate this experience as well as his brother George's wartime experiences into adventure literature. Here, however, one can observe his enthusiasm for "the new scientific appliances of war," an enthusiasm that will appear in both *The Mystery of the Sea* and *The Lady of the Shroud*.

Indeed, Stoker was fortunate to have experiences that he could translate easily into literature, but he also apparently spent a great deal of time doing research to make certain that his details were accurate. A number of scholars have documented Stoker's sources for *Dracula*, [9] but his own commentary in his own words about the research that went into *A Glimpse of America*, a comparatively slight work, suggests that he was equally scrupulous about his other works as well:

And there was no standard source from which an absolutely ignorant stranger could draw information. I found some difficulty then in buying a copy of an act of Congress so that I might study its form; and it was many months before I could get a copy of the Sessional Orders of Congress. However, before we left at the conclusion of our second visit I had accumulated a lot of books—histories, works on the constitution, statistics, census, school books, books of etiquette for a number of years back, Congressional reports on various subjects—in fact all the means of reference and of more elaborate study. When I had studied sufficiently—having all through the tour consulted all sorts of persons—professors, statesmen, bankers, &c.—I wrote a lecture, which I gave at the Birkbeck Institution in 1885 and elsewhere. This I published as a pamphlet in 1886, as *A Glimpse of America*. (I, 368)

In fact, the normally modest Stoker takes obvious pride in the fact that the explorer Henry Morton Stanley had praised this work for its accuracy:

I met . . . Dr. Parke, who had been with Stanley on his journey *Through the Dark Continent*. . . . He told me that it was one of the very few books that Stanley had brought with him in his perilous journey across Africa, and that he had told him that it "had in it more information about America than any other book that had ever been written." (I, 368–69)

Moreover, *Personal Reminiscences* is full of praise for other people, including Irving, who are scrupulous about their research.

Evidence of Stoker's willingness to perform thorough research is certainly evident in much of what he wrote. (A later section of this chapter will pay particular attention to the research that went into another of his nonfiction works, *Famous Impostors*.) Stoker undoubtedly gained significant exposure to the ideas of his own day simply by rubbing shoulders with many of the leading people of his day, a privilege that he gained because of his relationship with Irving:

The ordinary hospitalities of the Beefsteak Room were simply endless. A list of the names of those who have supped with Irving there would alone fill chapters of this book. They were of all kinds and degrees. The whole social scale has been represented from the Prince to the humblest of commoners. Statesmen, travellers, explorers, ambassadors, foreign princes and potentates, poets, novelists, historians—writers of every style, shade and quality. Representatives of all the learned professions; of all the official worlds; of all the great industries. Sportsmen, landlords, agriculturists. Men and women of leisure and fashion. Scientists, thinkers, inventors, philanthropists, divines. Egotists, ranging from harmless esteemers of their own worthiness to the very ranks of Nihilism. Philosophers. Artists of all kinds. In very truth the list was endless and kaleidoscopic. (I, 311–12)

And *Personal Reminiscences* strives to do some justice to this diversity:

The "First Night" gatherings on the stage of the Lyceum after the play became almost historic; the list of the guests would form an index to those of note of the time. . . . Occasionally, when opportunity permitted and memory served, I jotted down—often on my copy of the menu—the names of some of my fellow guests; and as I usually kept these interesting souvenirs, I am able to give a somewhat suggestive list. (I, 314–15)

Stoker follows this comment with twelve full pages, double columns of names, along with full chapters providing portraits of these people and their ideas. It is clear that Stoker watched them closely and listened to them carefully; and his brief portraits provide valuable insights to many of the important people of his day along with personal anecdotes about them. *Personal Reminiscences* provides little in the way of evaluation. For evidence of Stoker's own views, one must consult his other works.

Although Stoker was himself in poor health in the seven years remaining to him after the death of Henry Irving,[10] he continued to write: *Personal Reminiscences of Henry Irving* (1906), *Lady Athlyne* (1908), *The Lady of the Shroud* (1909), *Famous Impostors*,(1910), and *The Lair of the White Worm* (1911). Subsequent chapters will look at much of the fiction. The remainder of this chapter concentrates on Stoker's works that can be classified as nonfiction.

## A GLIMPSE OF AMERICA

Before moving to Stoker's later works, however, it is appropriate to take a brief aside to look at one early work, *A Glimpse of America*. Like so much of what Stoker wrote, it remains difficult to find and therefore relatively unknown. Because Stoker so frequently features American characters in his works (Quincey Morris in *Dracula*; Grizzly Dick in *The Shoulder of Shasta*; Marjory Anita Drake in *The Mystery of the Sea*, the American industrialist and his family in *The Man*; and the wealthy Ogilvies in *Lady Athlyne*), sets one novel (*The Shoulder of Shasta*) entirely in the United States, and obviously thinks about the political implications of the United States as a world power, it may be useful to understand his thoughts on the United States.

The book leads up to a grand finale in which Stoker expresses great "joy that England's first-born child has arrived at so noble a stature" (47). Indeed he comments on the advantages of close political alliance:

We have not, all the world through, so strong an ally, so close a friend. America has got over her childhood. The day of petty jealousy has gone by. . . . Our history is their history—our fame is their pride—their progress is our glory. They are bound to us, and we to them, by every tie of love and sympathy. . . . We are bound each to each by the instinct of a common race, which makes brotherhood and the love of brothers a natural law. (47–48)

Stoker suggests that the English have a great deal to learn from the United States.

In terms of the present study, however, it is especially appropriate to take note of Stoker's observations about science:

Not only is there throughout the United States a general educational effort, but, here and there, a tendency is manifested to achieve a high grade in special knowledge. For instance, the Massachusetts Institute of Technology is a very perfect high school of scientific effort. (28)

Praising the United States for its scientific training, Stoker also observes that education helps to break down the barriers between classes:[11]

The natural bridge between social and political life is education; and before we enter upon the latter domain it is well to understand the high place which education holds as a public need. . . . Suitable provision is made in nearly every State for public education. (26)

If access to education manages to obliterate class differences, technology also helps to conceal differences of origin:

A traveller, going through the country . . . by railways, steamboats, stages, and road-cars, could not possibly distinguish classes as at home, except when they are of very marked difference, or, of course, in the case of tramps, and other excretions of civilization. (14)

Because Stoker will address the issue of homelessness again, one might gather from this fact and from his treatment of other parasitic characters that he was bothered both by people who lived on society's margins and by people who were unwilling or unable to contribute to their society. *A Glimpse of America* continues:

The tramp is, in America, a class by himself, tolerated simply for the time. In the vast population . . . there is, of course, a percentage of incurable drones; their number is not many, but they form a dangerous element, since they have no home, and are without the responsibilities which regulate in some degree their fellows; consequently, they are at times treated with ruthless severity, when, for instance, some outrage has been committed, particularly when a woman has been the victim. . . . In some communities, tramps are warned off, and threatened with being "shot on sight," a summary process of the social law not holding a place in our code. (14–15)

It is interesting to note also that the tramp, like Dracula, is separated from the technology that Stoker so admires. He waxes positively effusive about American accomplishments and notes that "everywhere the constructive work is admirably done. The work of the stonemasons is really sound and good, and the plumbing is of the best" (18).

As is appropriate for someone who realized the dangers of fire, he is also fascinated with the efficiency of American fire brigades and fire stations:

It is almost incredible till one sees it done; but commonly, seven seconds after the gong has sounded the fire-escape is at full gallop in the street. The time sometimes is diminished so low as four seconds. Just fancy the value of every second when life is at stake. The men, and even the horses, seem to understand and act. (20)

One wonders how Stoker would have regarded American fire brigades in the years following the destruction of the Lyceum property.

Despite his enthusiasm, Stoker is aware that the United States is not without problems of its own:

We Londoners have opportunities of witnessing, in our daily life, the whole scheme of human existence. We have points of contact with as high a civilization as the earth affords; and also, I fear, with here and there, as complete a system of savagery as distinguished those aborigines who won a place in history by resting on the outside of Captain Cook. (5)

Here, as elsewhere in his writings, Stoker seems to associate civilization with scientific and technological progress, savagery with primitive people. The United States, it seems, had reached the summit of technological achievement and was, therefore, an appropriate model for the rest of the world.

## THE WORLD'S WORK (1907)

Stoker will continue to infuse everything he wrote with enthusiasm for scientific and technological developments. In 1907, he wrote two articles for a special Irish edition of *The World's Work* that reinforce the enthusiasm that readers often discern in his fictional works. "The Great White Fair in Dublin" focuses on the fair as a symbol of Irish pride in its present development from agriculture to industry. Indeed, while noting that Ireland is primarily an agricultural country, Stoker also points directly to the "wonderful things" that are being done to "start the island upon a new career of industrial progress" (571). Commenting specifically on the exhibits, he notes that the displays are "organised and arranged for the display of the direct and indirect results of learning, science and art, and illustrative of *that progress which follows in their wake*" (574, emphasis added). In fact, his description of the various displays directs the reader to the power that he associated with science and technology:

The 'Palace of Industries' . . . is mainly technical. The 'Palace of Mechanical Arts' is an immense building. . . . At the eastern end of it are power-producing appliances of different kinds . . . great engines and dynamos for producing the lighting of the Exhibition. The other sections of this great building are those of machinery in motion, engineering, and transportation. (575)

Though the article includes relatively little in the way of detail, Stoker's enthusiasm for the modern technical marvels that he sees is quite evident.

The second article, "The World's Greatest Shipbuilding Yard," takes Stoker's readers from Dublin to the more industrialized North of Ireland. Though Harland and Wolff was known for its technological innovations in shipbuilding, Stoker is more interested in "the magnitude, stability, and prosperity" that he witnesses in Harland and Wolff's shipbuilding yards (647), a focus appropriate for someone who spent his days making certain that the Lyceum operated smoothly. Nonetheless, as Coe explains in his history of engineering in Northern Ireland, Harland and Wolff was known for technological developments that resulted in record-breaking speeds *and* drastic reductions in fuel consumption as well as in more comfortable first-class accommodations:

The ship was the first of the modern type of ocean liner. Though it was claimed that T.H. Ismay of the White Star Line suggested moving the first-class accommodation amidships, there is no doubt that the revolutionary design as a whole was the product of the ingenuity of Harland & Wolff. The Queen's Island shipyard made the White Star Line, just as the White Star ships firmly established the reputation of Harland & Wolff as shipbuilders . . . until the market declined in the early 1960s, through the capture by the airlines of a substantial proportion of the passenger traffic across the oceans. (82)

"The World's Greatest Shipbuilding Yard" traces the transformation of raw materials to finished product; and Stoker, whose own work required strong managerial skills, waxes euphoric on the "omnipresent evidence of genius and forethought; of experience and skill; or organisation complete and triumphant" (650). Even more important, he observes that all this technological expertise is being used to benefit the human condition. The essay concludes with Stoker's celebration of human ingenuity: "As there are twelve thousand people employed . . . the payment of these varying accounts within *ten* minutes instances the perfection of business organisation, which can hardly be exemplified in a better or more fitting manner" (650).

Indirectly then, both articles in *The World's Work* present science and technology as means of relieving the poverty that Stoker elsewhere (for example, *The Snake's Pass*) associates with his native land. Just as he had Dick Sutherland in *The Snake's Pass* use science, technology, and Arthur Severn's capital to provide employment for the rural population, so these essays reveal the power of science and technology to produce progress in Ireland.

### "THE AMERICAN 'TRAMP' QUESTION" (1909)

Stoker, who had commented on tramps in *A Glimpse of America* returns to that topic in an article that he wrote for the *North American Review* in 1909. Titled "The American 'Tramp' Question and the Old English Vagrancy Laws," the essay reveals Stoker's willingness to perform detailed research, his impatience with those who were reluctant to work, and his confidence in scientific solutions. [12] The article opens by admitting the universality of the problem: "No age or country has been able to solve it satisfactorily, for the idle of each age and nation more or less adapt themselves to surrounding conditions"

(605). Stoker, who only two years earlier, had described the opportunities available to people who want to work, then proceeds to give a detailed history of the laws regarding vagrancy from the Middle Ages to his present.

Having examined the history of the problem, Stoker goes on to observe that tramps are a dangerous subgroup that threatens the well-being of the entire community:

But till this day those who will not work are practically regarded as a more or less dangerous class. Indeed, the passing of the "habitual criminals" Act has a common basis. When certain persons—or classes of persons—are manifestly dangerous to more peaceful and better-ordered classes of communities it is the essence of good government—indeed, a necessary duty to responsible officials—to keep them in restraint, or certainly under observation. In both civil and rural communities they are dangerous; in America as in England; to-day as well as in the time of "Good Queen Bess." In cities they are practically rogues; in the country vagabonds and sturdy beggars, whose presence is attended with fear if not with danger. (611–612)

Although the last sentence does suggest that the threat may be more perceived than actual, the essay as a whole provides valuable insights into Stoker's treatment of parasitic characters, including Dracula and Murdock, the villain in *The Snake's Pass*. Murdock dies unmourned by anyone, and Dracula is destroyed by a group that regards him as a threat to their well-being.

Although *Dracula* and *The Snake's Pass* are fiction and thus not necessarily political commentary, this article explains that political solutions are rapidly becoming a necessity: "The time is fast coming when something must be done regarding the wilfully-idle class. Already in Germany if they refuse to work they must starve" (613). Written at the same time as the utopian *The Lady of the Shroud*, a novel that celebrates hard work and a nation in which all the inhabitants are positively enthusiastic about work, "The American 'Tramp' Question" concludes that no punishment of parasites is too harsh. Indeed, Stoker, ever the cheerleader for technological solutions, here indicates that science can be used to monitor those whose decision not to work makes them a danger to their community:

As ear-marking with a "hot yron" be treatment of a drastic quality not acceptable to a less rude age, surely the resources of science are equal to some method of personal marking of an indelible quality. This step achieved, all idle persons, wandering and obviously undesirable to any ordinary intelligence, might in the first instance be arrested and tested as to the existence of modern ear-marking. If unable to show license or to account for themselves in any reasonable way they might be sent to a Labor Colony set far away in the heart of some fastness, there to be detained for a sufficient time to learn to be industrious in some form, and to have their physique brought by degrees up to the standard requisite for such work. It could be made apparent that there was no spirit of unkindness in such precautionary, and ultimately benevolent, doing. (614)

The solution is certainly more humane than the cited German plan of letting vagrants starve if they refuse to work. In fact, Stoker suggests that tramps might be trained to perform useful work.

Although a short piece, "The American 'Tramp' Question and the Old English Vagrancy Laws" is consistent with both Stoker's life and his longer works. It is almost a cliché to observe that his heroic protagonists are invariably hard working, as was Stoker himself. Because *The Man* is a romance that includes relatively few references to science or technology, it is not a major part of this study. *The Man* does include two characters (Harold An Wolf, the main male character, and Andrew Stonehouse, an ironmaster and contractor, as well as the father of the child whom Harold rescues) who reveal what hardworking individuals could achieve within a relatively short period. Here Harold uses work as an anodyne to emotional pain:

From daylight to dark labour never ceased; and for his own part he never wished that it should. In the wilderness, and especially under such conditions as held in Northern Alaska, labour is not merely mechanical. Every hour of the day is fraught with danger in some new form, and the head has to play its part in the strife against nature. In such a life there is not much time for thinking; certainly for brooding, which is thinking unduly of the past. (345)

Harold also puts his knowledge of science to good use in the American wilderness:

Game was plentiful, and he never seemed to want. The store of flora and fauna which he preserved grew largely. His geological specimens multiplied, and he began to feel that he was on the trail of fortune. Everywhere he went there were traces of gold, as though by some instinct he was tracking it to its home. (350)

As a result of his knowledge and his willingness to work hard, Harold amasses an enormous fortune in the gold fields within a relatively short period:

In the early days when everything had to be organised and protected Harold worked like a giant, and with a system and energy which from the very first established him as a master. But when the second year of his exile was coming to a close, and when Robinson City was teeming with life and commerce, when banks and police and soldiers made life and property comparatively safe, he began to be restless again. This was not the life to which he had set himself. He had gone into the wilderness to be away from cities and from men; and here a city had sprung up around him and men claimed him as their chief. (352)

While Harold is probably Stoker's hardest worker, even characters like Arthur Severn and Rupert St. Leger who inherit vast fortunes continue to work rather than rest on their investments.

Of course, Stoker also came from a family that prided itself on hard work. As mentioned earlier, his father retired after working fifty years for the Irish Civil Service. His mother, an ardent social reformer, worked hard within her own family and also worked to provide for those less fortunate. As a visitor to the Dublin Workhouse, she talked to destitute women and came up with a plan that sounds remarkably like what her son later advocated, training in basic skills and meaningful work. Finally, if no work was available locally, she advocated emigration:

In new countries there is a dignity in labour, and a self-supporting woman is alike respected and respectable. Why should the door of hope be closed on those poor women, and why refuse them the means of attaining that independence in other countries which they are debarred from in this? (cited by Belford, p. 27)

Although Charlotte Stoker's plan does not rely specifically on science, it is otherwise remarkably similar to her son's plan.

## FAMOUS IMPOSTORS (1910)

The last full-length non-fiction work that Stoker wrote is *Famous Impostors* (1910).[13] A collection of short reflections on various "impersonators, pretenders, swindlers, and humbugs of all kinds" (v), *Famous Impostors* is interesting for the light it sheds on other Stoker works. It is not especially interesting in its own right. Even though Stoker's preface promises to use the same strategies he would use as a novelist, he seems torn between the desire to tell the truth and the desire to entertain: "The author, nevertheless, whose largest experience has lain in the field of fiction, has aimed at dealing with his material as with the material for a novel, except that all the facts given are real and authentic" (v). I found myself disappointed that he was such a scrupulous adherent to truth.

If *Famous Impostors* is hardly a page turner, it provides insights on the various subjects that interested Stoker. It should come as no surprise that the man who created such notorious villains as Black Murdock, Dracula, and Lady Arabella was equally interested in cruel historical figures, among them England's Richard III, who "literally carved his way to the throne of England. It would hardly be an exaggeration to say that he waded to it through blood" (3). A second is Stefan Mali (Stephen the Little) who passed himself off in Montenegro as Czar Peter III of Russia. Although scholars continue to debate how much Stoker actually knew about the historical figure who was known as Vlad the Impaler, it is evident from Stoker's description in *Famous Impostors* that Stefan was very much like the original Vlad, for "early in his reign [he] had men shot for theft" (33).

Moreover, *Famous Impostors* centers on the subject of crime. Stoker notes in the preface that "the subject of imposture is always an interesting one" (v), and it goes without saying that much of what Stoker describes as imposture could be prosecuted as fraud. Continuing in the vein that he had learned from Lombroso and other early scientific criminologists, Stoker looks at criminals as weak individuals:

The true or natural criminal is essentially an opportunist. The intention of crime, even if it be only a desire to follow the line of least resistance, is a permanent factor in such lives, but the direction, the mechanism, and the scope of the crime are largely the result of the possibilities which open and develop themselves from a fore-ordered condition of things. (37)

The views held here approximate those held by nineteenth-century social scientists and reveal the extent to which Stoker was influenced by both contemporary science and by traditional moral views. Fearing always that the things he valued, including truth and human resolution, might be undermined by negative forces, Stoker openly presents the inherent weakness of most criminals.

Another crossover from his fictional world in *Impostors* is Stoker's interest in the Balkans, an area on which he had touched in both *Dracula* and *The Lady of the Shroud* as well as an area that would have been in the news during the period when Stoker was researching *Famous Impostors*. He comments on the man who ruled Montenegro at the time that Stefan Mali was posing as Peter III, Vladika Sava. What is interesting about Sava is his resemblance to Stoker's fictional Peter Vissarion who, in *The Lady of the Shroud*, abdicates his power over the Land of the Blue Mountains in favor of his more militarist son-in-law, Rupert St. Leger:

At the time Montenegro was ruled by Vladika Sava, who having spent some twenty years in monastic life, was unfitted for the government of a turbulent nation always harassed by the Turks and always engaged in a struggle for bare existence. (32)

In fact, Stoker comments on the warlike character of the Montenegrins who are "naturally so brave that cowardice is unknown amongst them" (34).

Stoker's interest in gender is also evident in *Famous Impostors*. Though he touches occasionally on men, such as the Chevalier D'Eon, who impersonate women, he is more interested in women who impersonate men. In most cases he argues that earlier historical periods had offered fewer opportunities to women:

It is not to be wondered at that such attempts are made; or that they were made more often formerly when social advancement had not enlarged the scope of work available for women. The legal and economic disabilities of the gentler sex stood then so fixedly in the way of working opportunity that women desirous of making an honest livelihood took desperate chances to achieve their object. (227)

Thus Stoker's treatment of gender is consistent with his generally Liberal belief in a progress brought about by science and rationality.

Believing that the scientific and technological civilizations of the United States and Western Europe are superior to all other civilizations, he also occasionally digs at other cultures. For example, writing of someone who had impersonated Sebastian, King of Portugal, he observes that  all the Latin races are "naturally superstitious" (24), an observation that he had made earlier of Don Bernardino in *The Mystery of the Sea*, a character who is explored further in Chapter 4.

Because *Famous Impostors* is primarily concerned with well-documented examples of imposture, Stoker's references to subjects that are usually considered Gothic are rare. Nonetheless, Stoker includes an entire section on witchcraft in which he once again is careful to note that witchcraft is the mistaken belief of an earlier stage of civilization, caused by "the superstitions of society which attributed powers of evil to innocent persons whose subsequent mock-trials and butchery made a public holiday for their so-called judges" (vi–vii). In fact, Stoker is careful to point out the cruelty associated with such superstitious beliefs. Stoker explains the human interest in a final Gothic topic, the legend of the Wandering Jew, "in a belief in the possibility of human longevity beyond what is natural and normal" (107). He indicates there is no scientific reason for such belief, though, and therefore suggests that belief in Gothic mystery comes from a primitive world.

On the other hand, if *Famous Impostors* rarely touches on Stoker's interest in the Gothic, it is full of Stoker's thoughts about science. Because of its subject matter, *Famous Impostors* generally focuses on fraudulent science, but Stoker also touches on genuine science or, in the case of Mesmer, a mixture of the two:

Although Frederic-Antoine Mesmer made an astonishing discovery which, having been tested and employed in therapeutics for a century, is accepted as a contribution to science, he is included in the list of impostors because, however sound his theory was, he used it in the manner or surrounded with the atmosphere of imposture. (95)

Stoker's interest in the scientific application of Mesmer's ideas had already appeared in *Dracula*, and he would incorporate his interest in Mesmer as a charlatan in his final novel, *The Lair of the White Worm*, as well. In fact, Stoker's final novel reinforces the same difference between magic and science that he notes here in *Famous Impostors*:

We of a later age, when electric force has been satisfactorily harnessed and when magnetism as a separate power is better understood, may find it hard to understand that the most advanced and daring scientists of the time—to whom Frederic-Antoine Mesmer was at least allied—were satisfied that magnetism and electricity were variants of the same mysterious force or power. (98)

Once again, Stoker focuses on the greater understanding brought about by a scientific inquiry that downplays mysterious elements.

In fact, Stoker associates the scientific desire for truth with a man who, in his own lifetime, had been accused of being a charlatan, Paracelsus, "a great and fearless scholar, as earnest as he was honest, as open-minded as he was great-hearted" (71). Indeed Stoker praises Paracelsus for having the "intellectual attitude . . . of a true scientist—denying nothing *prima facie* but investigating all" (73) and observes that he could have accomplished far greater things in a more scientific age:

Is it any wonder that when in this age after centuries of progress such absurd things are current Paracelsus is shewn in contemporary and later portraits with a jewel in his hand transcribed Azoth—the name given to his familiar daemon.

Those who repeat ad nauseam the absurd stories of his alchemy generally omit to mention his genuine discoveries and to tell of the wide scope of his teaching. That he used mercury and opium for healing purposes at a time when they were condemned; that he did all he could to stop the practice of administering the vile electuaries of the mediaeval pharmacopoeia; that he was one of the first to use laudanum; that he perpetually held—to his own detriment—that medical science should not be secret; that he blamed strongly the fashion of his time of accounting for natural phenomena by the intervention of spirits or occult forces; that he deprecated astrology; that he insisted on the proper investigation of the properties of drugs and that they should be used more simply and in smaller doses" (78)

Stoker concludes his tribute to Paracelsus by describing him as "an original investigator of open mind, of great ability and application, and absolutely fearless. He was centuries ahead of his time" (79).

One of the last sections of the odd compilation of anecdotes that Stoker titled *Famous Impostors* is a section on hoaxes. Though most of the stories here resemble April Fool or Halloween pranks, his discussion of "the famous Moon Hoax which was published in the pages of the New York *Sun* in 1835" (262) touches on the relationship between good science and good fiction. Stoker explains that the Moon Hoax "purported to be an account of the great astronomical discoveries of Sir John Herschel at the Cape of Good Hope, through the medium of a mighty telescope, a single lens of which weighed nearly seven tons" (262) and goes on to provide the details that made the hoax so believable:

There were hills of amethysts 'of a diluted claret colour'; mountains fringed with virgin gold; herds of brown quadrupeds resembling diminutive bison fitted with a sort of 'hairy veil' to protect their eyes from the extremes of light and darkness; strange monsters—a combination of unicorn and goat; pelicans, cranes, strange amphibious creatures, and a remarkable biped beaver. The last was said to resemble the beaver of the earth excepting that it had no tail and walked only upon its two feet. It carried its young in its arms like a human-being, and its huts were constructed better and higher than those of many savage tribes; and, from the smoke, there was no doubt it was acquainted with the use of fire. (263)

Although the Great Moon Hoax was an interesting story, Stoker concludes by noting that scientists must be interested in truth:

Whatever may have been his object, the work, as a hit, was unrivalled. For months the press of America and Europe teemed with the subject; the account was printed and published in many languages and superbly illustrated. But, finally, Sir John Herschel's signed denial gave the mad story its quietus. (265)

As a man who had spent the last five years writing for a living, Stoker obviously enjoyed a good story. However, as a man who knew and appreciated science, Stoker ultimately chose truth. According to Stoker, that truth would ultimately be responsible for bringing about a better world: "Back in the century that has elapsed historical research has been more scientifically organised and the field from which conclusions can be drawn has been enlarged as well as explored" (182). In fact, most of *Famous Impostors* offers readers the standard Liberal view that science was responsible for the progress that was enjoyed by Stoker's contemporaries.

Despite Stoker's celebration of science and his general belief that science would produce a better world, two brief passages in *Famous Impostors* suggest that Stoker continued to have some reservations about science. He notes at one point that "medical science has always been suspicious of, and cautious regarding, empiricism" (100) and thus seems to agree with *Dracula*'s Dr. Van Helsing that science may have serious limits.

In addition, Stoker suggests at another point that some matters are beyond the reach of scientific inquiry:

In an age more clear-seeing than our own and less selfish we shall not think so poorly of primitive emotions as we are present apt to. On the contrary we shall begin to understand that in times when primitivity holds sway, we are most in touch with the loftiest things we are capable of understanding, and our judgment, being complex, is most exact. (150)

This passage seems to celebrate a realm on which Stoker had touched in *Dracula*, *The Jewel of Seven Stars*, and *The Lady of the Shroud*, a realm that is not precisely Gothic but that is somehow beyond the scientific and rational world of the late nineteenth and early twentieth centuries. At least it seems to run counter to Stoker's usual enthusiasm about the benefits provided by scientific inquiry. These reservations about the direction that science was taking are most in evidence in *The Jewel of Seven Stars*, which is addressed in the next chapter.

## NOTES

1. Leonard Wolf, *A Dream of Dracula*. Boston: Little, Brown, 1972, 248.
2. Leatherdale, Ludlam, and Belford all observe that Charlotte had told her son about Irish folktales as well as about her experiences with the cholera epidemic in Sligo in 1832. Haining and Tremayne also suggest that Charlotte was responsible for her son's awareness of his Irish roots.
3. J.V. Luce, *Trinity College Dublin: The First 400 Years*. Dublin: Trinity College Dublin Press, 1992, 103. Because Americans are unlikely to be familiar with the term moderator, Luce defines it as a "candidate successful in the BA degree examination at honors level. He/she is said to have obtained a 'moderatorship'. This latter term is also applied to the various special course leading to the award" (228).
4. R.B. McDowell and D.A. Webb, *Trinity College Dublin 1592–1952: An Academic History*. Cambridge: Cambridge University Press, 1982, 273.
5. W.E. Coe, *The Engineering Industry of the North of Ireland*. Newton Abbot, Devon: David & Charles, 1969, 203–4.
6. Luce defines honors as follows:

Specialist undergraduate course and examinations at a higher level than the ordinary (pass) course were first instituted under Provost Lloyd in the early 1830s, and grew into the system that is now the norm. The College still retains the Latinate designation for them, in preference to 'honour'. (228)

7. Milbank's essay can be found in *Bram Stoker: History, Psychoanalysis and the Gothic*, edited by William Hughes and Andrew Smith. New York: St. Martin's, 1998, 12–28.
8. *Personal Reminiscences*, I, 32. Despite Stoker's disparaging comments, Ludlam observes that the "248-page volume did in fact come to be regarded in the civil service as a standard reference book" (63).
9. Tracking down the source materials for *Dracula* has become a veritable cottage industry. Among some of the more complete studies are the following: William Hughes, *Beyond Dracula: Bram Stoker's Fiction and its Cultural Context* (New York: St. Martin's, 2000); Clive Leatherdale, *The Origins of Dracula: The Background to Bram Stoker's Gothic Masterpiece* (Westcliff-on-Sea, Essex: Desert Island Books, 1987); and Elizabeth Miller, *Dracula: Sense and Nonsense* (Westcliff-on-Sea, Essex: Desert Island Books, 2000). Finally, Leslie Shepard, "The Library of Bram Stoker/ A Note on the Death Certificate of Bram Stoker," in Bram Stoker's dracula: Sucking through the Century, 1897–1997, edited by Carol Margaret Davison. Toronto: Dundurn Press, 1997), reports on the books that were in Stoker's library when it was sold after his death.

10. There has been a great deal of commentary on Stoker's health, including the speculation of his grandnephew and biographer, Daniel Farson, that he was suffering the ravages of tertiary syphilis and Belford's equally adamant claim that he was not. Despite this disagreement, practically all commentators agree that he did suffer at least two strokes during this period and that his health was extremely fragile at the end of his life.

11. Stoker's thoughts on class would provide material for another study. It is enough to note here that Stoker frequently uses marriage as a tool to join members of different classes and economic stations. In *Dracula,* however, Jonathan Harker overcomes relatively obscure origins by becoming the heir of his employer.

12. "The American 'Tramp' Question and the Old English Vagrancy Laws," *North American Review* 190 (1909), 605–14.

13. *Famous Impostors*, printed in the United States 1911. All references are to this edition and are included parenthetically in the text.

# Chapter 3
# Reservations about Science, Popular Egyptology, and the Power of the Natural World in *The Jewel of Seven Stars*

The first chapter in this study examines how Stoker confronted Jonathan Harker, a representative nineteenth-century Englishman, with a world that differs significantly from the seemingly rational and technologically advanced England that he ordinarily inhabited. Confident in his own abilities and in the strengths of his modern technological culture, Harker travels to Dracula's castle, located in a region where "every known superstition in the world is gathered" (30). The rest of *Dracula* pits Harker and a group of other modern Europeans against a being who is the physical and psychological embodiment of the dark and mysterious past of which he is suspicious, a creature who is both Renaissance warlord and a far more primal destroyer of human beings.[1] In a battle that only one side could win, the representatives of modernity, including scientists, lawyers, and technocrats, use the tools of nineteenth-century science and technology to destroy the forces of the primitive past. Though the conclusion to *Dracula* is not as simple as it has sometimes been made out to be, Stoker nonetheless seems to suggest that science and technology are positive forces that can overcome the mysterious evils associated with the past.

Stoker continued to be haunted by those mysterious Gothic powers that he embodies in *Dracula*: the mysterious powers associated with past periods; monstrous human beings, the source of whose evil is difficult to explain; and blurring of boundaries. However, the next novels that he wrote cannot be characterized as Gothic, for they include almost no events that might be characterized as supernatural, and they also seem to emphasize the rational powers of the modern world. Most importantly, they present the world as more or less comprehensible rather than as a place of great mystery. *Miss Betty*, published the year after *Dracula*, takes place during the first years of the eighteenth century but addresses issues of gender and nationalism that were almost as relevant to Stoker and his contemporaries as science and technology. *The Mystery of the Sea* (1902), which is set in Stoker's present, continues to brood over the power of the past and, like *Dracula*, suggests that those who understand science and technology are most capable of handling the social and political problems of the day. In fact, most of Stoker's fiction seems to exude confidence that science and technology can correct the problems of the past and provide for a more comfortable future.

With *The Jewel of Seven Stars*, which he published six years after *Dracula*, Stoker returns to the conflict between the modern technological age and the power of the mysterious past. *Jewel*, however, is a very different kind of novel. Not only are the forces generally associated with the Gothic presented as being much more powerful, but they are also presented as overwhelming. The result is that the forces of the present are absolutely annihilated by Queen Tera, whose mummy is resurrected by a small group of scientists and Egyptologists. Unlike *Dracula*, which concludes with the representatives of the modern community complacently celebrating their conquest, *Jewel* seems to end with the annihilation of these modern characters. [2] Malcolm Ross, the sole survivor, wraps up the novel after the deaths of his companions concludes by suggesting that no hope remains:

I did what I could for my companions; but there was nothing that could avail. There, in that lonely house, far away from aid of man, naught could avail.

It was merciful that I was spared the pain of hoping. [3]

Even more frightening, perhaps, is the sense that an incomplete knowledge of science makes the scientists willing accomplices in their own destruction.

One of the few critics to address the place of science in *The Jewel of Seven Stars* is Robert Edwards, [4] whose ideas on the limitations of science are very similar to those that I plan to present in this chapter. Edwards even observes that "the scientific apparatus of the present is powerless" and that, as in Dracula, the "past and present are . . . in perpetual competition." Dracula successfully blends "Whig and scientific historical narratives and methodology . . . to defeat the authentic, genealogical aspect of the past." In *Jewel*, however, "initial, uncomprehending hostility to the authentic forces of the past is overcome for a while." Edwards observes that the plan is to synthesize "all these elements—Whig, scientific and genealogical—into an overarching, transcendent and all-explaining 'meta-narrative' in which all contradictions and opposition will finally be resolved." However, the reappearance of the uncanny demonstrates the impossibility of achieving such a goal. "The ultimate synthesis does not and cannot come to pass" (112). Not only is there no synthesis, there is absolutely nothing at the end of *The Jewel of Seven Stars* but the promise of absolute annihilation. Indeed, William Hughes notes in *Beyond Dracula* that *Jewel* is uncharacteristically bleak for Stoker: "The 1903 conclusion, in which all but Ross die, is pervaded by a hopelessness unique in Stoker's published fiction" (36). Also characterizing the bleak first ending as "untypical of Stoker, who customarily tidies things up," Leatherdale refers to the ambiguities of the 1903 conclusion:

The fate of Tera, Margaret and the men is capable of multiple interpretation. In particular, there is no mention of Silvio. Some critics have suggested that apocalyptic endings were unfashionable in the first years of this century. Either way, the open-endedness of Stoker's conclusion made it easy to change for later editions. (250)

Though Leatherdale's observation that apocalyptic endings were unfashionable makes a certain amount of sense, it is also possible that Stoker's publishers encouraged him to write happy endings. For example, Hughes, who characterizes the original ending as bleak, refers to another less-than-happy conclusion, the unpublished first draft of *Miss Betty, Seven Golden Buttons* (81). In this ending the hero dies on his quest rather than return to marry the heroine, and she learns of his reformed character when she is an old woman only through a galley slave whose freedom he had purchased. In the published version of *Miss Betty*, the hero returns to England and marries the heroine.

Although both Ludlam and Farson refer to the change in *Jewel*, neither provides specific information on the reasons behind the change. Thus, we can only wonder whether Stoker decided to alter the ending or whether his publisher encouraged him to modify it. The change in the conclusion also required him to eliminate Chapter 16, "Powers—Old and New," the chapter in which Ross expresses most of his concerns about science. (For years, most reprints continued to print the sanitized "happy" ending in which Ross marries Margaret). Thanks to several recent editions of *Jewel* (Oxford University Press and The Dracula Library) that include both conclusions, it is now possible to examine the differences in the two conclusions.

Even without the apocalyptic conclusion, however, *The Jewel of Seven Stars* is consistently more ambivalent about the mysterious powers that are generally labeled Gothic and less optimistic about the power of modern science. In fact, Ross, a character who in many ways resembles Jonathan Harker, muses throughout the novel about the continued power of the past. Unlike characters who are confident about the ability of modern science to control and manipulate the past, he is the only character to survive Tera's destructive powers.

The remainder of this chapter examines the mysterious powers that Stoker associates with the past and the hope of his scientific characters that they can understand and channel those powers. In particular, it explores Stoker's awareness of some of the scientific and cultural developments that were taking place around the turn of the century (including developments in biology, paleontology, and archeology), his fascination with technology, and his apprehensions about various primitive forces, including certain powers that he associated with people of color and women.

*The Jewel of Seven Stars* includes four characters who might be considered scientists: the archeologists Eugene Corbeck and Abel Trelawny, and the physicians Doctor Winchester and Sir James Frere. Corbeck, Trelawny, and Winchester are present throughout the novel, but Frere is called in only briefly as a consultant. Frere refuses to work on the case unless Margaret is willing to provide a more controlled, scientific environment in which to work:

Doctor Winchester informs me that you are not yourself free in the matter, but are bound by an instruction given by your Father in case just such a condition of things should arise. I would strongly advise that the patient be removed to another room; or, as an alternative, that those mummies and all such things should be removed from his chamber. Why, it's enough to put any man into an abnormal condition, to have such an assemblage of horrors round him, and to breathe the atmosphere which they exhale. (66–67)

When Margaret refuses to meet his conditions, Frere disappears from the work, and Leatherdale observes that Stoker's brother (frere) had also been knighted and that Frere might be Stoker's tribute to his older brother (p. 65, note 14). That Frere is not as foolish as the other supposed scientists might be an additional tribute to his brother. One doubts that the careful Frere would have followed so blindly in the attempt to resurrect the mummy of Queen Tera.

Dr. Winchester, the Trelawny family physician, is described as a young man. His extreme youth and lack of experience provides reasons that Margaret feels compelled to call in a more experienced physician, someone who has devoted himself to "this branch of science" and who would have "more knowledge and experience" in these matters (63). Youth and lack of experience also explain why Winchester becomes such a "yes man" as the novel progresses. In fact, while he initially suspects Margaret of the attack on her father, he has stopped questioning anything by the end of the novel. Thus he is available at the conclusion to help the Trelawnys move from the London home to Cornwall where the Great Experiment takes place. He is also one of the companions (along with Margaret, Trelawny, and Corbeck) that Ross finds at the end "sunk down on the floor . . . gazing upward with fixed eyes of unspeakable terror" (250). Had he been more willing to apply the scientific method to the Great Experiment, he might have survived.

Eugene Corbeck, much like Van Helsing, is an expert in a number of fields. Describing himself as a "Master of Arts and Doctor of Laws and Master of Surgery of Cambridge; Doctor of Letters of Oxford; Doctor of Science and Doctor of Languages of London University; Doctor of Philosophy of Berlin; Doctor of Oriental Languages of Paris," he adds that he has "some other degrees, honorary and otherwise" (88–89). A veritable encyclopedia of esoteric information on hieroglyphics as well as the history of both ancient and modern Egypt, Corbeck reveals Stoker's knowledge of Egyptology, an interest he might have picked up from his personal acquaintance with either Sir William Wilde or Sir Richard Burton. Wilde had toured Egypt in 1838 and had brought a mummy back to Ireland with him, and Burton had found prehistoric stone implements in Egypt as John David Worthham explains in *The Genesis of British Egyptology 1549–1906.* [5] Best known today for translating the *Arabian Nights* and for exploring Central Africa and traveling to Mecca, Burton was known to his contemporaries for his archeological work in Egypt. Like the British geologist A.J. Jukes Browne, Burton knew of John Lubbock's discovery of prehistoric remains, and he began to search for others at Giza. After finding prehistoric flint objects and acquiring others from archeologists that he met in Egypt, he published "a description of them and a defense of Lubbock's earlier discoveries" in 1879 (91). Stoker's fascination with Burton is evident in *Personal Reminiscences.*

Despite Corbeck's academic qualifications, however, he seems to be at Trelawny's beck and call when he returns to England after spending several years seeking the lamps that had been stolen from Queen Tera's tomb. During Trelawny's trance, Corbeck is important for filling Ross and the reader in on background information, including the tomb of Queen Tera. Like Dr. Winchester, however, he fails to question Trelawny's plan to aid in Tera's resurrection even though, unlike the physician, he is personally aware of Tera's potential power. Indeed having visited her tomb on two occasions, he had witnessed the devious serdab, which had been designed to kill potential tomb robbers:

With a loud click, a metal figure seemed to dart from close to the opening of the serdab; the stone slowly swung back to its place, and shut with a click. The glimpse which I had of the descending figure appalled me for the moment. It was like that grim guardian which according to the Arabian historian Ibn Abd Alhokin, the builder of the Pyramids, King Saurid Ibn Salhouk placed in the Western Pyramid to defend its treasure: "A marble figure, upright, with lance in hand; with on his head a serpent wreathed. When any approached, the serpent would bite him on one side, and twining about his throat and killing him, would return again to his place." (151)

Because of his experience with various Egyptian tombs, Corbeck was able to avoid the grisly fate of that earlier tomb robber though he is ultimately unable to avoid an equally grisly fate at the hands of Queen Tera. After describing his adventures in Egypt and revealing his knowledge of the power of the ancient world, Corbeck falls into silence. Though present to assist in the packing and present at the Great Experiment, he has not learned enough from his previous experiences to urge caution.

Careful to demonstrate that most of his so-called scientific characters have undergone thorough academic training, Stoker provides practically no information on Trelawny's professional background. In fact, the extreme differences in Corbeck and his employer reveals that Stoker was probably aware of the fact that not all archeologists had the kind of specific scientific training that he gives to Corbeck. Worthham suggests the wide variety of people who were interested in Egypt. Worthham notes that eighteenth-century visitors to Egypt made detailed descriptions of "all the ancient structures along the Nile" and even described ruins "that lay some distance from the Nile in the desert" and explored "the Egyptian remains in the delta on the north and in Nubia and the Sudan on the far south." During the same period, travelers also became interested in "making copies of hieroglyphic inscriptions and of the paintings that they found on the sides of obelisks and on the walls of temples and tombs." Although their efforts to transcribe this material were rarely accurate, it nonetheless revealed a growing awareness of the "potential importance of such activities" (35–36). Thus Worthham suggests a growing professionalism among archeologists.

William Chapman observes, however, that most nineteenth-century archeologists were amateurs rather than professionals in "Toward an Institutional History of Archaeology: British Archaeologists and Allied Interests in the 1860s." [6] Chapman observes that throughout the mid-Victorian period there was no concept of professionalism as we now understand it. British archaeologists of that time were technically amateurs. Some, including John Lubbock and John Evans, were wealthy businessmen. Others were landed gentry or, like William Greenwell, country clergymen (p. 160).

Stoker too might be considered an amateur Egyptologist if one were to judge from his library. Indeed Hughes mentions that Stoker's private library (which was sold at Sotheby's on July 7, 1913) included a number of books on Egypt:

Budge's *Egyptian Ideas of the Future Life* (1900); *Egyptian Magic* (1899); *Easy Lessons in Egyptian Hieroglyphics* (1899–1902); *The Mummy* (1893); *The Book of the Dead: The Papyrus of Ani in the British Museum* (1895); A History of Egypt . . . (9 vols. 1902) as well as 'Flinders Petrie's 1895 *Egyptian Tales Translated from the Papyri* (British Library: SC Sotheby 7/7/1913). (186)

Hughes reinforces the amateur nature of Stoker's Egyptology by noting that Stoker "may have read John Greaves's *Pyramidographia* of 1752— the only work on ancient Egypt cited by title in *The Jewel of Seven Stars*—at the British Museum," but that the major influence on the novel is that of Dr. E.A. Wallis Budge, "Keeper of Egyptian and Assyrian Antiquities at the British Museum as well as the "author of several popular though scholarly works on Egypt" (38).

For all its moments of technical accuracy, *The Jewel of Seven Stars* expresses a *popular* Egyptology, that of the travel narrative and the non-academic journal. Egypt in the novel is typified by the spectacle of death rather than the drudgery of life, its focal points being the tomb and the mummy rather than the potsherd. (38)

It is possible that Stoker had these books on Egyptology in his library as research or as a way to continue his own exploration of a topic that had fascinated him since his youth in Dublin. One can hardly criticize his amateur status. The nineteenth century was still a period in which many of the fields that we now consider either science or social science moved from amateur status to professional fields requiring college or university training.

Although Trelawny seems to be an amateur archeologist, what is even more important is his wealth and the power that stems from that wealth. Indeed, every detail that Stoker includes about his background suggests wealth rather than academic preparation. Even though Trelawny seems to fill the Van Helsing position as self-proclaimed leader of the group, he assumes that position because of his wealth rather than because of his knowledge. He is thus unlike Van Helsing and even Corbeck. In fact, if one were to pursue the parallel to *Dracula,* he is more like Arthur than like Van Helsing. For example, Ross describes him as living in "a great house" (22) on Kensington Palace Road and later characterizes the Trelawny home as "a great grey stone mansion of the Jacobean period" (202). Because of his wealth, Trelawny has been able to acquire a vast collection of Egyptian artifacts. Indeed, Ross, seeing the home for the first time, describes it in language that conjures up a museum rather than a home:

The room was a large one, and lofty in proportion to its size. In its vastness was place for a multitude of things not often found in a bedchamber. In far corners of the room were shadows of uncanny shape. More than once as I thought, the multitudinous presence of the dead and the past took such hold on me that I caught myself looking round fearfully as though some strange personality or influence was present. (46)

The metaphor is an important one as it suggests an important transformation taking place over the course of the nineteenth century, as collectors became gradually more scientific, moving from mere acquisition to knowledge. Certainly, Stoker had known both kinds of individuals. As a young man in Dublin, he had conversed with Sir William Wilde about the artifacts Wilde had seen in Egypt; he praised both Irving and the set designer Edward Abbey[7] for their historical accuracy; and he apparently spent a great deal of time conducting research for his own books. Furthermore, he could not have been oblivious to the nineteenth-century attempt to collect and codify the artifacts of ancient civilizations as well as zoological specimens from all over the world. That movement is described in a fascinating essay by David K. van Keuren.[8]

The Museum Movement in nineteenth-century Britain had its origin in the early decades of the century, experienced steady growth from the 1830s to the early 70s, and rapidly escalated thereafter. . . . the majority of collections were in local and natural history, with British archeology and antiquities somewhat less numerous. Collections in anthropology (both physical and cultural) and in medicine were less common. (270–71)

Of course, the motivation behind such collections varied from the desire to demonstrate one's wealth and power to the desire to understand other human beings.

If Trelawny's London dwelling is as much a museum as a home, the conclusion of the novel takes place in his ancestral home in Cornwall, a dwelling that is also charged with metaphoric significance. Stoker's description suggests that the Trelawny family is much older, the reference to the walls and the need for defense suggesting something of at least medieval origin: "Of old it was fenced in by a high stone wall, for the house which it succeeded was built by an ancestor of mine in the days when a great house far away from a centre had to be prepared to defend itself" (197).

Further evidence of his wealth is the fact that he has filled his house in London with priceless Egyptian antiquities, so many in fact that he needs to hire a special train to transport them to his ancestral home. He has also managed to electrify his ancestral home despite its geographical remoteness (and the fact that he has chosen to live in London rather than in Cornwall) at a time when electricity is not yet the norm. [9]

Whereas Ross and Winchester are presented as professional men and Corbeck is able "to get a living of a sort" (89) out of tomb hunting, all this emphasis on wealth suggests that Trelawny is independently wealthy and therefore able to fund his own explorations or to send people like Corbeck off in his place. Corbeck certainly defers to his employer:

I have been several times out on expeditions in Egypt for your Father; and I have always found it a delight to work for him. Many of his treasures—and he has some rare ones . . . he has procured through me, either by my exploration or by purchase—or—or—otherwise. (89)

Thus he is presented as a powerful and perhaps not overly scrupulous individual, one more accustomed to command than to listen to others and learn from them.

Two contemporary literary critics have commented on Trelawny's desire for control. In "Eruptions of the Primitive into the Present: *The Jewel of Seven Stars* and *The Lair of the White Worm*," [10] David Seed cites Nicholas Daly's argument that "the role of the museum was to bring under control the flood of exotic artifacts, Egyptian and otherwise, which swept into Britain during the second half of the nineteenth century" (189). Trelawny may want to control artifacts, and he certainly seems determined to exert control over the people around him. Suspecting that he may fall into a trance or catalepsy, he leaves strict instructions on what others should do while he is thus incapacitated; he treats his own daughter less as a human being than as a beautiful possession; and he consistently tells other people what to do and how to act. It would be surprising if such control did not extend to his studies as well. Explaining that "science, and history, and philosophy may benefit; and we may turn one old page of a wisdom unknown in this prosaic age" (170), he suggests that he is searching for knowledge. Despite his emphasis on the benefits to the present, readers ought to question whether he is more interested in control than in understanding. For example, he is eager to gain access to that wisdom by resurrecting Queen Tera, whose mummy he has brought with him back to England. His confusion of science, pseudoscience, and magic is evident in the fact that he sometimes characterizes the knowledge that he hopes to acquire as scientific knowledge, sometimes as magic: "'The experiment which is before us is to try whether or no there is any force, any reality, in the old Magic'" (172). That he is not really a scientist is evident in his repetition of the phrase, "We shall see! We shall see!" (189, 193). Scientific discoveries may indeed depend on some luck, but Trelawny seems to be operating in the dark and violating his own experiences.

His confusion is especially evident in the scene in which he and his followers unwrap the mummy of Queen Tera. Beginning the unwrapping, he observes that they may learn about the Egyptian science of embalming:

Later on we must try and find out the process of embalming. It is not like any that I know. There does not seem to have been any opening cut for the withdrawing of the viscera and organs, which apparently remain intact within the body. Then, again, there is no moisture in the flesh; but its place is supplied with something else, as though wax or stearine had been conveyed into the veins by some subtle process. (242)

The apparent desire for scientific knowledge is certainly a red herring, however. Indeed, the scene in which the three men (Ross, because of his love for Margaret, decides not to be present) unwrap the body of the dead queen is more voyeuristic than scientific, and one wonders exactly what Trelawny hoped to learn by the endeavor. Furthermore this scene and the earlier scene in which they destroy the cat mummy are as cruel as the rape like scene of Lucy Westenra. Trelawny professes that they will learn much from the experience: "We are all grave men, entering gravely on an experiment which may unfold the wisdom of old times, and enlarge human knowledge indefinitely; which may put the minds of men on new tracks of thought and research" (237).

Many readers will wonder whether Trelawny and his minions are being merely prurient, however. In fact, at about the time I was mulling over the treatment of women "patients" by male scientists, I ran across the term "medical rape" in Judith Walkowitz's City of Dreadful Delight: Narratives of Sexual Danger in Late Victorian London. [11] Used to describe the way that women felt about the treatment of suspected prostitutes under the Contagious Diseases Acts and the fact that medical men were given the authority to examine these women, it also describes the power structure in *Dracula* and *The Jewel of Seven Stars*, a structure that gave male scientists power over women:

To the women, the Acts also constituted a powerful drama of sexual politics, entailing the male "medical rape" of working class women and an inspiring example of female heroism in the figure of Josephine Butler, who rallied middle-class women to the defense of their "fallen sisters." (159–60)

Margaret's discomfort and the fact that Ross refuses to participate in the unwrapping reinforce the voyeuristic nature of this metaphoric rape.

Ross quickly recognizes that the participants learn very little from the exercise:

Then, and then only, did the full horror of the whole thing burst upon me. There, in the full glare of the light, the whole material and sordid side of death seemed staringly real. . . . What was before us was Death, and nothing else. All the romance and sentiment of fancy had disappeared. The two elder men, enthusiasts who had often done such work, were not disconcerted; and doctor Winchester seemed to hold himself in a business-like attitude, as if before the operating-table. But I felt low-spirited, and miserable, and ashamed. (238)

That Ross emphasizes shame rather than knowledge is interesting, for it reveals how little he learns from the scientific aspects of the experiment.

There is also the possibility that Stoker used Ross's shame to reveal how unscientific Trelawny is. Worthham's study indicates that they would have learned very little from the endeavor because unwrapping mummies was commonplace by the time *Jewel* was published. He notes that the "most authoritative" treatment of Egyptian embalming practices in the nineteenth century was Thomas Joseph Pettigrew's *History of Egyptian Mummies* (1834). A surgeon and author of a number of both professional and popular books, Pettigrew became interested in mummies in 1820 when he helped Giovanni Belzoni unwrap and dissect a mummy:

From then until the end of 1852 he either assisted at or conducted regularly scheduled public examinations of mummies. Many of these exhibitions were attended by as many as six hundred people. (94)

Worthham adds that the advent of new technology allowed archeologists to learn more about mummies without destroying them. Pettigrew's methods left many questions unanswered, but his *History of Egyptian Mummies* "remained the best account of Egyptian mummification" until the end of the century when Dr. Grafton Elliot Smith used "more modern equipment, including X-ray machines" to study them (95). It is interesting that Trelawny mentions Xrays as well as other kinds of rays but apparently never considers their usefulness for studying mummies. Perhaps this absence is another indication of his scientific shortsightedness.

There are other significant gaps in Trelawny's fields of interest, gaps that may signify exactly how much of an amateur he is. For example, he seems unaware that other scientists are using new technologies to advance their knowledge of ancient Egypt, and he frequently blends science with pseudoscience. At one point, he specifically mentions astronomy, which in old Egypt "developed to an extraordinary height," and links it to astrology, for which he hopes to find some scientific basis: "And it is possible that in the later developments of science with regard to light rays, we may yet find that Astrology is on a scientific basis. Our next wave of scientific thought may deal with this" (174). A final scientific discipline is acoustics, which was "an exact science with the builders of the temples of Karnak, of Luxor, of the Pyramids" but "a mystery to Bell, and Kelvin, and Edison, and Marconi" (175). Thus, Trelawny seems to suggest that contemporary science can build on scientific knowledge that had been lost for some time. This belief would seem to link Trelawny to the progressive notions found in *Dracula*.

What is especially interesting about science in *The Jewel of Seven Stars* is the fact that it is ultimately unsuccessful. Though Van Helsing and the other scientific and professional men in *Dracula* are frequently obtuse, they are nonetheless presented as successful in their quest to destroy the vampire. Scientists, engineers, and even amateurs with some knowledge of science are generally presented as entirely capable in Stoker's other fiction. *Jewel* is thus anomalous in that the scientific figures here are presented as blind, dense, and ultimately unsuccessful.

Perhaps the failures of the scientists in *Jewel* become most evident by comparison to other characters, most notably the members of the criminal justice system, another group that became increasingly professional and dependent on new technological tools of crime detection during the second half of the nineteenth century. Called in at the beginning of the novel to investigate the attack on Professor Trelawny are Superintendent Dolan, a senior police officer, and Sergeant Daw, a detective affiliated with the Criminal Investigation Division (CID) of Scotland Yard. Although Daw doesn't look for fingerprints,[12] Stoker does have him examine the crime scene with a magnifying glass, evidence of the applied science used in police work. Moreover, although the kind of scientific proof of which Daw typically speaks is not exactly scientific in the sense that it could be replicated by other independent investigators, it does resemble science to the extent that it adheres to certain conventions and is not entirely mysterious and unpredictable. Daw describes his process:

I thought, therefore, that if you had it once in your mind that somebody else held to such a possibility, you would by degrees get proof; or at any rate such ideas as would convince yourself, either for or against it. Then we would come to some conclusion; or at any rate we should so exhaust all other possibilities that the most likely one would remain as the nearest thing to proof, or strong suspicion, that we could get. (77)

Aside from ruling out the cat as the being responsible for the attack on Trelawny, however, Daw is utterly ineffectual in solving the mystery.

Daw also investigates the theft of the lamps from Corbeck's hotel room and is no more effective at solving this mystery than he is at determining who had attacked Trelawny. Indeed, when Trelawny awakens from the mysterious trance and the lamps just as mysteriously reappear, Daw expresses his relief at being taken off the case:

I'm glad the case is over. . . . We'll be told officially . . . that it was an accident, or sleep-walking, or something of the kind, to satisfy the conscience of our Record Department; and that will be the end. As for me, I tell you frankly, sir, that it will be the saving of me. I verily believe I was beginning to get dotty over it. There were too many mysteries, that aren't in my line, for me to be really satisfied as to either facts or the causes of them. Now, I'll be able to wash my hands of it, and get back to clean, wholesome criminal work. Of course, sir, I'll be glad to know if you ever do light on a cause of any kind. And I'll be grateful if you can ever tell me how the man was dragged out of bed when the cat bit him, and who used the knife the second time. (163–64)

His relief demonstrates that he is uncomfortable with the kinds of mysteries with which he is confronted at the Trelawny home.

In addition to the fact that many characters in *Jewel* had been trained in various scientific and/or pseudoscientific fields, they are, like so many of the characters in Stoker's other novels, fascinated by new technology. One of the first examples is the respirator that Ross uses to help him stay awake while he watches at Trelawny's side. Leatherdale's edition of *Jewel* includes an interesting note on respirators:

Stoker is not speaking of military gas-masks, introduced in World War I nor . . . the modern medical ventilator. To counteract the effects of smog and other causes of bronchial ailments companies . . . manufactured a range of inhalers and respirators . . . made of metal, celluloid, or plain gauze. . . . Respirators covered the nose and mouth, if not the whole face, and were tied around the head or behind the ears. They were sufficiently in demand to be stocked by local pharmacists. In the interests of decorum, smaller models were designated 'for ladies.' (p. 47, note 35)

This respirator, which Ross purchases from a chemist's shop (in U.S. parlance, a drugstore), is relatively "low-tech" in comparison to many of the other examples.

The electricity in Trelawny's Cornwall home is "worked by a set of turbines moved by the flowing and ebbing tide, after the manner of the turbines at Niagara" (227), a development that "came into service in 1895," a date confirmed by the Web page of the George Westinghouse Museum. Their account demonstrates the same enthusiasm for electrical power as Stoker's novel:

The fixed specifications eventually agreed upon were: alternating current, two-phase, 25 cycles, 2200 volts at a speed of 250 revolutions per minute, 5000 electrical horsepower. Seven manufacturers . . . were asked to bid. . . . The result was that in October 1893, a contract was executed with the Westinghouse Company for three 5000-horsepower dynamos. . . . The first 5000-horsepower hydroelectric unit was tested in April 1895, and in the autumn of that year the commercial distribution and sale of electric power from Niagara Falls began.

It would be difficult for those whose recollection does not go back to those days to realize the great and wide-spread interest aroused by this step in power development. The first Niagara hydroelectric installation was a brilliant engineering    achievement

. . . accepted generally. . . . as the demonstrated solution of the problem of developing hydraulic power for transmission and distribution and its utilization for practically every purpose to which power is applicable. [13]

Leatherdale's footnote indicates that turbines "were all the rage at the turn of the century" because The Niagara Power Station was built in 1895 "to exploit the immense waters of the falls" (227). The equipment in Trelawny's home is thus state of the art and, although unlikely in an ordinary dwelling, entirely within the range of what was plausible at the time Stoker wrote.

However, if the turbines that Trelawny has installed in his home fall within the range of what was possible at the time, much of the other science to which he alludes is more speculative. The conclusion to the Great Experiment is entirely dependent on Trelawny's interpretation of various properties of light. He hopes to open the Magic Coffer and resurrect Queen Tera by filling the lamps around the sarcophagus with cedar oil, an oil "which was much used in the preparation and ceremonials of the Egyptian dead" as well as an oil with "a certain refractive power which we do not find in other oils" (188) and lighting them. Stoker, of course, was aware of how new these fields are, as he has Trelawny admit that he is treading on a highly speculative field, mentioning recent discoveries by Rontgen and the Curies. (Rontgen had discovered Xrays in 1895; the Curies had isolated radium and polonium in 1898.) Trelawny makes these recent discoveries appear almost more Gothic than scientific, however:

The discoveries of the Curies and Laborde, of Sir William Crooks and Becquerel, *may have* far-reaching results on Egyptian investigation. This new metal, radium—or rather this old metal of which our knowledge is new—*may have* been used thousands of years ago in greater degree than seems possible to-day. (194, emphasis added)

Leatherdale's footnote on this particular passage suggests that the reference to Laborde (1878–1968) reveals the extent to which Stoker kept up with the science of his day because Laborde was not widely known: "He co-wrote a paper with Pierre Curie on the heating effects of radium, published . . . c. 1900. . . . The fact that Stoker writes 'the Curies and Laborde' suggests he knew the existence of that paper, and may even have read it." (p. 194, note 19)

On the other hand, the repetition of "may have" (like the earlier repetition of "We shall see! We shall see!") suggests speculation on Trelawny's part. He does not have the knowledge generally expected of scientific discourse. Furthermore, although he apparently has some knowledge of Xrays, he seems not to know that one of his contemporaries, Dr. Grafton Elliot Smith, had already used Xrays to study mummies. Thus his Great Experiment seems to rely more on Gothic mystery than on scientific forces. The excised Chapter 16 concludes by having Ross comment on science, pseudoscience, and occult mysteries: "These scientific, or quasi-scientific discussions soothed me. They took my mind from brooding on the mysteries of the occult, by attracting it to the wonders of nature" (195). The confusion may soothe Ross, but what is genuinely scientific with other disciplines may also be part of the reason that the scientists here are so totally unsuccessful.

Although *The Jewel of Seven Stars* is far less confident about the ability of modern science and technology to overcome, even to control, mysterious forces, it follows many of the same patterns established by Stoker's other fiction. In fact, like *Dracula*, it opens with a narrator's acute awareness of dark mysterious forces when Ross is called to the home of a young woman acquaintance. Ross, who presents himself throughout *Jewel* as a capable professional man, quickly realizes that he is out of his element here when he becomes aware of things he can neither hope to understand nor control:

One might think that four or five thousand years would exhaust the olfactory qualities of anything; but experience teaches us that these smells remain, and that their secrets are unknown to us. To-day they are as much mysteries as they were when the embalmers put the body in the bath of natron. . . . [Stoker's ellipsis]
   All at once I sat up. I had become lost in an absorbing reverie. The Egyptian smell had seemed to get on my nerves—on my memory—*on my very will*. (46, emphasis added)

Like Jonathan Harker, Ross recognizes that he is not in control and that he cannot understand the mysterious powers with which he is confronted. Other characters frequently note that the present age actually has less knowledge of these mysterious forces than did the ancients. For example, Dr. Winchester observes that the ancient Egyptian priests knew how to "arrest the natural forces of decay," knowledge which is "not understood in this later and more prosaic age" (81). The emphasis is on the mysterious power associated with the past.
   The concrete embodiment of that past, Tera is presented as a creature of magic rather than of science. Furthermore, like Dracula, she had studied with the foremost experts of her time and had become knowledgeable in various occult fields:

She had been an apt pupil; and had gone further than her teachers. . . . She had won secrets from nature in strange ways; and had even gone . . . down into the tomb herself, having been swathed and coffined and left as dead for a whole month. (137)

There is even the suggestion that she has managed to overcome natural law, that she is not really dead but merely in a state of suspended animation. For example, her wrist bleeds when a grave robber attempts to steal her hand, and her uncovered body shows none of the usual signs of having been mummified. Given his desires to control those around him, there is every reason to suspect that Trelawny might want to learn from her ability to control the forces of nature, life, and death.
   Despite Trelawny's repeated assurances that there is no danger in their plan and that the present age can gain beneficial knowledge from its encounter with the past, Ross remains skeptical, frequently noting that the mummy had in the past often been linked to violent activities. The careful reader is inclined to share in Ross's misgivings, and the novel itself focuses on very real acts of violence in Tera's past. The following passage, from a seventeenth-century Dutch text written by Nicholas van Huyn of Hoorn and later used as a resource by Trelawny and his associates, recounts the first instance of violence associated with it. Here the victim is a Bedouin who, after wrenching off the mummy's hand to use for a charm, is found strangled. Because of her peculiar seven-fingered hand, there is no doubt that Tera was responsible for this violence: "There were seven; and all

parallel, except the thumb mark, as though made with one hand. This thrilled me as I thought of the mummy hand with the seven fingers" (124). Musing over the mummy's past, Ross reflects on other violence associated with it:

In the history of the mummy . . . the record of deaths that we knew of, presumably effected by her will and agency, was a startling one. . . . Nine dead men, one of them slain manifestly by the Queen's own hand! And beyond this again the several savage attacks on Mr. Trelawny in his own room, in which . . . she had tried to open the safe and to extract the Talisman jewel. (216)

Ross is especially concerned about Tera's power because of her uncanny connection with the woman with whom he has fallen in love. Not only was Margaret born on the day that her father discovers Tera's tomb, but she had always resembled Tera more than she resembled her own mother. Furthermore, as the novel progresses, Tera seems to take possession of Margaret. Ross muses about the source of this mysterious power, often identifying it with long-forgotten Egyptian religion: "If the Egyptian belief was true, . . . then the 'Ka' of the dead Queen and her 'Khu' could animate what she might choose. In such case Margaret would not be an individual at all, but simply a phase of Queen Tera herself; an astral body obedient to her will!" (213).

Like the vampires in *Dracula* who seem to exercise profound control over their modern victims, Queen Tera may be controlling Margaret. Alternatively, she may have even possessed the younger woman. This possession is especially problematic because, as Ross observes, that control may not be in the direction of progress: "It might be that that other individuality was of the lower not of the better sort! Now that I thought of it I had reason to fear" (216).

Though there are obvious similarities between Tera and the vampires in *Dracula*, there are some subtle, but important differences. Tera is powerful like the vampires, but she is less identified with the animal world than they are and is instead presented as an extremely independent female force, a circumstance on which several critics have commented. Arata, for example, notes that the "heroines" of several Stoker novels—Queen Tera, Princess Teuta (in *The Lady of the Shroud*), and Lady Arabella (in *The Lair of the White Worm*) represent "the eruption of archaic and ultimately dangerous forces in modern life" and notes that "fear of women is never far from the surface of these novels" (86). Lisa Hopkins puts a slightly different spin on Stoker's apprehensions about women in a fascinating essay.[14] She observes that Tera and Teuta are threatening because their characterization is pervaded with the "association with motherhood—which is, as always in Stoker's writings, figured at the subliminal level as inherently monstrous" (135). Reinforcing her point, Hopkins points to the structuring pun on mother/mummy (135). It's a clever pun, but I see very little evidence that Tera is a maternal figure (though Mina and Lucy clearly are in *Dracula*.) Indeed Tera is often frightening because she has usurped power usually allotted only to men. Ross, however, is more perplexed by the changes he sees taking place in Margaret:

I never knew whether the personality present was my Margaret—the old Margaret whom I had loved at the first glance—or the other new Margaret, whom I hardly

understood, and whose *intellectual aloofness* made me an impalpable barrier between us. (211, emphasis added)

In describing the difference in the Margaret that he had grown to love and the
changed Margaret, Ross notes especially her growing independence and
amorality and the decrease in her loving care. As a result, she seems to be more
intelligent but less feminine, more aloof and less dependent on him or on any
other man—characteristics most uncommon for socially acceptable women in
the nineteenth century:

In spite of her profession of ignorance Margaret knew a good deal about them [her
father's Egyptian artifacts]. . . . She was a remarkably clever and acute-minded girl,
and with a prodigious memory; so that her store of knowledge, gathered unthink-
ingly bit by bit, had grown to proportions that many a scholar might have envied.
(98–99)

Because Stoker leaves open-ended the question of whether Margaret is possessed
by Tera, it is unclear whether Margaret's knowledge is her own or a man-
ifestation of Tera's control. Certainly, Tera had been known in her own time for
her ability to usurp male powers and privilege:

Prominence was given to the fact that she . . . claimed all the privileges of kingship
and masculinity. In one place she was pictured in man's dress, and wearing the
White and Red Crowns. In the following picture she was in female dress, but still
wearing the Crowns of Upper and Lower Egypt, while the discarded male raiment lay
at her feet. In every picture where hope, or aim, or resurrection was expressed there
was the *added symbol of the North.* (137, emphasis added)

The entire passage focuses on Tera's power, power that subverts nineteenth-
century notions of distinctly separate genders, and furthermore suggests that
Tera had achieved active powers that nineteenth-century thinkers associated only
with males. David Glover observes that the power associated with women is
something that Stoker's contemporaries might have learned from their study of
ancient Egypt:[15]

One of the most provocative of contemporary archaeological findings was that
ancient Egypt was a matrilineal society. According to Flinders Petrie (one of Stoker's
sources for *The Jewel*), "all property belonged to the woman; all that a man could
earn or inherit, was made over to his wife; and families always reckoned back further
on the mother's side than the father's." Since the general historical trend was toward
"men's rights," Petrie argued that "this system" was one which "descends from
primitive times." But other writers were less likely to see this as a regressive
phenomenon. In her lecture "The Social and Political Position of Women in Ancient
Egypt" (c. 1890), Amelia Edwards—one of Egyptology's major fund-raisers and an
indefatigable popularizer of the subject—liked to place particular emphasis upon
the fact that thousands of years ago Egyptian marriages were subject to a 'rule of
contract' that gave women far more economic and legal freedom than their modern
British sisters." (89–90)

Certainly, Stoker weaves into his portrait of Queen Tera an extraordinary degree
of power and influence.

Furthermore, the reference to the North also suggests, as with *Dracula*, what Arata characterizes as reverse colonialism, this time of ancient Africa coming to conquer England. Judith Wilt goes so far as to describe Stoker's novel as "a popular nightmare arising out of 'The African Question' of the last Victorian decades." [16] Elsewhere Stoker tends to associate Africans, including Oolanga in *The Lair of the White Worm* and the reprobate kidnapper in *The Mystery of the Sea*, with the most unredeemed specimens of humanity, As Joseph Bristow observes in *Empire Boys: Adventures in a Man's World*,[17] Stoker's racism was common among his contemporaries:

The image of the African, in particular, had been increasingly distorted since the earliest phases of colonial slavery. As the nineteenth century wore on, evangelists, explorers, and anthropologists produced writings that put together a picture of Africa as the most savage place in the world, averting their gaze from the highly organized composition of many African societies. It has to be remembered that as wars were successively waged in practically every part of the continent, ethnologists were measuring African heads to establish a hierarchy of racial types. In France, anthropometry and, more particularly, craniometry began with Paul Broca's investigations of 1861. Francis Galton's hereditarian interests in measuring skulls and bodies were put on public display in the laboratory he established at the International Exposition of 1884. (130)

According to Patrick Brantlinger, in *Rule of Darkness: British Literature and Imperialism, 1830–1914*, [18] Stoker could have acquired some of his negative views of Africa and Africans from his acquaintance with Sir Richard Burton:

The missionary idea that Africa could be redeemed for civilization was more than some explorers were willing to grant. Burton believed that the African was "unimprovable." "He is inferior to the active-minded and objective . . . Europeans, and to the . . . subjective and reflective Asiatic. He partakes largely of the worst characteristics of the lower Oriental types—stagnation of mind, indolence of body, moral deficiency, superstition, and childish passion." [Sir Richard Burton, *The Lake Regions of Central Africa*, 2 vols. (1861; New York: Horizon, 1961; Brantlinger's ellipsis), 2:326] (182)

Brantlinger also connects Burton's views to the science of his day:

The racist views held by Burton and [Samuel White] Baker were at least as close to the science of their day as the somewhat less negative views of the missionaries. Burton, as a member of the Anthropological Society, agreed with its founder James Hunt that the Negro race probably formed a distinct species. In contrast, most Darwinians held that the races of mankind had a common origin and . . . believed the unity of human nature. . . . The development of physical anthropology and ethnology as disciplines concerned with differences among races strengthened the stereotypes expressed by explorers and missionaries. Evolutionary anthropology . . . suggested that Africans, if not nonhuman or a different species, were such an inferior "breed" that they might be impervious to "higher influences." (184–85)

Another scholar, Nancy Stepan, also connects the racism in *Jewel* to contemporary scientific theories in "Biological Degeneration: Races and Proper Places":[19]

Racial biology . . . was a science of boundaries between groups and the degen-
erations that threatened when those boundaries were transgressed. As slavery was
abolished and the role of freed blacks became a political and social issue, as
industrialization brought about new social mobility and class tensions, and new
anxieties about the "proper" place of different class, national, and ethnic groups in
society, racial biology provided a model for the analysis of the distances that were
"natural" between human groups. Racial "degeneration" became a code for other
social groups whose behavior and appearance seemed sufficiently different from
accepted norms as to threaten traditional social relations and the promise of
"progress." By the late nineteenth century, the urban poor, prostitutes, criminals,
and the insane were being construed as "degenerate" types whose deformed skulls,
protruding jaws, and low brain weights marked them as "races" apart, interacting
with and creating degenerate spaces near at home. (98)

Robert Tracy examines Stoker's racial fears in terms that are closer to home in
"Loving You All Ways: Vamps, Vampires, Necrophiles and Necrofilles in
Nineteenth-Century Fiction." [20]

For LeFanu and Stoker, both members of the Protestant Anglo-Irish ruling class of
nineteenth-century Ireland, these legends were at once local folklore and metaphors
for their class's anxieties about the unhyphenated Irish, who were emerging from
centuries of suppression to demand political and economic power. The Anglo-Irish
feared intermarriage with the Irish, which would lead to racial degeneration, and the
loss of power which would inevitably follow letting the Irish gain ownership of
land. These anxieties underlie such works as *Carmilla* and *Dracula*. (p. 38)

No matter how one tends to justify the racist views, it seems obvious that these
views were often connected to what passed as science in Stoker's day.

In the end, Gothic mystery seems to triumph over scientific predictability,
and Ross, the only survivor of the Great Experiment, concludes the novel with
horror. How are twentieth-century readers to explain the reasons for Stoker's
radically different treatments of the relationship between science and the Gothic
in Stoker's novels? One reason for this difference may simply be the various
sources of inspiration. Certainly *Jewel* seems to be influenced by Egyptian
archeology, which, as Worthham notes, achieved "an amazing popularity" in
nineteenth-century England (92–93). Not only did Archibald Henry Sayce, professor of Assyriology at Oxford, spend seventeen years in Egypt (beginning in
1879 and therefore covering the period in which Stoker was reading and
accumulating material for his novels), but he sent letters to popular magazines
and kept the British public informed of the work that archaeologists were
carrying out in Egypt.

In addition, Stoker knew Burton personally. Not only did Burton write about
his experiences, but his works on archeology reinforced John Lubbock's
progressive ideas. Lubbock, a neighbor and friend of Darwin's, had founded a
new intellectual field, prehistoric archeology, and had also translated Darwin's
theories into the human realm as Christopher Chippindale observes:[21]

Despite the inconsistencies of savage virtue and vice, Lubbock sees a pattern of
progress from savages—slaves to their wants, neither noble nor free—to civilized
persons whose lives are spent, thanks to printing, in communion with the greatest

minds. . . . Lubbock ends with a peek at the future and sees how mankind always progresses towards less pain and more happiness as science abolishes the evil that comes from ignorance and sin: "Utopia . . . turns out . . . to be the necessary consequences of natural laws." (28–29)

In fact, Chippindale underlines the progressive ideas found in Lubbock's writing by saying that the central idea of *The Origin of Civilisation and the Primitive Condition of Man* is "a social, moral, and cognitive progression of savages that must advance steadily from the beginning in just the same manner as technology develops" (29). Such beliefs in progress are generally consistent with Stoker's beliefs.

Although Stoker generally seems to share the progressive belief in the power of science and technology over primitive forces, *The Jewel of Seven Stars* introduces a dark and discordant suggestion, sometimes hinted at in *Dracula* as well, that the modern age is not strong enough to either understand or to overcome the Gothic past. That the past was associated with savagery and violence could have been found in many places, including works in evolutionary biology and archeology. Worttham's book on Egyptology, for example, suggests that a work by one of Stoker's contemporaries, Sir William Matthew Flinders Petrie, could have provided a source for the violence Stoker includes in *Jewel*. Comparing his findings at different sites, Petrie concluded that a major social revolution must have taken place in Egypt during the period of the Old Kingdom. This upheaval, which was "marked by systematic destruction of tombs, sarcophagi, statues, and other royal relics . . . Petrie imaginatively compared . . . to the excesses of the mob during the French Revolution" (117–18). Stoker, who often incorporated references to Egyptology in his works, owned a copy of Petrie's *Egyptian Tales* of 1895. Certainly the destruction of Tera's tomb and her conflict with the priests is consistent with Petrie's findings.

Evidence suggests that Stoker was acquainted with Petrie's work. That he was concerned with the impact of mysterious forces that he frequently associated with the past is, however, evident in almost everything he wrote. That his fiction usually focuses on modern characters who triumph over characters whose savagery or primitiveness connects them with the past is equally evident. This confidence in science and technology to overcome such primitive forces would appear to link him to other nineteenth-century progressionists who believed that human beings were moving toward a better and more civilized future. In fact, one of the things that makes *The Jewel of Seven Stars* so anomalous is the fact that it includes no suggestion that progress is inevitable or even that science and technology can control the forces of the past. When Trelawny and his allies use the information that Tera had left them to resurrect her mummy, she simply destroys them instead of offering to share her knowledge. Moreover, she presumably goes on to wreak havoc on England as a whole. Unlike *Dracula*, which suggests the growth of the bourgeoisie and implies genuine progress for the future, *The Jewel of Seven Stars* hints only at death and utter annihilation from which no future can spring.

Stoker ultimately modified this horrifying conclusion to make it less bleak and hopeless. That Stoker was willing to make this change and essentially change a tragedy into a comedy may be evidence of his own uncertainty about the way the world was going or simply of his need for money. Biographical information suggests that the failure of the Lyceum had a devastating impact on Stoker. In fact, Skal suggests that *Dracula* is better written than most of Stoker's other works because Stoker was financially secure during the period when he wrote it and therefore had more time to work on it.

Although it is hard to explain the reason for it, *The Jewel of Seven Stars* is consistently more ambivalent about the powers of modern science to overcome ancient evils than any of Stoker's other novels. It is also the only one of his novels that did not originally conclude happily.

*The Jewel of Seven Stars* is anomalous in one other way: the attention that Stoker pays to the mysterious Other that is nature. The denouement of *Jewel* might arguably be due to natural forces rather than occult ones. As the scientists wait inside for resurrection, a fierce storm rages outside. Just as the forces emerge from the now-opened coffer, nature emerges triumphant:

In the heart of this mist . . . was something like a hand holding a fiery jewel flaming with many lights. As the fierce glow of the Coffer met this new living light, the green vapour floating between them seemed like a cascade of brilliant points—a miracle of light!

But at that very moment there came a change. The fierce storm, battling with the shutters of the narrow openings, won victory. . . . In rushed a fierce blast which blew the flames of the lamps to and fro, and drifted the green vapour from its course. (247)

Soon after that, all the lights fade, and Ross is left alone. It is almost as though human beings—despite their professional training, their science, and their wealth—are entirely irrelevant. Their plans are snuffed out by a conflict between occult forces and natural forces.

That Ross alone remains raises additional questions. Is he saved because he is the only character in *Jewel* who is reluctant to participate in the unrolling of the mummy? Because Stoker needs a narrative perspective to wrap up the story? Because Ross is presented as a more skeptical character, one who never places his faith entirely with science? Because, as Leatherdale suggests, Ross is the only character who places his life "in the hands of God"? (228) [22] These questions suggest other ways *Jewel* remains anomalous among Stoker's works.

In only one other work, *The Watter's Mou'*, [23] does Stoker allow nature to triumph over human beings, this time, however, in an entirely naturalistic way. In fact, this short work, which takes place in Stoker's beloved Cruden Bay, focuses almost entirely on the power of nature, including human nature. Nature, for example, is strong enough to carve rocks: "As one sees this natural mouth of the stream in the rocky face of the cliff, it is hard to realise that Nature alone has done the work" (189). If nature can carve away rocks, it can also impact human lives as well, ultimately destroying the lovers William Barrow and Maggie MacWhirter. Here Maggie finds herself faced with that power:

All this time she took something of inspiration from the darkness and the roar of the storm around her. She was not yet face to face with danger, and did not realise, or try to realise, its magnitude. In such a mystery of darkness as lay before, above, and around her, her own personality seemed as nought. Truly there is an instinct of one's own littleness which becomes consciously manifest in the times when Nature puts forth her might. (191)

Ultimately here, as in *Jewel*, nature triumphs. Looking at the material that was excised from the conclusion to *Dracula* suggests that Stoker may have originally intended for nature to be more powerful in that novel as well. Seeing the "terrible convulsion" that occurs at Dracula's death, Harker focuses on a natural cataclysm. Although the longer passage was quoted in Chapter 1, the following excerpt is worth quoting again because of the emphasis on the power of nature: "From where we stood it seemed as though the one fierce *volcano* burst had satisfied *the need of nature* and that the castle and the structure of the hill had sunk again into the void" (cited by Belford, 268). Indeed, this natural power is beyond anything that the scientists do.

Though nature serves as an important backdrop in works as otherwise dissimilar as *The Snake's Pass*, *The Watter's Mou'*, *The Shoulder of Shasta*, *The Mystery of the Sea*, *The Man*, and *Snowbound*, and though Stoker often focuses on nature's power, his human characters ultimately triumph in all but *The Watter's Mou'* and *Jewel*.

Comparing *The Jewel of Seven Stars* to Stoker's other works suggests that his attitudes to the mysteries that he could not begin to understand and his visions for the future were complex and ambiguous, expressing the range of possibilities available to people at the turn of the century. In particular, his novels suggest that Stoker was aware of the scientific and cultural developments that were taking place around the turn of the century, that he was fascinated with technological developments and apprehensive about various primitive forces, including certain forces that he associated with women and other minority groups. [24] The brother of three physicians and a man who experienced poor health at several points in his life, Stoker creates physicians and scientists who are complex and interesting but also ultimately unable to solve the problems put before them, including Renfield's madness and Trelawny's catalepsy. His punishment of independent women (in *Dracula* and *The Man*), people of color (Africans in *The Mystery of the Sea* and *Lair of the White Worm* and Native Americans in *The Shoulder of Shasta*) and other supposedly primitive people (including the Turks in *The Lady of the Shroud*) who step outside the boundaries of their gender, class, or national grouping certainly make him appear both racist and sexist by contemporary standards, though such groupings were typical for people of Stoker's own day. Most important, these complex and occasionally ambiguous responses identify Stoker as a man of his time. Faced with the possibilities that science and technology sometimes seemed to hold out and with the violence and irrationality that he and his contemporaries often associated with the past and with primitive people closer to home, Stoker sometimes saw the future as full of infinite possibilities for improvement, sometimes as totally at the mercy of primitive forces, and sometimes offering human beings a range of possible responses much as Stoker's own age had done. Although Stoker and most of his works embody the power of the modern scientific and technological age, *The Jewel of Seven Stars* is his single greatest tribute to the mysterious power of the  Gothic even in the modern world.

## NOTES

1. Stephen D. Arata notes that *Dracula* "addresses a series of cultural issues, particularly those involving race, specific to the 1890s" (84) and thus links Stoker's novel to the scientific theories of his day. Arata's essay can be found in "The Occidental Tourist: *Dracula* and the Anxiety of Reverse Colonization," *Victorian Studies* 33 (Summer 1990), 621–45; in *The Critical Response to Bram Stoker*, edited by Carol A. Senf, p. 84. Westport, Ct: Greenwood, 1993.

2. Although vampire literature is an accepted subgenre of Gothic fiction, the mummy has never gained equivalent popularity. Among the fictional works featuring mummies that Stoker might have known was one that his friend Conan Doyle had written in 1894, "Lot No. 249," which appeared in *Round the Red Lamp: Being Facts and Fancies of Medical Life.*

3. Bram Stoker, *The Jewel of Seven Stars*, annotated and edited by Clive Leatherdale. Westcliff-on-Sea, Essex: Desert Island Books, 1996, 250; all subsequent references will be to this text and will be included parenthetically in the text.

4. Robert Edwards, "The Alien and the Familiar in *The Jewel of Seven Stars* and *Dracula*," in *Bram Stoker: History, Psychoanalysis and the Gothic*, edited by William Hughes and Andrew Smith, pp. 96–115. London: Macmillan Press Ltd.: 1998.

5. John David Worthham, *The Genesis of British Egyptology 1549–1906*. Norman: University of Oklahoma Press, 1971.

6. Chapman's essay is found in *Tracing Archaeology's Past: The Historiography of Archaeology*, edited by Andrew L. Christenson, pp. 151–162, Carbondale: Southern Illinois University Press, 1989.

7. In *Personal Reminiscences*, Stoker observes of Abbey's designs:

In his designs Abbey brought home to one the *cachet* of medieval life. What he implied as well as what he showed told at a glance the conditions and restrictions--the dominant forces of that strenuous time: the fierceness and cruelty; the suspicion and distrust; the horrible crampedness of fortress life; the contempt of death which came with the grim uncertainties of daily life. In one of his scenes was pictured by inference the life of the ladies in such a time and place in a way which one could never forget. It was a corner in the interior of a castle, high up and out of reach of arrow or catapult; a quiet nook where the women could go in safety for a breath of fresh air. Only the sky above them was open, for danger would come from any side exposed. (II, 83)

8. David K. van Keuren, "Museums and Ideology: Augustus Pitt-Rivers, Anthropological Museums, and Social Change in Later Victorian Britain," *Energy and Entropy: Science and Culture in Victorian Britain. essays from Victorian Studies*, edited by Patrick Brantlinger, pp. 270–88. Bloomington: Indiana University Press, 1989.

9. One of Leatherdale's footnotes drew my attention to the relative novelty of electricity:

There is no mention of electric lights in *Dracula* . . . but they feature prominently in *The Jewel*. . . . Indeed the climax depends upon them. Stoker is referring to carbon filament lamps, which illuminated affluent households at the turn of the century. (p. 21, n. 14)

On the other hand, one would expect Trelawney's London home to be electrified. It is more surprising to learn that his home in Cornwall has been completely electrified.

10. David Seed, "Eruptions of the Primitive into the Present: *The Jewel of Seven Stars and The Lair of the White Worm*," in *Bram Stoker: History, Psychoanalysis*

*and the Gothic*, edited by William Hughes and Andrew Smith, pp. 188–204. London: Macmillan Press Ltd.: 1998.

11. Judith Walkowitz, *City of Dreadful Delight: Narratives of Sexual Danger in Late Victorian London*. Chicago: University of Chicago Press, 1992.

12. According to the entry on "Law Enforcement" in *Victorian Britain: An Encyclopedia*, fingerprinting would have been in use in 1903; and Stoker, because of his background in law and his interest in crime, would have known it. The entry notes that Scotland Yard adopted Francis Galton's system of identifying criminals by their fingerprints in 1894 and replaced Alphonse Bertillion's anthropomorphic measurement system. Galton's *Fingerprint Directories*, which was published in 1895, was the "first system of digital classification to appear in print. Edward Richard Henry, who became CID commissioner in 1901, also developed a fingerprint system; it was adopted by the Indian government in 1897" (437).

13. http://www.georgewestinghouse.com/chapter8.html (consulted July 20, 2000).

14. "Crowning the King, Mourning his Mother: *The Jewel of Seven Stars* and *The Lady of the Shroud*," in *Bram Stoker: History, Psychoanalysis and the Gothic*, edited by William Hughes and Andrew Smith, pp. 134–50. London: Macmillan Press Ltd.: 1998.

15. David Glover, *Vampires, Mummies, and Liberals: Bram Stoker and the Politics of Popular Fiction*. London and Durham: Duke University Press, 1996.

16. Judith Wilt, "The Imperial Mouth: Imperialism, the Gothic and Science Fiction," *Journal of Popular Culture* 14 (1981), 618–28.

17. Joseph Bristow, *Empire Boys: Adventures in a Man's World*. London: Harper Collins Academic, 1991.

18. Patrick Brantlinger, *Rule of Darkness: British Literature and Imperialism, 1830–1914*. Ithaca: Cornell University Press, 1988.

19. Nancy Stepan. "Biological Degeneration: Races and Proper Places," in *Degeneration: The Dark Side of Progress*, edited by J. Edward Chamberlin and Sander L. Gilman, pp. 97–120. New York: Columbia University Press, 1985.

20. Robert Tracy. "Loving You All Ways: Vamps, Vampires, Necrophiles and Necrofilles in Nineteenth-Century Fiction," in *Sex and Death in Victorian Literature*, edited by Regina Barreca, pp. 32–59. Bloomington: Indiana University Press, 1990.

21. "'Social Archaeology' in the Nineteenth Century: Is It Right to Look for Modern Ideas in Old Places?" in Christenson, *Tracing Archaeology's Past*, pp. 21–33. (The quotation is from Lubbock's *The Origin of Civilisation and the Primitive Condition of Man*, 1865:492 [Chippindale's ellipses], in Christenson, *Tracing Archaeology's Past*, pp. 21–33.

22. Leatherdale seems to suggest the final conclusion, reminding readers in a footnote that Ross is one of Stoker's most religious characters:

Whilst Stoker's fictional heroes often give thanks to God, it is unusual for him to have them kneel in prayer. The act of kneeling humbles oneself before God, while giving thanks acknowledges God's providence. (p. 224, n. 6)

23. *The Watter's Mou'* in *The Bram Stoker Bedside Companion: 10 Stories by the Author of Dracula*, edited by Charles Osborne, pp. 166–224. New York: Taplinger Publishing Company, 1973.

24. The collection of essays edited by J. Edward Chamberlin and Sander L. Gilman, *Degeneration: The Dark Side of Progress* (New York: Columbia University Press, 1985), is devoted to this alternate view:

The present collection of essays is an attempt to sketch . . . this force which complements the idea of progress in the nineteenth and early twentieth centuries. We have selected the term "degeneration" for it; and like "progress," it is a term widely employed in numerous and often contradictory contexts. There is no one area in which the concept of degeneration is dominant. It permeates nineteenth-century thought with a model (or a series of models) for decline, and it permeates nineteenth-century feeling with images of decay. Its roots are . . . embedded in biological models and images, but its import soon incorporated, not to say overwhelmed, the purely biological character of the paradigm. It borrows or subverts other terms, such as decadence, but it remains for the nineteenth century the most frightening of prospects, as well as at times the most enthralling. (Preface, vii)

# Chapter 4
# Technological Salvation in *The Snake's Pass*, *The Mystery of the Sea*, *Lady Athlyne*, *The Lady of the Shroud*, and *The Lair of the White Worm*

Although it is usually appropriate to begin at the beginning, Stoker's first published book, *The Duties of Clerks of Petty Sessions in Ireland* (1879), is more concerned with the daily activities of a particular group of individuals, and his first fictional book, *Under the Sunset* (1882), is a collection of fairy tales. Stoker's first novel, *The Snake's Pass*, is, however, full of references to science and technology. Indeed, the two young heroes, Arthur Severn and Dick Sutherland, emerge victorious from their conflict with the usurious Black Murdock, a naturalistic predecessor to the supernatural Dracula and Queen Tera, precisely because their knowledge of science enables them to anticipate the movements of the shifting bog. Another realistic predator appears in *The Watter's Mou'* (1894), Solomon Mendoza "of Hamburg and Aberdeen . . . who had the reputation of being as remorseless as he was rich" (169) and who encourages the father of the heroine to try smuggling to keep his fishing boat.

## THE SNAKE'S PASS (1890)

In *The Snake's Pass*, [1] his young scientific characters triumph, and Stoker also leads the reader to believe that their understanding of technology will ultimately enable them to transform the beautiful but impoverished landscape of Western Ireland into a Utopia. In fact, the novel concludes with the picture of progress brought about by technological knowledge:

Each few months I ran over to the Knockcalltecrore, which Dick was transforming into a fairyland. The discovery of the limestone had, as he had conjectured, created possibilities in the way of building and of water-works of which at first we had not dreamed. The new house rose on the table-rock in the Cliff Fields. A beautiful house it was, of red sandstone with red tiled roof and quaint gables, and jutting windows and balustrades of carven stone. The whole Cliff Fields were laid out as exquisite gardens, and the murmur of water was everywhere. (246)

Such progress is the direct result of Severn's English money and Sutherland's technical knowledge.[2] In fact, Stoker points out that Sutherland is a graduate of the Irish College of Science while Norah's brother Eugene is studying engineering in Scotland.

*The Snake's Pass* weaves together several plots: the victory of science/technology/capital over superstition and greed, the ancient myth of the King of the Snakes, a more recent myth of lost treasure,[3] and a rather conventional love story. In *The Snake's Pass*, Arthur Severn tells of his visit to Ireland, a visit that turns into a lifelong stay when he falls in love with Norah Joyce, and purchases land on which they discover the lost treasure. Arthur's old school friend Dick Sutherland is an engineer and geologist hired by Murdock to explore the bog on his property and on Farmer Joyce's property in hopes of recovering the treasure. Contemptuous of Murdock's greed, Sutherland none-theless warns him that his house is in danger of being overtaken by the shifting bog, which Daly characterizes as "the central figure in *The Snake's Pass* for what we might designate as the Anglo-Irish anxiety of origins: the resistant texture of the bog makes much more sense when we recognize it as the figure in the text for the colonial past" (60). Additional material on the bog appears in the next chapter. Murdock, who refuses to listen to the engineer's warning, is eventually drowned when the bog shifts once again and overtakes his house, a dramatic end that is fully as convulsive as was the end that Stoker initially imagined for *Dracula*:

For a while the superior size and buoyancy of the roof sustained it, but then it too began slowly to sink. . . . And then came a mighty roar and a gathering rush. The side of the hill below us seemed to burst. Murdock threw up his arms. . . . Then came the end of the terrible convulsion. With a rushing sound, and the noise of a thousand waters falling, the whole bog swept, in waves of gathering size, and with a hideous writhing, down the mountain-side—to the entrance of the Shleenanaher—struck the portals with a sound like thunder, and piled up to a vast height. And then the millions of tons of slime and ooze, and bog and earth, and broken rock swept through the Pass into the sea. (230)

This spectacular conclusion and the equally dramatic conclusions of other Stoker works often result in the destruction of primitive characters. More sophisticated characters sometimes cause these spectacular conclusions but almost always benefit from them.

In fact, *The Snake's Pass* is full of references to the ways that science and technology can produce progress. A relatively minor character, Norah's brother Eugene is studying engineering with George Henshaw, the great engineer. Because the area in which the story takes place is beautiful but relatively impoverished, this decision is evidently a way to better himself. No longer able to make a living from the land, the Irish had been emigrating for some fifty years before Stoker wrote his novel, and the decision that Eugene and his father make about his future career is typical of the time. Coe describes the period in *The Engineering Industry of the North of Ireland*:

After the potato famine not only were many workers compelled to leave the land, but many of those who served their needs were also thrown out of work, and engineering firms had no difficulty in recruiting the unskilled and semi-skilled workers who then formed at least a third of the labour force. (172)

Eugene is perhaps more skillful than the workers that Coe describes, but he is equally interested in improving his lot through work in engineering rather than agriculture.

Stoker's interest in science and technology is most evident, however, in Dick Sutherland. Dick, who has also fallen in love with Norah Joyce but is unable to win her heart, is the real hero of the story. Significantly he is the also the character who best understands science and technology and is willing to use them to transform the world. His old school chum Art notes that Dick's work exploring the bog results in a spectacular transformation of the landscape:

Dick was in great spirits; his experiment with the bog had been quite successful. The cutting had advanced so far that the clay wall hemming in the bog was actually weakened, and with a mining cartridge, prepared for the purpose, he had blown up the last bit of bank remaining. The bog had straightway begun to pour into the opening, not merely from the top, but simultaneously to the whole depth of the cutting. (119)

If Dick's desire to understand the nature of bogs [Stoker has him include a long discussion on the fact that Ireland is "an Island almost infamous for bogs" (56)] reveals his interest in science, his plans to reclaim the land reveal his interest in technological developments:

Let us once be able to find the springs that feed the bog, and get them in hand, and we can make the place a paradise. The springs are evidently high up on the hill, so that we can not only get water for irrigating and ornamental purposes, but we can get power also! Why you can have electric light, and everything else you like, at the smallest cost. And if it be, as I suspect, that there is a streak of limestone in the hill, the place might be a positive mine of wealth as well! We have not lime within fifty miles, and if once we can quarry the stone here we can do anything. (178)

A similar transformation takes place at the end of *The Lady of the Shroud* (1909), where Rupert St. Leger, recently crowned king of the Land of the Blue Mountains, undertakes elaborate public works projects to produce another technological paradise in a formerly primitive place. In fact, in *The Snake's Pass*, Sutherland notes that the government should undertake similar public works projects throughout Ireland:

Sutherland gave me a rapid but masterly survey of the condition of knowledge on the subject of bogs. . . . He told me of the extent and nature of the bog-lands—of the means taken to reclaim them, and of his hopes of some heroic measures being ultimately taken by Government to reclaim the vast bog of Allen which remains as a great evidence of official ineptitude. (55–56)

Reclaiming the land in Ireland would help reduce the poverty of the Irish agricultural worker, a poverty that Stoker had observed firsthand when, as Inspector of Petty Sessions, he accompanied the magistrate's court to areas where there was no permanent court. Such familiarity with rural Ireland ultimately resulted in two books, one a work of nonfiction, *The Duties of Clerks of Petty Sessions in Ireland*, the other of fiction, *The Snake's Pass*.

Stoker's faith in scientific/technological progress was certainly not uncommon in its day. For example, A.P.M. Fleming and H.J. Brocklehurst, in *A History of Engineering* (1925), [4] point to a belief remarkably like Sutherland's in the

Charter of the Institution of Civil Engineers. Here engineering is defined in a way that evokes its power to improve the human condition:

art of directing the great sources of power in nature for the use and convenience of man, as the means of production and of traffic in states, both for external and internal trade, as applied in the construction of roads, bridges aqueducts, canals, river navigation, and docks for internal intercourse and exchange, and in the construction of ports, harbours, moles, breakwaters, and lighthouses; and in the art of navigation by artificial power for the purposes of commerce; and in the construction and adaptation of machinery; and in the drainage of cities and towns. (1)

Like Stoker, the writers of this charter imagine the many ways that engineering, a field that unites science and technology, might transform their world.

If Dick Sutherland is the character who has the knowledge of science and technology necessary to transform the world, Arthur Severn's name suggests that transformative power. His name  evokes the Severn Tunnel, a project that, according to  L.T.C. Rolt's *Victorian Engineering,* [5] is "worthy to rank beside the greatest achievements of the pioneers" (251). Rolt explains that the directors of the Great Western railway had long recognized the need for a crossing of the Severn but also that "such was the breadth of the estuary and so fierce its tidal currents that they were daunted by the magnitude of the task" (252). Though an act for a Severn Tunnel Railway was passed in 1872 and work on the tunnel began in 1873, it took more than twelve years to complete the project. The Severn Tunnel was finally opened for use in December 1886, a mere four years before Stoker published *The Snake's Pass.*

In contrast to Sutherland and Severn and even the peasant Phelim Joyce, who plans to use the treasure they find on his land for the good of Ireland, is Black Murdock, the usurious Gombeen Man. Murdock is interested in finding the lost treasure only to advance his own cause. His utter selfishness is revealed when Arthur asks a crowd of peasants to define the local term gombeen man:

He's a man that linds you a few shillin's or a few pounds whin ye want it bad, and then niver laves ye till he has tuk all ye've got—yer land an' yer shanty an' yer holding' an' yer money an' yer craps; an'  he would take the blood out of yer body if he could sell it or use it anyhow! (26)

A total parasite—the reference to bloodsucking does after all make him an early predecessor to Dracula—Murdock is interested in science and technology—he does, after all, hire Sutherland to help him locate the treasure that he believes had been buried on his land—only when they advance his own selfish cause. So blinded by his desire to find the treasure, he ignores Sutherland's warning that his house is in the way of the shifting bog, and his failure results in the spectacular death that I quoted at the beginning of the chapter. Like the villainous figures in so many of Stoker's other novels (including Dracula and Lady Arabella and Edgar Caswall in *The Lair of the White Worm*), he fails precisely because he is incapable of adapting to the modern world, a world that is rapidly being transformed by science, technology, and capital, a world moreover in which the mysterious evils usually associated with the Gothic are being brought under control. And, like theirs, his end is spectacular even if it is the result of natural rather than technological forces.

This study began with a question about Stoker's ideas on the relationship between science/technology and Gothic mystery. Observing Stoker's consistent interest in science, I wondered whether he saw in contemporary science/technology a way of overcoming the seemingly insurmountable human problems that Gothic literature depicts in characteristically exaggerated form. Clearly *The Snake's Pass* presents Sutherland and Severn as superior to the superstitious Murdock. Nonetheless they are powerless to prevent the accident that eventually takes his life even if Sutherland does predict it. The ultimate power is still nature even though Stoker definitely celebrates science and technology in *The Snake's Pass*.

Similarly *The Snake's Pass* provides one more field in which science and technology are helpless, a field that is equally mysterious and perhaps equally spectacular. When Arthur Severn sees Norah Joyce for the first time, he falls violently in love, as he here reveals to Dick:

"I don't know. I don't know anything about her, except this Dick, that I love her with all my heart and soul!" I could not help it—I could not account for it—but the tears rushed to my eyes, and I had to keep my head turned away from Dick lest he should notice me. He said nothing, and when I had surreptitiously wiped away what I thought were unmanly tears of emotion, I looked round at him. He, too, had his head turned away and, if my eyes did not deceive me, he too had some unmanly signs of emotion. (90)

That their love concludes the novel is perhaps one more bit of evidence for the power of those mysterious things usually considered Gothic. The villainous Murdock is gone, literally swept away by the forces of nature, while the heroes are putting their science and technology to good use reclaiming Ireland from the bogs. What remains, however, is something equally incapable of being controlled by technology. Perhaps, after all, it is appropriate that Dick Sutherland, the heroic engineer, does not in the end win the girl of his dreams. Even though science and technology can often harness the forces of nature, they have not yet been proven effective in matters involving the human heart.

*The Snake's Pass* is followed by *The Watter's Mou'* (1894), one of several Stoker works that takes place at his beloved Cruden Bay; *The Shoulder of Shasta* (1895), one of the novels that features both American characters and an American setting; *Dracula* (1897); *Miss Betty* (1898), Stoker's only historical novel; and *The Mystery of the Sea* (1902), another work that explores the landscape of Cruden Bay. Although these works demonstrate Stoker's willingness to experiment with a variety of genres, only *Dracula* and *The Mystery of the Sea* combine the Gothic with an interest in science and technology.

## THE MYSTERY OF THE SEA (1902)

Less demonstrably Gothic than *Dracula*, *The Mystery of the Sea* is interested in revealing a world where both science and mystery can exist side by side. Moreover, like both *The Snake's Pass* and *Dracula*, *Mystery* includes characters who are affiliated with the worlds of science and technology. Indeed, if the plot is indicative, *Mystery* suggests that Stoker may have even gained more faith in science, for here he allows his scientific character to win the girl of *his* dreams. On the other hand, including two characters who are capable of Second Sight and having the heroine's rescue depend on it as well as on his physical strength and technological prowess reveals that Stoker has not totally abandoned Gothic mystery for scientific certainty. This unique combination of scientific plausibility and Gothic mystery foreshadows *The Jewel of Seven Stars* and *The Lair of the White Worm* as well as *The Lady of the Shroud*, a novel that ultimately abandons Gothic mystery for politics.

Out of print in the United States and therefore less known than some of Stoker's other novels, *The Mystery of the Sea* is interesting for its characterization as well as for its combination of science and mystery. Although it is dangerous to assume that a writer necessarily shares the values and beliefs that he gives to his central characters, it is tempting to assume that Archibald Hunter, the hero and narrator of *The Mystery of the Sea*, is a mouthpiece for Stoker because there are so many similarities in the two. Although Glover describes Dick Sutherland as "one of Stoker's early fictional self-portraits" (page 162, note 33) Archie Hunter in *The Mystery of the Sea* is an even more obvious self-portrait. Belford, for example, points to several similarities including their enthusiasm for train travel, their affection for Cruden Bay, and the fact that Stoker has Archie live in two of the places he himself had lived, the Kilmarnock Arms and Whinnyfold, the latter where he wrote *The Mystery of the Sea*. She is careful to mention one important difference: whereas Archie builds a house at Cruden Bay, Stoker remained a renter.

Some of the biographical parallels are even more subtle. *The Mystery of the Sea* opens with Archie's arrival "at Cruden Bay on my annual visit" (1) and even suggests a time framework that connects Stoker and his character: "The last week in June of next year, 1898, found me back in Cruden," (29) the solitary fishing village on the Scottish coast that Stoker and Irving had first explored in 1888 during their research for Macbeth and where Stoker completed *Dracula*, put the finishing touches on *Miss Betty*, and wrote *The Mystery of the Sea*. Additional details link the two, including the fact that, like his creator, Archie had been an invalid and that both are writers. At least Archie confesses, "I was supposed to be an author" (146). By the time Stoker wrote *Mystery*, there was no doubt that he was a writer, even if he spent the bulk of his time managing the Lyceum rather than writing.

More apropos to this study is the fact that Archie seems to share Stoker's enthusiasm for both technology and for pure science. In fact, Archie is as enthusiastic about bicycles as Jonathan Harker is about trains and Lord Athlyne is about fast automobiles. [6] When he and Marjory ride bicycles through Scotland, Archie expresses his almost erotic enthusiasm for the machine: "Oh, but that ride was delightful. . . . Down the falling road we sped almost without effort, our wheels seeming to glide on air" (81). A kind of late-nineteenth-century "techno-nerd," he buys two of the finest revolvers he can get when he realizes that the woman he loves is in danger of being kidnapped, and waxes eloquent describing the equipment that he will use to dig for the buried Spanish treasure:

I had the very latest American devices, including a bit-and-brace which one could lean on and work without stooping, and diamond patent drills which could, compared with ordinary tools of the old pattern, eat their way into rock at an incredible rate. My ground was on the gneiss side of the geological division. Had it been on the granite side of the line my labour and its rapidity might have been different. (129)

He is equally delighted with the equipment that will enable him and Marjory to explore the cave safely and with his own technological ingenuity:

First I  rigged up a proper windlass over the hole into the cave; and fixed it so that any one could manipulate it easily and safely from above. It could be also worked from below by aid of an endless chain round the axle. I hammered the edges of the hole somewhat smoother, so that no chance friction might cut the rope; and I fixed candles and lanterns in various places, so that all the light which might be necessary could be had easily. (146)

His description suggests that Archie believes he has covered all the necessary bases and that technology can solve even the most complex problems.

Even more of a techno-nerd than Archie, Marjory Anita Drake is an ideal mate for him.  When Archie rides up to the castle where she and her guardian are staying, he finds her "with her Kodak on the sweep outside, taking views of its various points" (154). He also learns from a member of the American Secret Service that the wealthy heiress had previously used technology to attempt to solve a real political problem. As with *The Lady of the Shroud*, Stoker is unashamed of using real political situations even in his most Gothic works. In fact, the conflict between Marjory and Don Bernardino stems from their conflicting allegiances during the Spanish-American War, a war that was taking place at the same time the novel supposedly took place. Stoker even provides one literal date, "the last week in June 1898" (29), the date at which Archie returns to Cruden Bay. The *Maine* had been blown up on February 15, and Teddy Roosevelt's famous charge up San Juan Hill would take place on July 1. The treaty ending the war and allowing Archie and Marjory to accompany the body of Don Bernardino back to Spain would take place on December 10, 1898.

Marjorie justifies her patriotism by recounting Spanish atrocities in Cuba:

At the time the reports kept crowding in of the Spanish atrocities on the *reconcentrados*; when public feeling was rising in the United States, this girl got all on fire to free Cuba. To this end she bought a battle ship that the Cramps had built for Japan. She had the ship armed with Krupp cannon which she bought through friends in Italy; and went along the Eastern coast amongst the sailors and fishermen till she had recruited a crew. Then she handed the whole thing over to the Government as a spur to it to take some action. (88)

Once again, it is clear that Stoker has done his homework, for the reference to the *reconcentrados* is highly topical. General Valeriano Weyler y Nicolau was a successful Spanish general who planned to repress the Liberation Army and restore political order in Cuba by separating the peasants from the insurgents. To this end he had troops herd the peasants into reconcentration camps, which were disorganized and where  disease and malnutrition spread rapidly. Over 300,000 people died as a result of Weyler's Reconcentration Policy. While his plan was supported by the Spanish Conservative government, it earned him the name of the "Butcher" and angered many liberal Americans. Marjory's sentiments link her with the group that wished to liberate Cuba from Spanish control. Marjory assembles a veritable arsenal of technological equipment to assist the quest for freedom. She even buys a battle ship, which she gives to the American government and equips with the latest weaponry.

As Chapter 2 discusses, Stoker was notedly enthusiastic about technology of all kinds. His memoir of Henry Irving even includes a section that describes his appreciation of the American cruiser *Chicago* that he and his employer had been invited to visit in May 1894. Perhaps even more important to his portrayal of the naval battle in *Mystery*, however, is an experience during 1880 when he and Irving were on a short holiday:

We went down on the beach and picked out a likely looking boat. . . . The boatman was very deaf, but as he seemed also dumb we regarded him as a find. He hoisted his sail and we began to steal away from shore. Behind us was a lot of shouting, and many people ran down on the beach gesticulating and calling out. We could not distinguish what they said; but we were both so accustomed to hear people shouting at Irving that we took it that the present was but another instance of clamorous goodwill.

We had got away from shore about half a mile when suddenly there was a terrific sound close to us, and the boat was thrown about just as a rat is shaken by a dog. (II, 266–67)

The explanation becomes clear when they return to shore. Their boat had been in the middle of an "an attack on Fort Monckton—the low-lying fort which guards the mouth of the harbour of Portsmouth—by the *Glatton*, then the most up-to-date of our scientifically equipped ships. We appeared to have come right over the mine-bed" (II, 268). Even this close call, however, does not seem to diminish Stoker's enthusiasm for technological innovations. In fact, he is positively thrilled to be able to witness the mock battle later that day from the safety of Fort Monckton, and he remembers the experience more than twenty years later when he crafts the battle scenes for *Mystery*.

His enthusiasm for science in *Mystery* is perhaps less dramatic but equally evident. Indeed,  Archie solves many of the problems posed in the novel because of his knowledge of science and scientific process. The first indication of his scientific awareness comes when he decodes the cipher:

I knew something of secret writing, for this had in my boyhood been a favourite amusement with me. At one time I had been an invalid for a considerable period and had taken from my father's library a book by Bishop Wilkins. . . . Herein were given accounts of many of the old methods of secret communication, ciphers, string writing, hidden meanings, and many of the mechanical devices employed in an age when the correspondence of ambassadors, spies and secret agents was mainly conducted by such means. (53)

Once Archie has taught Bacon's biliteral cipher to Marjory, they use it to communicate to one another after she is kidnapped. Here is one of the few opportunities to glimpse Stoker's training in mathematics. Although Joseph S. Bierman commented on the complex mathematical punning in "When 7 Went Mad," [7] there is no commentary on Stoker's use of cipher in *The Mystery of the Sea* aside from his friend Arthur Conan Doyle who complimented Stoker on the use of cipher: "I've done a bit in cryptograms myself, but that knocks me out" (cited by Belford, 296).

If scientific certainty helps the two young lovers to communicate over vast distances and spans of time, it also helps Archie to discover the buried treasure near his house. Remembering what the Spanish don's papers had revealed about the cave where the treasure was buried, Archie applies his knowledge of geological formations:

The one guiding light as to locality in the Don's narrative was the description of the cave 'the black stone on the one hand and the red on the other.' Now at Broad haven the gneiss and the red sienite join, and the strata in places seem as if welded together or fused by fire. (166)

It is only a matter of time until Archie discovers the missing treasure.

If Archie and Marjory frequently employ either science or scientific principles to lead them to the truth, it is one of the novel's less scientific characters, Don Bernardino, who comments on the place of science in the modern world: "It is manifest to me that in these days of science nothing can long remain hidden, when once a clue has been found" (197).

Throughout *Mystery* Stoker uses the contrast between Archie and Marjory, scions of the future, and Don Bernardino, a representative of the past, to demonstrate what the future will be like. Everything about Don Bernardino suggests that, like Dracula, he is an anachronism. Archie describes his physical appearance as "despite his modern clothes, just such a picture as Velasquez would have loved to paint, or as Fortuny might have made to live again" (159). His litany of names also links him to the feudal past: "In my own land, the land of my birth, the cradle of my race, I am called Don Bernardino Yglesias Palealogue y Santordo y Castelnuova de Escoban, Count of Minurca and Marquis of Salvaterra!" (159). Furthermore, like Dracula, he seems to be a kind of evolutionary throwback as well, one who resembles an animal when he becomes angry, his eyes like "a cat in the dark; a narrow slit with a cavern of fire within" (193) and his mouth like a dog or wolf: "As he spoke, the canine teeth began to show" (194). [8] Stoker also reinforces that Don Bernardino is a relic of the past rather than a symbol of the future by having him die without issue. At the novel's end, his body is returned to the past when Archie and Marjory, who represent a scientific and technological future, accompany his body back to Spain and lay it "amongst the tombs of his ancestors" (270).

There are other evolutionary throwbacks in the novel, several of them reminding readers of *Dracula*, where Stoker uses the theories of Lombroso and Nordau to reinforce that criminals are "a survival of the primitive man and the carnivorous animals." [9] The fates of these criminals are more grim than that of Don Bernardino, however, their bodies being found either "terribly mangled" or "swallowed in the sea" (269).

Although Don Bernardino and the criminals in *Mystery* are primitives, they are not necessarily Gothic. Indeed, much of the novel's Gothic mystery resides in one of literature's truly unique characters, Stoker's Gormala MacNiel. An elderly woman who is gifted with Second Sight (the ability to see into the future), she is, according to Haining, modeled on an actual person:

It was during one of these holidays in 1901 that he had a strange encounter with an old woman on the seashore. The woman was believed by the local people to have supernatural powers and was generally avoided. As a result of their meeting, Bram created a story, 'The Seer', which appeared in *The London Magazine* of November 1901. Doubtless Bram augmented the scraps of supernatural lore which he learned in Cruden Bay with further research in London, but it did make for an evocative story about the ancient belief in 'Second Sight.' [10]

Gormala haunts Hunter throughout the novel, frequently reminding him of his own occult abilities and reinforcing for the reader that science cannot provide the answer to everything. In fact, without Gormala, Archie would not have been able to swim to the boat where Marjory was held captive and rescue her. The rescue scene is full of mysterious details, for the dying Gormala advises Archie to use her powers:

"I'm done this time, laddie; the rocks have broke me when the roadie gav way. Listen tae me, I'm aboot to dee; a' the Secrets and the Mysteries 'll be mine soon. When the end is comin' haud baith my hands in ane o' yours, an' keep the ither ower my een. The, when I'm passin' ye shall see what my dead eyes see; and hear wi' the power o' my dead ears. Mayhap too, laddie, ye may ken the secrets and the wishes o' my hairt." (250)

Stoker uses the previous scene to remind the scientific Archie and the reader that the world is a mysterious place, beyond the reach of normal science:

All the time there was to me a dual consciousness. Whatever I saw before me was all plain and real; and yet I never lost for a moment the sense of my own identity. I knew I was on shore amid the rocks under the cliff, and that Gormala's dead body was beside me. . . . But there was some divine guiding principle which directed my thought—it must have been my thought, for my eyes followed as my wishes led, as though my whole being went too. They were guided from the very bow of the ship along the deck, and down the after hatchway. I went down, step by step, making accurate and careful scrutiny of all things around me. (252)

Having never been on the ship where Marjory is held captive, Archie can see the layout of the ship, details that enable him to rescue her more easily. However, though the scene is important to the plot of the novel, Archie's musings also remind readers of the same dualism that is so often evident in Stoker's works, a dualism that includes what is plain and real as well as what is mystical and incomprehensible.

While it may be going too far to argue that Stoker is himself convinced of the connection between science and the ineffable world, Archie frequently makes the connection. Thinking about Gormala, the normally scientific and rational Archie observes: "My own intellectual attitude to the matter interested me. I was not sceptical, I did not believe; but I think my mind hung in poise" (12). His own experiences ultimately convince him of the existence of a much larger world:

Even a few hours of experience had taught me much; for now that my mind was bent on the phenomena of Second Sight the whole living and moving world around me became a veritable diorama of possibilities. Within two days from the episode at the Pier head I had had behind me a larger experience of effort of occult force than generally comes to a man in a lifetime. When I look back, it seems to me that all the forces of life and nature became exposed to my view. A thousand things which hitherto I had accepted in simple faith as facts, were pregnant with new meanings. I began to understand that the whole earth and sea, and air—all that of which human beings generally ordinarily take cognisance, is but a film or crust which hides the deeper moving powers or forces. With this insight I began to understand the grand guesses of the Pantheists, pagan and Christian alike, who out of their spiritual and nervous and intellectual sensitiveness began to realise that there was somewhere a purposeful cause of universal action. An action which in its special or concrete working appeared like the sentience of nature in general, and of the myriad items of its cosmogony. (15)

As is plainly evident from the rest of the novel, Archie never leaves behind his faith in science and technology. He does, however, recognize that other strong forces are at work: "The fates were at work upon us. Clotho was spinning the thread which was to enmesh Marjory and myself and all who were in the scheme of the old prophecy of the Mystery of the Sea and its working out" (105).

Like *The Snake's Pass* and *Dracula*, *The Mystery of the Sea* ends with the deaths of its Gothic characters, Gormala and Don Bernardino, and with the representatives of progress looking ahead to a brighter future, a progress that is reinforced by the U.S. victory over Spain in the Spanish-American War. Like *Dracula*, *The Mystery of the Sea* leaves readers with a sense that in a conflict between the old ways and the new, the new ways will inevitably triumph. A brief episode at the beginning of the novel suggests that traditional ways are being supplanted when Archie asks the fisherman Lauchlane Macleod (whom Archie rather significantly identifies as an anachronism, a son of the Vikings[11]) his opinion about "the decline of the herring from the action of the trawlers in certain waters:"

He gave it, and it was a decided one, uncompromisingly against the trawlers and the laws which allowed them to do their nefarious work. . . . When he had pointed out that certain fishing grounds, formerly most prolific of result to the fishers, were now absolutely worthless he ended his argument:
'And, sure, good master, it stands to rayson. Suppose you be a farmer, and when you have prepared your land and manured it, you sow your seed and plough the ridges and make it all safe from wind and devastatin' storm. If, when the green corn be shootin' frae the airth, you take your harrow and drag it ath'art the spring' seed, where be then the promise of your golden grain?' (90)

There is no doubt in Lauchlane Macleod's mind that technological advances, in this case the use of a fishing net for dragging along the sea bottom, produce immediate successes.[12] His analogy to farming, however, is a reminder that such immediate success may undermine future success. It is a subtle reminder of the cost of many scientific discoveries and technological developments and thus undermines some of the confidence that both Archie and the reader might have.

Moreover, *The Mystery of the Sea*, like *Dracula*, recognizes both the forces of tradition and the fact that science has not yet gained total control over the modern world. In many ways, Gormala, like Dracula, her more obviously Gothic predecessor, remains the most powerful figure in the novel. Remnants of the past, both, even in death, continue to exert their presence over the present as Regenia Gagnier observes of Dracula:

Defeated by the modern age, he yet lives on with all the 'aura'—presence through time and space—of art.
This . . . ambivalence is hardly surprising when one remembers that Stoker spent ten years as a civil servant . . . worked as clerk, newspaper editor, reporter and writer . . . and after 1878 managed the Lyceum Theatre in London. To his penchants for sexual fantasy and sensational fiction he opposed what he knew best, management and information technique and technology. His monument to modern industry nonetheless reveals a longing for a mythic and imaginative art. (152)

Practical man that he was, Stoker celebrates the scientific and professional present while nonetheless looking at the heroic past. *The Mystery of the Sea,* like *Dracula*, is unable to relinquish the mysterious and heroic past entirely. It concludes only when Archie and Marjory return the "golden figure of San Cristobal which Benvenuto had wrought for the Pope" (and which had come to England with the Armada) to stand "over the Spaniard's tomb in the church of San Cristobal in far Castile" (270). Just as the Treaty of Paris concludes the Spanish-American War, Marjory's act mends a long-standing conflict that had begun with her ancestor, Sir Francis Drake, and Don Bernardino's.

## THE LADY OF THE SHROUD (1909)

A mere seven years later when Stoker wrote *The Lady of the Shroud,* he seemed more inclined to relinquish the mystery associated with the Gothic and to seek scientific and technological solutions. The change must not have come altogether easily, however, as the plot and structure of this remarkable novel reveal. Initially it seems to be a kind of sequel to *Dracula*, complete with another vampire, at least two characters who are gifted with Second Sight as well as a number of references to earlier Gothic literature. For example, Rupert orders an airplane from Whitby and notes that it is unshipped at Otranto. (Although both Whitby and Otranto are real geographical places, they would also be associated with the Gothic in the minds of many readers because Walpole's *The Castle of Otranto* is often considered the first Gothic novel and because Dracula enters England at Whitby.) Later his cousin explains that his mother prefers to live at Carfax (also the name of Dracula's first English residence) in Kent. The scene right before Rupert sees Teuta for the first time literally reverberates with Gothic details even though Rupert undermines the Gothic with a hint of scientific skepticism:

Owls hooted in the forest; bats taking advantage of the cessation of the rain, flitted about silently, like shadows in the air. But there was no more sign of moving ghost or phantom, or whatever I had seen might have been—if, indeed, there had been anything except imagination. (69)

Despite the suggestion that his mind may have been playing tricks on him, the scene might have come from almost any Gothic novel. No wonder that the reader, familiar with Gothic conventions, is likely to assume that Teuta is a vampire. However, the novel, which begins with a report of a vampire sighting in *The Journal of Occultism* (Stoker's fictionalized version of the mouthpiece produced by the Psychical Research Society)[13] and features Rupert's midnight marriage to his supposed vampire bride, concludes with a unified Balkan Federation, which Glover characterizes as "Stoker's liberal utopia in its fullest, most developed form" (52). Glover also puts Stoker's novel into a literary perspective by citing Krishan Kumar, *Utopia and Anti-Utopia in Modern Times:* [14]

For the end of the nineteenth century saw a revival of literary utopias, a trend both inspired by and in reaction against precisely the sorts of spectacular . . . technological achievements, like photography or the airplane, that Stoker loved to feature in his novels. At opposite poles, stories of "advanced mechanical civilizations jostled those of simple, back-to-nature utopias," and on this spectrum *The Lady of the Shroud* is positioned neatly in the middle. (53)

Gothic mystery is thus replaced by political and technological certainty.

Victor Sage, in "Exchanging Fantasies: Sex and the Serbian Crisis in *The Lady of the Shroud*," speaks for many readers when he observes that science is no substitute for the loss of Gothic mystery[15] and that "once she has ceased to be a credible supernatural vampire, Teuta turned into the dullest of matrons and loses all her power as a fictional propaganda weapon" (132). Despite the loss of power, *The Lady of the Shroud* [16] is important because it reveals that Stoker has gained confidence in the power of science and technology.

Even though the novel ultimately abandons all pretense of being a Gothic work, the opening is appropriately mysterious even though Gothic mystery, even here, is coupled with the scientific desire to understand that mystery. The report of the supposed vampire sighting is prepared by "Mr Peter Caulfield, whose reports of Spiritual Phenomena in remote places are well known to the readers of 'The Journal of Occultism'" (1). Caulfield is careful to add that the phenomenon he describes was verified by three independent witnesses—Captain Mirolani and "two of his officers, Signori Falamano and Destilia" and that "none of them had either knowledge or experience of Occult matters," whereas he had spent over thirty years making a "special study of the subject and have gone to and fro over the earth investigating to the $n$th all records of reported Spiritual Phenomena" (2). Caulfield's description of his procedure suggests that it was similar to the stated aims of the Psychical Research Society, which was founded in 1882, to "investigate that large body of debatable phenomena designated by such terms as mesmeric, psychical and spiritualistic" and to do so "without prejudice of prepossession of any kind, and in the same spirit of exact and unimpassioned enquiry which has enabled Science to solve so many problems, once not less obscure nor less hotly debated." [17] Thus both "The Journal of Occultism" and the Psychical Research Society employ scientific procedures to examine all kinds of mysterious phenomena.

In *Rule of Darkness: British Literature and Imperialism, 1830–1914*, Brantlinger looks at the scientific aspects of the Society for Psychical Research, paying particular attention to the work of Andrew Lang, who served as its president but whose "opinions about psychic phenomena always retain a healthy skepticism stopping short of supernatural explanations." Brantlinger adds that Lang "favors instead explanations in terms of extraordinary, hitherto unidentified mental powers, including the power of 'unconscious cerebration' to create illusions of ghosts or spirits and to perform telepathic feats. If we assume that psychic phenomena do occur, then the theory that they emanate from the subconscious is the chief alternative to what Lang calls "the old savage theory" of "the agency of the spirits of the dead." [18] Brantlinger observes, however, that some of Lang's contemporaries "moved . . . away from an early skepticism toward increasing and occasionally absolute faith in occult phenomena, including demonic invasions and possessions of reality."

A.J. Balfour . . . Conservative prime minister from 1902 to 1905, produced several "metaphysical" essays—*A Defence of Philosophic Doubt* (1879), *The Foundations of Belief* (1895), and others—that make the case for faith by sharply dividing science and religion. Balfour argues that the two are separate, equally valid realms; the methods and discoveries of science cannot invalidate those of religion. That his sympathies lie with religion is obvious. In his presidential address to the Society for Psychical Research in 1894, Balfour expresses his joy that the society's work demonstrates "there are things in heaven and earth not hitherto dreamed of in our scientific philosophy." (241–42)

Looking at various of Stoker's works reveals that he too mulled over the origin of mysterious phenomena. In fact, I began this study to try to understand Stoker's peculiar juxtaposition of the mysteries usually included in Gothic literature and the certainty presented in nineteenth-century views on science.

In his protagonist, Rupert St. Leger, Stoker creates a character who is interested in occult phenomena but who is also skeptical by nature AND by training. Like Stoker himself, Rupert obviously feels pulled in both directions. Coming to the romantic Land of the Blue Mountains, he is pulled in the direction of the occult and mysterious: "It was natural enough that my thoughts should tend towards something uncanny—the belief that this place is haunted, conveyed in a thousand ways of speech and inference" (68). He couples this tendency with a strong dose of skepticism, however, noting that he had "investigated and reported on too many cases for the Psychical Research Society to be ignorant of the necessity for absolute accuracy in such matters of even the minutest detail" (67). Thus, when he suspects that his lovely midnight visitor is a vampire, he carefully weighs the evidence rather than jumping to a conclusion:

Briefly, the evidence in favour of accord between the facts of the case and the Vampire theory were:
   Her coming was at night—the time the Vampire is, according to the theory, free to move at will.
   She wore her shroud—a necessity of coming fresh from grave or tomb, for there is nothing occult about clothing which is not subject to astral or other influences.
   She had to be helped into my room—in strict accordance with what one sceptical critic of occultism has called 'the Vampire etiquette'. (78)

Evidence suggests that his visitor is a vampire, but Rupert, casting all logic aside, falls in love with her nonetheless. He is saved by the fact that, this time, the truth is truly stranger than fiction, for, as *The Lady of the Shroud* makes clear, Teuta had merely used the legend of the vampire to conceal herself from potential kidnappers. Thus, halfway through the novel, Stoker entirely abandons the Gothic for the scientific and technological present.
   In the previous paragraph, I confidently announced that Stoker had totally abandoned the mystery associated with the Gothic. There are two significant exceptions—the gift of Second Sight shared by Rupert and his aunt Janet MacKelpie and the fact that, beyond all logic, Rupert falls in love with the supposed vampire. At one point Rupert considers the talent that he had observed in his aunt and wonders whether he too might have the gift as well:

Could not I as well as Aunt Janet have a little Second Sight! I went towards the window, and, standing behind the curtain, listened. Far away I thought I heard a cry, and ran out on the Terrace; but there was no sound to be heard, and no sign of any living thing anywhere; so I took it for granted that it was the cry of some nightbird, and came back to my room. (140)

When, on the next page, Rupert learns that Teuta had been kidnapped by the Turks, the reader suspects that he had indeed heard her cry the night before and that the generally rational Rupert is indeed gifted with Second Sight. This circumstance confirms an earlier observation that Rupert had made about the power of instinct: "We humans place far too little reliance on instinct as against reason; and yet instinct is the great gift of Nature to all animals for their protection and the fulfillment of their functions generally" (70).

Although instinct is not precisely Gothic, it may seem mysterious, even overwhelming, to people who believe that the world can be categorized and understood. Moreover, the power that Rupert associates with instinct is linked—at least indirectly—with the fact that even Stoker's most rational characters often fall in love at first sight. Reading various criticism of Stoker's novels, I gather that I am not the only reader to be overwhelmed by his enthusiasm for love at first sight. Nonetheless, his emphasis on the mysterious power of love is a characteristic found in practically everything that he wrote and is, moreover, recognition of the fact that science and technology do not control everything. Of course, Rupert and many of Stoker's other heroes are throwbacks in other ways as well. Described on several occasions as resembling his Viking ancestors, he also bears "himself as a Paladin of old, his mighty form pausing for no obstacle" (153). On some levels at least, it seems that Stoker would like to preserve the best of the heroic past and join it to the scientific and technological present.

Whereas Stoker continues to remind readers of the emotional bond between Rupert and Teuta, much of the rest of *The Lady of the Shroud* is a testimony to the transformative power of technology. Indeed Rupert almost immediately begins to think about using technology to transform the Land of the Blue Mountains:

We have such a fine head of water here, and the climate is, they tell me, usually so lovely that we can do anything in the gardening way. If it should ever turn out that the climate does not suit, we shall put a great high glass roof over it, and *make* a suitable climate. (55, emphasis in original)

Rupert also comments on the rich natural resources of the Blue Mountains, which are "as yet undeveloped . . . trees of splendid growth . . . mineral wealth of many kinds" (214). It is clear that, as Arthur Severn does in *The Snake's Pass*, Rupert plans to use technology to develop these natural resources:

Thither came by various rails of steep gradient, by timber-shoots and cable-rails, by aerial cables and precipitating tubes, wealth from over ground and under it; for as our Land is all mountains, and as these tower up to the clouds, transport to the sea shall be easy and of little cost when once the machinery is established. As everything of much weight goes downward, the cars of the main tunnel of the port shall return upward without cost. We can have from the mountains a head of water under good control, which will allow of endless hydraulic power, so that the whole port and the mechanism of the town to which it will grow can be worked by it. (214–15)

Unlike Severn, who manages a relatively small parcel of land in Western Ireland, King Rupert and Queen Teuta hope to use technology to bring the entire Land of the Blue Mountains into the modern era.

Though there is some evidence of the use of technology for industrial and commercial growth, much of the technology in *Lady* is used for military purposes. Recognizing that his adopted homeland is surrounded by hostile (or potentially hostile) forces, Rupert uses his wealth to provide it with an army, navy, and even an air force and to supply arms for "every man and woman—even the children—of our land to take a part in its defence should such be needed" (82). These arms include "fifty thousand of the newest-pattern rifles, the French Ingis-Malbron, which has surpassed all others, and sufficient ammunition to last for a year of war" (82).

As was evident in Chapter 2, Stoker had gained some vicarious experience with military matters through his brother George's experiences during the Russo-Turkish War and through his own experiences with various members of the armies and navies of England and the United States. Additionally, his travels had also caused him to be interested in various kinds of ships, and Rupert's navy includes the most technologically sophisticated ships available:

She is the last word in naval construction—a torpedo yacht. A small cruiser, with turbines up to date, oil-fuelled, and fully armed with the latest and most perfect weapons and explosives of all kinds. The fastest boat afloat to-day. Built by Thorneycroft, engined by Parsons, armoured by Armstrong, armed by Krupp. (116)

Stoker had evidently done his homework prior to outfitting his hero. Of the manufacturers that Rupert mentions, Thorneycroft and Krupp are still in business. Thorneycroft still manufactures engines for small boats, and Krupp is still in the business of making steel and arms, though the family company became a corporation in 1968. The company supported Prussia's and Germany's military ventures in the nineteenth and twentieth centuries, and Stoker would undoubtedly have associated the name with the fact that the company was the chief supplier of arms to the German Empire.[19]

Even more impressive is the fact that Stoker is already thinking of an air force that can be launched from armored aircraft carriers. Though the United States and various European countries did have some aircraft ready for combat by World War I, Stoker's aircraft, along with the crablike submarine that destroys the Turkish warship, are fanciful creations rather than accurate depictions of what was available at the time. Observing that the Wright brothers had made their most successful flights only in "the last months of the previous year" and that "only as the book was published did Bleriot successfully fly the Channel," Ludlum comments on how prophetic Stoker's plans were and notes that Stoker "had already given his Land of the Blue Mountains a royal air force" (159). Ludlum adds that Stoker had no doubt of the airplane's "ultimate power. His fantastic last scene . . . written more than five years before the start of World War I, now reads prophetically" (159–60).

Stoker's military machinery, though prophetic, is also highly imaginative. The airplane involved in the dramatic rescue of Teuta's father, for example, hovers quietly over the tower in which he is held prisoner. The description of exactly what the submarine does is equally fanciful:

The ship was . . . full in view. As I looked, she gave a queer kind of quick shiver, prow and stern, and then sideways. It was for all the world like a rat shaken in the mouth of a skilled terrier. . . . I noticed that nothing was stirring. The men who had been at the guns were all lying down; the men in the fighting-tops had leaned forward or backward, and their arms hung down helplessly. Everywhere was desolation—in so far as life was concerned. . . . It was evident that some terrible shock had been given to the mighty war-vessel. (184–85)

Exactly what that shock was the reader never learns. Despite the lack of absolute accuracy, however, it is clear that Rupert St. Leger is, like Archie and Marjory in *The Mystery of the Sea*, a techno-nerd who always wants the latest and best in the way of technological gadgetry.

Given European military history subsequent to 1909, the novel ends on an ominous note with the following exchange between Rooke, the Lord High Admiral of the Land of the Blue Mountains, and the Western King:

"It must need some skill to drop a letter with such accuracy." With imperturbable face the admiral replied:
    "It is easier to drop bombs, Your Majesty." (258)

Stoker, of course, could not have imagined the carnage of twentieth-century warfare. In addition, Stoker makes it clear that, in spite of his preparations for war, Rupert is working toward a negotiated peace that would make such arms unnecessary.

If Stoker sometimes plays "fast and loose" with the facts regarding technological development, he also incorporates enough historical truth to make his entirely fictional Land of the Blue Mountains believable. Because of its mountainous terrain and its border on the Adriatic, where Teuta's coffin is first sighted, it resembles both Albania and Montenegro and is in danger of being annexed from all sides:

Greece, Turkey, Austria, Russia, Italy, France, had all tried in vain. . . . Austria and Greece, although united by no common purpose or design, were ready to throw in their forces with whomsoever might seem most likely to be victor. Other Balkan states, too, were not lacking in desire to add the little territory of the Blue Mountains to their more ample possessions. Albania, Dalmatia, Herzegovina, Servia, Bulgaria, looked with lustful eyes on the land, which was in itself a vast natural fortress, having close under its shelter perhaps the finest harbour between Gibraltar and the Dardanelles. (33)

To add to the potential confusion, Stoker associates Teuta with Serbia, a landlocked country during the period that Stoker describes: "For the Voivodin Teuta of Vissarion must be taken as representing in her own person the glory of the old Serb race, inasmuch as being the only child of the Voivode Vissarion, last male of his princely race" (145). In addition, a letter from Roger Melton to Rupert mentions the "'Balkan struggle' of '90" (32). There was however no specific episode in 1890 to which Stoker is referring.

Because I am not an expert on either Balkan history or on British public policy regarding the Balkans and therefore run the risk of making what is a confusing political situation even more confusing, I am going to return to the relevant fact here. Stoker obviously believed that the judicious use of technology could help to alleviate even complicated political issues.[20] Rupert envisions a unified Balkan Federation:

My own dream . . . was to make 'Balka'—the Balkan Federation—take in ultimately all south of the line drawn from the Isle of Serpents to Aquileia. . . . Of course, it involved Austria giving up Dalmatia, Istria, and Sclavonia, as well as part of Croatia and the Hungarian Banat. . . . Each of these integers would be absolutely self-governing and independent, being only united for purposes of mutual good. I did not despair that even Turkey and Greece recognizing that benefit and safety would ensue without the destruction or even minimizing of individuality, would, soon or later, come into the Federation. (240–41)

Judging from Rupert's plans for the Land of the Blue Mountains, I gather that the "mutual good" of which he is thinking would include trade, industry, and commerce. A sound military defense of the kind he had already put in place for his adopted homeland would undoubtedly be necessary. And here, Stoker's history is more accurate:

True it is that the Turk, after warring for a thousand years, is fading into insignificance. But from the North . . . have crept towards our Balkans the men of a mightier composite Power. Their march has been steady; and as they came, they fortified every step of the way. Now they are hard upon us, and are already beginning to swallow up the regions that we have helped to win from the dominion of Mahound. The Austrian is at our very gates. Beaten back by the Irredentists of Italy, she has so enmeshed herself with the Great Powers of Europe that she seems for the moment to be impregnable to a foe of our stature. There is but one hope for us—the uniting of the Balkan forces to turn a masterly front to North and West as well as to South and East. (221)

Having established this federation, Stoker clearly believes that the unified Balkan states need only to use technology to create a brand new world.

## THE LAIR OF THE WHITE WORM (1911)

*The Lady of the Shroud* seems to leave the Gothic entirely behind, and *Famous Impostors*, Stoker's next book, published the following year, is almost entirely concerned with real world events. In his last novel, *The Lair of the White Worm*, published in 1911, Stoker might be said to return to the Gothic with a vengeance although the mystery is definitely tied up with science and technology.

Unlike the other novels with which this chapter has been concerned, which are set in Stoker's present and are full of the technological marvels of the fin de siècle, *The Lair of the White Worm* is set earlier in the nineteenth century. (Internal evidence suggests that it takes place some time between 1820 and 1850):

The first Caswall in our immediate record is Edgar . . . who came into his kingdom just about the time that George III did. He had one son of about twenty-four. There was a violent quarrel. . . . the son left the house. . . . He never came back to the house again. . . . It was only due to the watchfulness of the lawyers that the birth and death of a new heir was ever made known. . . . the great-grandson of the Edgar whose son had left him. [21]

The earliest conceivable date for the quarrel would therefore be 1760, the date at which George III took the throne. Figuring a generation as twenty years would make the novel's present 1820. If a generation is considered to be thirty years, the novel's present would be 1850, and 1850 or even later is more likely because the novel opens with a discussion of travel by rail between London and Stafford. Such travel would have been entirely possible in 1850 because of the railroad mania of the 1830s and 1840s.

Dating *Lair* precisely is unnecessary and may be impossible because of the lack of specific dates. What is appropriate to note is that the novel takes place in England before science and technology are well established in the mind of the ordinary citizen. Furthermore, it seems to take place during a period of transition when people can travel both by carriage and by rail and when many people do not understand the dangers of lightning and electricity. Certainly, the fiery conflagration at the conclusion occurs because Lady Arabella and Edgar Caswall are ignorant of science. Equally important, the scientific figures in the novel are amateurs rather than professionals. Sir Nathaniel de Salis is a professional diplomat and an amateur scientist, the "President of the Mercian Archaeological Society. . . . He is also our local geologist and natural historian . . . and knows all the old legends" (12), a man typical of the amateur archeologists of his day as they are described by A. Bowdoin Van Riper in *Men among the Mammoths: Victorian Science and the Discovery of Human Prehistory*: [22]

The rapid proliferation of archaeological societies reflected this growing interest in the past and its material remains. Of the two national and forty-one county archaeological societies founded in England between 1830 and 1880, half were established during the fifteen years between 1840 and 1855. The new societies made archaeology a nationwide enterprise for the first time in Britain. (15)

Van Riper also notes that nineteenth-century archeologists, like Sir Nathaniel, adopted scientific techniques from geology:

The founders of the new subdiscipline and its research tradition—John Evans, John Lubbock, Augustus Pitt-Rivers, and William Boyd Dawkins . . . came from disparate intellectual backgrounds but shared . . . a belief that it could best be studied by using techniques borrowed from geology. (186)

Woven into the plot of *Lair* is evidence of Stoker's own interest in geology, including references to earlier geological periods ("The condition of things we speak of belongs to the geologic age . . . when the struggle for existence was so savage that no vitality which was not fc :nded in a gigantic form could have even a possibility of survival" [54]) and to the connection between geology and industrialization:

Stafford owes much of its wealth to the large deposits of the rare china clay found in it from time to time. These deposits became in time pretty well exhausted; but for centuries Stafford adventurers looked for the special clay as Ohio and Pennsylvania farmers and explorers looked for oil. Anyone owning real estate on which clay can be discovered strikes a sort of gold mine. (253)

Ultimately it is Adam Salton's knowledge of geology that enables him to destroy the White Worm and increase his already substantial fortune, a further indication that knowledge of geology is important to *Lair* (and also to *The Snake's Pass* and *The Mystery of the Sea*).

Similarly, in both *The Snake's Pass* and *The Mystery of the Sea*, knowledge of geological formations ultimately produces great riches. In *Dracula*, on the other hand, interest in geology is almost irrelevant:

The very place, where he have been alive, Un-Dead for all these centuries, is full of strangeness of the geologic and chemical world. There are deep caverns and fissures that reach none know whither. There have been volcanoes, some of whose openings still send out waters of strange properties, and gases that kill or make to vivify. Doubtless, there is something magnetic or electric in some of these combinations of occult forces which work for physical life in strange way; and in himself were from the first some great qualities. (378)

In fact, a little knowledge of geology merely adds to the Gothic mystery of *Dracula*.

In addition to his academic training in science, Stoker could also have gained some knowledge of archeology from his friendships with the Wilde family in Dublin and with Sir Richard Burton. (Stoker's relationship with the two of them is explored in greater detail in the previous chapter.) Clearly the first half of the nineteenth century was still a period when a person might be interested in a number of radically different fields rather than a specialist. It was also a period in which the juxtaposition of science and legend does not seem as peculiar as it does today.

Adam Salton, the youthful protagonist, is also presented as an amateur. Reared in Australia, he is a rancher (whose horse farm has more than a thousand head) with knowledge of historical research (he had written a lecture on the Romans in Britain), "farriery and such mechanics as come into travel" (30), and explosives. (Like Richard Sutherland, the civil engineer in *The Snake's Pass*, he is familiar with the use of explosives, especially as explosives can be used to reclaim previously unused land. In the case of Adam Salton, however, Stoker is guilty of an anachronism when he has him inform Sir Nathaniel of the explosion at Hell Gate in New York [257], for John Newton (1823–1895) did not work on Hell Gate until the 1880s. A general and engineer who had fought and engineered at Antietam, Fredericksburg, Chancellorsville, and Gettysburg, Newton had used thousands of pounds of explosives to make the passage through Hell Gate safer.) [23]

Like so many of Stoker's heroes, Adam Salton is a technocrat who looks to the future rather than to the past. His opponents, on the other hand, are rooted in the ancient past. Edgar Caswall is, like Dracula, connected to this past in various ways. Although he did not literally live in the past, he is a primitive being nonetheless whose "cold, hard nature" resembles the "dominant, masterful nature" (18) that Sir Nathaniel associates with the Romans.

Even more primitive is the sinister Lady Arabella March who has the ability to transform into a primeval serpent; thus, like Dracula, she is literally a relic from the past though a past infinitely more distant and less human than his. Her home, Diana's Grove, is the site of an enormous well hole that has concealed the White Worm for centuries as well as a dwelling that reveals connections to the historical past, "a Roman temple, possibly founded on a pre-existing Druidical one. Its name implies the former, and the grove of ancient oaks suggests the latter" (24).

As he had done with *Dracula,* Stoker manages to integrate the past with the present by having these representatives of the primitive past (along with another primitive, Caswall's African servant, Oolanga) impact the modern world. In *Lair,* Edgar Caswall returns to claim his family dwelling, and the White Worm (for reasons that Stoker never adequately explains) returns after centuries of dormancy to wreak havoc on the countryside. The only explanation offered suggests that, like Dracula, she had been resting for a period. She "has been in the habit of sleeping for a thousand years at a time. . . . However, be all that as it may, her ladyship is now nightly on the prowl . . . in her own proper shape that she used before the time of the Romans" (218).

Although Lady Arabella is frequently presented as a human temptress (daughter of an impoverished gentleman, she had married for money once before and apparently hopes to use her feminine wiles to attract another wealthy husband), she is more monster than human being. Initially attracted to her beauty, Adam is soon repelled by her behavior: He watches her shoot one mongoose, charm a second, rip a third to pieces with her bare hands, and finally drag Oolanga to his death in the well hole. This last scene is graphic and designed to emphasize Lady Arabella's inhuman nature:

She moved forward . . . with her bare hands extended, and had just seized  him, when . . . the king-cobra-killer flew at her. . . . she caught hold of it, and . . . actually tore it in two. . . . In another instant she had seized Oolanga, and . . . drawn him . . . down into the gaping aperture. (174)

The precise relationship between human woman and monster is a complex one that Stoker doesn't even attempt to explain, and Mimi Watford Salton observes that most modern people wouldn't believe in Lady Arabella's transformation if she told them. Much like Jonathan Harker at the conclusion to *Dracula*, she almost disbelieves her own eyes:

The more Mimi thought . . . the more puzzled she was. Adam had actually seen Lady Arabella coming from her own house on the Brow, yet he—and she too—had last seen the monster . . . wallowing in the Irish Sea. . . . On either side of her was a belief impossible of reception. . . . And yet . . . in old days there had been monsters . . . and certainly some people had believed in just such mysterious changes of identity. (245)

The contrast between proof and belief might shed some light on our discussion of Stoker's use of science. Unfortunately, as in *Dracula*, the surviving characters do not follow normal scientific protocol. They neither publish the results of their experiments nor feel compelled to explain their decisions to anyone; and the novel concludes with an apocalyptic explosion that destroys both Diana's Grove and Castra Regis. Once again, the scientific and technological forces of the present (Adam Salton, his uncle, and Sir Nathaniel) triumph over the forces of the past, in this case a primeval serpent rather than a Renaissance warlord/supernatural being.

In fact, the appropriately named Adam Salton sees himself as a new kind of man. An Australian, he prides himself on his technological understanding, as we see in the following scene when he repairs Lady Arabella's broken carriage: "'All right, I am a workman. . . . I am an Australian, and, as we have to move about fast, we are all trained to farriery and such mechanics as come into travel'" (30). Like Lord Athlyne who repairs his own automobile and Rupert S. Leger who flies his own airplane (indeed like Stoker himself who delighted in getting the Lyceum Company from place to place in the most efficient way possible and who, therefore, like Mina and Jonathan Harker, memorized train and boat schedules), Adam has allied himself with more advanced technological thinkers.

Neither Edgar Caswall nor Lady Arabella has any interest in science. Edgar even has an opportunity to learn about electricity from his Franklinesque kite-flying experiments, but he is finally more superstitious than scientific:

He took a personal interest in the keeping of the great kite flying. He had a vast coil of string . . . which worked on a roller fixed on the parapet of the tower. There was a winch for the pulling in of the slack of the string; the outgoing line was controlled by a racket. . . . Edgar began to attribute to it, in his own mind, almost human qualities. It became to him a separate entity, with a mind and a soul of its own. (107).

Thus, the kite becomes a deity for Edgar, an object of belief, rather than the subject of a scientific experiment, an object of knowledge. Another scene, in which Edgar opens a chest that had been left to his grandfather by Mesmer, also makes it clear that he is driven more by intuition, a mysterious and unpredictable force, than by reason:

He was conscious of being still asleep, and of acting rather in obedience to some unseen and unknown command than in accordance with any reasonable plan to be followed by results which he understood and was aiming at. . . . His fingers seemed to have acquired a new and exquisite subtlety and even a volition of their own. Then he brought some force to bear—how or where, he knew not,—and soon the room was filled with the whirr of machinery moving at great speed. (116–17).

Even though he has apparatus that might be used in scientific experiments, Edgar does not use it for the advancement of science. In fact, much like *Dracula*'s Lucy Westenra, Edgar is powerful but largely unconscious of the source of that power; and Sir Nathaniel draws the reader's attention to Edgar's lack of awareness when he observes the potential hazards of kite flying during a thunderstorm: "Kite flying on a night like this from a place like the tower of Castra Regis is, to say the least of it, dangerous. . . . It is bringing the lightning into where he lives" (302). Truly, Edgar's kite does ultimately bring fire and destruction to himself and his dwelling.

The destruction of Diana's Grove, Lady Arabella, and the White Worm also stems from Lady Arabella's fascination with things she does not understand. A fortuitous bolt of lightning strikes Castra Regis, but Lady Arabella had previously unrolled a spool of magnesium ribbon (again for reasons that Stoker does not explain) that she found at the castle and provided the trail that carried that fire to the dynamite that Adam had placed around Diana's Grove. Perhaps the real response here is not to question why Lady Arabella does what she does but to observe that her actions are not based on either science or reason and that her destruction ultimately stems from her failure.

The destruction of Castra Regis and Diana's Grove is spectacular:

Then a broad ribbon of fire seemed to drop on the tower of Castra Regis just as the thunder crashed. By the glare of the lightning he could see the tower shake and tremble and finally fall to pieces like a house of cards. . . . With inconceivable rapidity running along the ground in the direction of Diana's Grove, [it] reached the dark silent house, which in the instant burst into flame at a hundred different points. (314)

As a result of this explosion, almost nothing remains of these remnants of the past at the novel's conclusion: "Castra Regis was a shapeless huddle of shattered architecture. . . . As for Diana's Grove, they looked in vain for a sign which had a suggestion of permanence" (319–20).

Since both Lady Arabella and Caswall and their dwellings are associated with the past, it would appear that the end of *The Lair of the White Worm* signifies the triumph of science and technology over the past as well as the ascent of a professional middle class over the remnants of a feudal aristocracy. A number of studies show that nineteenth-century science was connected to the rise of the professional middle class. One of the best, Desmond's *Archetypes and Ancestors*, [24] reveals the antiaristocratic movement of science in the 1850s.

Stoker's interest in science seems to be similarly democratic. Hereditary privilege virtually disappears in both *Dracula* and *Lair*. Even Lord Godalming, an aristocrat, is allied with the middle class, whereas Adam Salton, who has inherited a great deal of money, is definitely middle class. Furthermore, in *Lair*, as elsewhere in Stoker's fiction, representatives of Western civilization triumph over forces that Stoker and his contemporaries regarded as primitive (and therefore inferior): white men over black men, dynamite over dinosaurs, the scientific middle class over remnants of the aristocracy, men's women over women alone. Oolanga, who dies relatively early in the novel, is presented as humanity at its most primitive, a "savage, with . . . all the hideous possibilities of a lost-devil-ridden child of the forest and the swamp—the lowest and most loathsome of all created things which were in some form ostensibly human" (34–35). He is thus deliberately contrasted with Adam Salton and Sir Nathaniel, who represent humanity at its most sophisticated and scientific.

Like the original endings to both *Dracula* and *The Jewel of Seven Stars*, the conclusion to *The Lair of the White Worm* combines natural energies with human power. That Salton's fuse is ignited by lightning even suggests that natural forces collaborate with technology to destroy evil. Indeed the conclusion to *Lair* suggests this connection, noting that it almost seems "as if Nature herself had tried to obliterate the evil signs of what had occurred, and to restore something of the aesthetic significance of the place" (322).

Tied to this sense that science, perhaps combined with nature, will conquer forces of the past is an examination of both race and gender, with both women and people of color being treated as primitive beings. In fact, no one—Adam, Lady Arabella, Edgar, Sir Nathaniel, or even Stoker himself—is overly concerned by Oolanga's horrifying death. What is somewhat surprising is that Mimi Watford Salton is celebrated by Stoker even though she is also presented as a woman of color (whereas her father was English, her mother had been Burmese). Unlike Oolanga, however, Mimi totally accepts the tenets of Western civilization, and she is accepted by the proponents of Western civilization. There seems no danger of her reverting to some primitive behavior. Certainly, the success of the dark-skinned Mimi suggests that skin color is less important than ideology.

However, if Oolanga represents the primitive African ("hideously ugly, with the animal instincts developed as in the lowest brutes; cruel, wanting in all the mental and moral faculties—in fact, so brutal as to be hardly human" [36]), Lady Arabella is more complex. As far as appearances go, the human Lady Arabella does not look monstrous: "The girl of the Caucasian type, beautiful, Saxon blonde, with a complexion of milk and roses, high-bred, clever, serene of nature" (36). Lady Arabella has another dimension to her character, however. Even as they prepare to destroy the White Worm, Sir Nathaniel and Adam consistently describe it in terms that combine femininity with primitive power:

I never thought this fighting an antediluvian monster was such a complicated job. This one is a woman, with all a woman's wisdom and wit, combined with the heartlessness of a *cocotte* and the want of principles of a suffragette. She has the reserved strength and impregnability of a diplodocus. We may be sure that in the fight that is before us there will be no semblance of fair-play. (206)

This passage emphasizes Lady Arabella's primitive strength and independence and furthermore puts them in political terms that would have been immediately relevant to Stoker's contemporaries. In her introduction to *Daughters of Decadence: Women Writers of the Fin-de-Siècle*,[25] Elaine Showalter examines some of these stereotypes and observes that the New Women writers "were threatening daughters of decadence" who attacked marriage and reproduction. She observes that "*Punch* never wearied of the chance to caricature New Women in cartoons, or to parody their fiction." She then quotes one particularly outraged reviewer:

Emancipated woman in particular . . . loves to show her independence by dealing freely with the relations of the sexes. Hence the prating of passion, animalism, "the natural workings of sex", and so forth, with which we are nauseated. Most of the characters in these books seem to be erotomaniacs. [Hugh Stutfield, 'Tommyrotics', *Blackwood's Magazine*, 157 (June 1895), p. 836]. (ix–x)

Lady Arabella resembles the suffragette or other forward New Woman.

If Lady Arabella's characterization suggests a negative stereotype of the New Woman or the suffragette, Mimi, the only woman to survive, is definitely a more traditional woman who has linked her fortune to Adam. Both her cousin Lilla, who had chosen to battle wills with Edgar, and Lady Arabella, who had attempted to control her own destiny and those of the world around her, are dead. Mimi, like Mina Harker in *Dracula*, is in every way a man's woman—a woman who has accepted the conventional wisdom of patriarchal civilization including its embrace of law and technology. Early in the novel, the wise old Sir Nathaniel warns Adam against falling in love with Lady Arabella and tells him that Mimi would be an acceptable wife: "She is indeed a very charming lady. I do not think I ever saw a girl who united in such perfection the qualities of strength of character and sweetness of disposition" (189). Ultimately, the novel suggests that the monstrous female must be destroyed before the world is safe for Mimi. The novel concludes with a return to domesticity and the expectation that Adam will use his already substantial fortune to produce a profit from the white clay he had discovered on Lady Arabella's property.

The more I read Stoker's novels, the more I am convinced that he counters Gothic and mysterious threats with science, that he incorporates both the scientific thought of his day (including material that we would now classify as social science), and that he uses this material to examine both his fear of regression/devolution and his fear that women are an inferior and dangerous presence. Moreover, in the majority of his novels, Stoker has his male protagonists use science/technology to overcome the powers that he associates with the primitive past.

Furthermore, *The Lair of the White Worm* provides an excellent opportunity to see Stoker as typical of his day in that he saw the incredible power of the past and hoped that science and technology would ultimately enable human beings to solve problems that had come to them from the past. Recognizing his optimism about science and technology does not mean that readers have to share it, however. Nor does it mean that we must share his willingness to destroy those who do not agree with him, for there is no doubt that the science that Stoker celebrates comes at an immense cost.

Included in that cost is the annihilation of everyone that the self-described scientists and technocrats see as primitive. These representatives of modernity do not see any horror in the trail of death and destruction that they leave behind them: for example, the deaths of Lucy Westenra, Dracula, the three vampire-brides in Dracula's castle, and even Quincy Morris as well as the deaths of Arabella, Edgar Caswall, and Oolanga. They do not even see that their condescending treatment of the people that they regard as primitive forces these individuals to deny much of what it means to be fully human. A century later, we can no longer share Stoker's confidence in the positive power of science and technology.

## NOTES

1. Bram Stoker, *The Snake's Pass*, 1890; rpt. Dingle, Co., Kerry, Ireland: Brandon, 1990.

2. One of the few people to write on *The Snake's Pass*, Nick Daly interprets the novel somewhat differently, looking at it as an example of literature that is apprehensive about colonial relations—"Irish Roots: The Romance of History in Bram Stoker's *The Snake's Pass*," *Literature and History* 4 (1992), 42–70. Daly observes:

*The Snake's Pass* develops a more uneasy thematics of imperial vision. Arthur, as a tourist, spends a great deal of his time in visually consuming Ireland; in his eyes the colonial territory is abstracted into a series of reassuring prospects. (48)

Daly goes so far as to identify "the immediate colonial context" as "the late nineteenth-century Land War that shattered the power of the Anglo-Irish as a class" (55) and comments that the novel provides "an imaginary solution to a political problem, landlord-tenant conflict, that it renders invisible" (56).

3. Haining and Tremayne suggest that Bram may have learned about the lost treasure from his mother:

Whether Charlotte was also responsible for the basis of this story is uncertain. Charlotte could well have picked up stories of the 1798 uprising in Sligo for, during that year, a French army under General Joseph Amable Humbert had landed in Killala, Co. Mayo, not far from Sligo, in an effort to help the Irish insurgents establish their republic. Charlotte identified the 1798 insurgent, George Blake, one of those who joined Humbert as her mother's brother. George was captured on 8 September 1798, after the battle at Ballinamuck. . . and immediately hanged (45–46).

4. A.P.M. Fleming and H.J. Brocklehurst, *A History of Engineering*. London: A. & C. Black, Ltd, 1925.

5. L.T.C. Rolt, *Victorian Engineering*. London: Penguin, 1970.

6. Lord Athylene describes his new automobile lovingly as a "beauty," capable of doing "sixty miles an hour easily" (Bram Stoker, *Lady Athlyne*. New York: Paul R. Reynolds, 1908, 124). The scene in which he and Joy Ogilvie take an unchaperoned drive to Scotland suggests that the sheer speed of the automobile is almost an aphrodisiac though, of course, that technological power comes at a price. On their way back from Scotland, Lord Athylene is arrested for speeding. Colonel Ogilvie then threatens to shoot him, thinking that Athylene had compromised his daughter's honor and reputation.

7. Joseph S. Bierman, "*Dracula*: Prolonged Childhood Illness and the Oral Triad," *American Imago* 29 (1972), 186–98.

8. William Hughes comments on Don Bernardino's appearance in an extremely interesting essay: "'Militant Instinct': The Perverse Eugenics of Bram Stoker's Fiction," *Bram Stoker Society Journal* (1994), 11–19.

9. Cesare Lombroso, "Criminal Anthropology: Its Origin and Application," *The Forum* 20 (1895), 35. Furthermore, as Daniel Pick reminds us in *Faces of Degeneration: A European Disorder, c. 1848–c. 1918.* (Cambridge: Cambridge University Press, 1989), science provides the solution to such criminal degeneration:

Lombroso's work insisted that science was not a symptom of degeneration, but a means of regeneration. If he denied the validity of grand metaphysical ideas, he was nonetheless profoundly idealistic in his desire to serve the nation through the scrupulous impartiality of his social theory. Lombroso's language sought to purge itself of extravagant metaphor, to produce a pure medium of description. He counterposed the artistic expressions, handwriting, fiction, of the delinquent and the law-abiding, the insane and the sane. (116–17)

10. Peter Haining, ed. *Shades of Dracula: Bram Stoker's Uncollected Stories.* London: William Kimber, 1982, 124.

11. Nicholas Daly comments on Stoker's use of "Viking," noting that it "seems to function as the common ideal of manhood":

Stoker uses "Viking" as a term of approbation in his *Personal Reminiscences of Henry Irving* as well as in his novels. This usage may owe something to the earlier adventure novels of Charles Kingsley, though perhaps also to the growing interest in Anglo-Saxon culture. In *The Snake's Pass,* where the connections of present and past heroism are heavily emphasized, the wedding of Arthur and Norah takes place in the "grand old church" at Hythe, "where the bones of so many brave old Norseman rest after a thousand years.'"(69)

Certainly Stoker does link "Viking" with a kind of heroic masculinity as Daly suggests. As *The Mystery of the Sea* reveals, however, the noble Viking is an anachronism, to be replaced by people like Archie, no less heroic certainly but scientific and professional as well.

12. It is interesting to speculate on the source of Stoker's information about herring. Perhaps he simply kept his ears open to the discussion of the people around him. Even though many readers lack enthusiasm for his use of dialect, there is no question that Stoker had a good ear for speech patterns. And, as Farson observes, Cruden, where Stoker spent so many vacations, was "also known as Port Erroll, a fishing village that depended on the local herring industry" (93).

13. Although Stoker seems to have made up this journal, a similarly titled journal, *The American Theosophist; A Journal of Occultism,* was published by the Theosophical Society between 1899 and 1914. I am grateful to Anne Garrison of the Georgia Tech Library for locating this information.

14. Krishan Kumar, *Utopia and Anti-Utopia in Modern Times*. Oxford: Basil Blackwell, 1987, 65.

15. Victor Sage, "Exchanging Fantasies: Sex and the Serbian Crisis in *The Lady of the Shroud*," in *Bram Stoker: History, Psychoanalysis and the Gothic*, edited by William Hughes and Andrew Smith, pp. 116–33. London: Macmillan Press Ltd.: 1998.

I once made a similar point in "*The Lady of the Shroud*: Stoker's Successor to *Dracula*," *Essays in Arts and Sciences* (1990), 82–96:

> *The Lady of the Shroud* is especially interesting, however, as a revised version of *Dracula*, which adapts the mythic figure of the vampire only to eliminate the uncanny and disturbing psychological characteristics so often associated with this figure. Thus, while the earlier novel raises troubling questions about individual identities and personal relationships, the later novel adapts many of the same formulas to produce merely a novel of suspense.

16. Bram Stoker, *The Lady of the Shroud*, 1909; reprint. Dover, NH.: Alan Sutton Publishing, Inc., 1994.

17. The information comes from Alan Gauld, *The Founders of Psychical Research*, (New York: Schocken, 1968, 138). I am indebted to Stephanie Moss for bringing this information to my attention in "Bram Stoker and the Society for Psychical Research," p. 85 in *The Shade and the Shadow: Papers Presented at "Dracula 97." a Centenary Celebration at Los Angeles, August 1997*, edited by Elizabeth Miller. Westcliff-on-Sea, Essex: Desert Island Books, 1998, 82–92.

18. Andrew Lang, "Psychical Research," *Encyclopedia Britannica*, 11th ed, 22:544–47. cited in Brantlinger (Ithaca: Cornell University Press, 1988), p. 240–41.

19. My thanks to Mary-Frances Panettiere, of the Georgia Tech Library, for pointing me to *The British Shipbuilding Industry, 1870–1914* written by Sidney Pollard and Paul Robertson in 1979 (VM299.7 .G7 P64), which explains that Thorneycroft was a yard on the Thames where ships were built. The Parsons Marine Steam Turbine Co. Ltd. patented and produced a successful engine design. The Engine Works of Sir W.G. Armstrong, Whitworth and Co. manufactured armored decks among other things. Harvey and Krupp created a process of heavy plate manufacturing and more.

20. At least two recent articles specifically deal with Stoker's treatment of Balkan politics. Victor Sage, "Exchanging Fantasies: Sex and the Serbian Crisis in *The Lady of the Shroud*," 116-133. Sage comments directly on the fact that Stoker had "two different but related propaganda aims . . . asserting the Masculine values of protective instinct and natural chivalry . . . to challenge the 'liberal' approach to Britain's foreign policy in the Balkans." He adds that *The Lady of the Shroud* "plays on traditional (but apparently outdated) British fears of Turkey and further suggests to the reader the desirability of Serbian expansion against Austria-Hungary, in the wake of the latter's annexation of Bosnia in 1908" (116). A second treatment of Stoker and "The Eastern Question" is Eleni Coundouriotis, "*Dracula* and the Idea of Europe," *Connotations* 9 (1999/2000), 143-159.

In addition, reading a lecture printed on the Web by Steven W. Sowards (http://www.lib.msu.edu/sowards/balkan/lect10.htm) made me think that Stoker's confusion about the Balkans may have mirrored England's somewhat inconsistent policy toward the Balkans at the end of the nineteenth century. It is especially relevant to think about the relationship between Stoker and Gladstone:

> British Balkan interests derived from interests in the Eastern Mediterranean. Given Britain's position as the most industrialized European state in the early 1800s, economic interest played a large role. . . . Britain needed to secure the shipping lanes to India. Those trade routes passed

through areas . . . that were nominally Turkish. . . . Britain also had humanitarian interests in the Balkans: with the most developed system of representative government in Europe (and the most influential popular press), London cabinets were under pressure when Ottoman misrule led to atrocities, uprisings and repression. Britain's strategic and humanitarian interests in the Ottoman parts of the Balkans tended to conflict. In 1876, William Gladstone . . . wrote a pamphlet called "The Bulgarian Horrors and the Question of the East" condemning the massacres which the Turks carried out in suppressing the latest Balkan revolt. After that year, no British cabinet could completely support the sultan. In 1853, Britain had gone to war rather than see Russian influence grow in the Balkans; when the Russians invaded and defeated Turkey in 1877-78, Britain stood by. . . . In 1878 Britain took control of the island of Cyprus, and in 1883 occupied Egypt and the Suez Canal. After that, the need to intervene on the Balkan mainland waned, although Britain did keep an eye on Greece and Russia's privileges at the Straits.

21. Bram Stoker, *The Lair of the White Worm*. London: Rider and Son, 1911, 15–17. All future quotations will be to this edition and will be included in the text.
22. A. Bowdoin Van Riper, *Men among the Mammoths: Victorian Science and the Discovery of Human Prehistory*. Chicago: University of Chicago Press, 1993, 15.
23. Henry Koeppel of the Georgia Tech Library located the relevant information on Hell Gate in *Encyclopedia Brittanica*, 11th edition, on August 6, 1998: <http://www.wbaifree.org/fish/hellsgate/hellgate.html>. The entry reveals the constructive impact of Newton's destruction:

His most important work . . . was the improvement of the Hudson River, and especially the removal of the obstructions to shipping in the dangerous entrance to the East River. . . . Under two of the largest obstructions . . . shafts were sunk from the shore, and tunnels were bored in every direction. In these tunnels thousands of pounds of explosives were placed, and the rocks blown into fragments.

24. Adrian Desmond, *Archetypes and Ancestors: Paleontology in Victorian London 1850–1875*. Chicago: University of Chicago Press, 1982.
25. Elaine Showalter, *Daughters of Decadence: Women Writers of the Fin-de-Siècle*. (New Brunswick, NJ: Rutgers University Press, 1993).

# Chapter 5
# The Place of Science in Stoker's Fiction and the Place of Science Fiction in the Stoker Oeuvre

After examining practically everything that Bram Stoker wrote, this study swings back to reconsider many of the questions with which I began, most of them moving to the larger question of science and technology in his work and whether that science might cause him to be considered as either an early writer of science fiction or as a writer who dabbled in a number of different genres as well as a writer of Gothic novels and adventure tales. Because Stoker is generally identified only as the author of *Dracula*, he is practically never associated with science fiction. Indeed, *Merriam Webster's Encyclopedia of Literature* [1] provides a broad definition of science fiction as a genre that includes both "a careful and informed extrapolation of scientific facts and principles" and as literature that ranges "into far-fetched areas flatly contradictory of such facts and principles." Despite the breadth of its definition, the *Webster* entry concludes with the positive assertion that *Dracula* is not science fiction:

In either case, plausibility based on science is a requisite, so that such a precursor of the genre as Mary Shelley's gothic novel *Frankenstein* (1818) is science fiction, whereas Bram Stoker's *Dracula* (1897), based as it is purely on the supernatural, is not. (1004)

Science fiction writer and historian Brian Aldiss agrees that *Dracula* is not science fiction. [2] In fact, of the people who mention science fiction and *Dracula* in the same breath most do so only to argue that *Dracula* is not an example of science fiction. Although the present study does deal with *Dracula* and even examines the science in that novel, it is also careful to remind readers that Stoker wrote sixteen other books—novels, romances, and works of nonfiction— plus numerous short stories, articles, and reviews and also that many of these works are not remotely Gothic or include only a few Gothic elements. Thus the question of whether or not Stoker can be considered a science fiction writer ought not to rest on *Dracula*.

For example, his first signed work, "The Necessity for Political Honesty," was published in Dublin in 1872 by James Charles & Son. *The Snake's Pass* (1890), *The Watter's Mou'* (1894), *The Shoulder of Shasta* (1895), *The Mystery of the Sea* (1902), *The Man* (1905), *Lady Athlyne* (1908), and *The Lady of the Shroud* (1909) combine sentimental romance with adventure. *The Duties of Clerks of Petty Sessions in Ireland* (1879), *A Glimpse of America* (1886), *Personal Reminiscences of Henry Irving* (1906), and *Famous Impostors* (1910) are nonfiction. *Under the Sunset* (1882), a collection of short stories, includes some stories that might be classified as Gothic along with several fables and other fantasy pieces; *Snowbound* (1908), another collection of short stories, alternates between a realistic frame tale and stories in a variety of genres that are designed to reveal the character of their tellers. *Miss Betty* (1898) is a historical novel. Indeed, of the seventeen books that he wrote, only *Dracula* (1897), *The Jewel of Seven Stars* (1902), and *The Lair of the White Worm* (1911) can be definitely classified as Gothic.

Furthermore, although the scholarly emphasis on *Dracula* tends to connect Stoker to the fin de siècle Gothic, Stoker's works span a period of forty years. His first published work, an unsigned review for the *Dublin Mail*, appeared in 1871, and his last, *The Lair of the White Worm*, in 1911. (There is also the posthumous collection of stories on which Stoker was working when he died, *Dracula's Guest—And Other Weird Stories*. This collection was published in 1914 and includes the much discussed story, "Dracula's Guest.") Thus, his written works go well beyond the fin de siècle to include works written within both the Victorian and Edwardian periods.

That *Dracula* is an example of Gothic literature is not in question. Nor is its tremendous popularity. Not only has it remained in print since its first publication in 1897, but English editions of *Dracula* are currently available through most major publishers, including Bantam, Broadview, Dover, Everyman, Modern Library, Norton Critical, Oxford World's Classics, Penguin, Signet, and Tor. It has also been translated into a number of other languages as well as interpreted and re-interpreted both on the stage and in film. As a result, many people who have never read Stoker's novel are more or less familiar with Dracula, its Gothic villain. Most of Stoker's other works, on the other hand, are either unavailable or are available only to people who have access to research libraries. Thus, one can conclude that Stoker is remembered today primarily for his contribution to the Gothic.

On the other hand, *Dracula* and much of what Stoker wrote features plausible scientific material. The real issue of this study, of course, is the way he integrates scientific assurance with Gothic mystery and awe and the question of whether or not his use of science might cause him to be classified as a writer of science fiction.

According to many standard definitions of science fiction, most of what Stoker wrote is too early to be classified as science fiction. For example, science fiction writer and critic James Gunn observes, in the introduction to *Anatomy of Wonder 4*, that science fiction began as a literary genre "in 1926 when Hugo Gernsback published *Amazing Stories* . . . the first SF magazine." Gunn adds, however, that previously "what is now classified as science fiction had been produced as scattered examples of travel stories, satires, utopias, extraordinary voyages, and scientific romances" before Gernsback brought together "the Poe inspiration, the Verne technological innovation and adventure." [3] In other words, Gunn observes that science fiction emerged as a distinct genre only in the 1920s but that some of the characteristics that people associate with the genre had existed earlier. John Sutherland makes a similar point, observing that the term science fiction "is a twentieth-century invention" but that "the genre's roots are found in the earlier century." [4] Some of the more significant forerunners that Gunn mentions are the utopias (and the conclusion to Stoker's *Lady of the Shroud* definitely makes it an example of this genre), and the technological innovation that Gunn associates with Verne is also evident in Stoker's works as well, including *The Snake's Pass*, *The Mystery of the Sea*, *Dracula*, *Lady Athylene*, and *Snowbound*. Furthermore, Gunn adds that "science fiction emerged not from the pulp tradition but from the tradition of popular science" (xix). Because the science in so many of Stoker's works can be classified as plausible or nearly plausible, one can see a definite connection to the field of popular science.

   Gunn is interested in twentieth-century science fiction, but Paul Fayter explores the specific connection between Victorian science and science fiction at the end of the nineteenth century. [5]

Contrary to repeated claims that modern science fiction was created in the American pulps of the 1920s, the genre was an offspring of the nineteenth-century Age of Science. According to Wells, the century underwent two major transformations, one technological, the other intellectual and spiritual. First was the appearance of new forms of transportation, especially railroads, which were symbolic of a host of engineering marvels with material benefits and other social transformations. Second was the crisis signaled by Thomas Malthus's *Essay on the Principles of Population* (1798), and climaxing in Charles Darwin's *Origin of Species* (1859). (257)

Indeed, because Fayter's definition of science fiction is not "limited to secular or future fiction" but is broadly "described as the literature of social change as initiated or mediated by technology and science" (258), it is certainly broad enough to include a great deal of what Stoker wrote, including *A Glimpse of America*, *The Snake's Pass*, *The Shoulder of Shasta*, *Dracula*, *The Mystery of the Sea*, *The Jewel of Seven Stars*, *The Man*, *Lady Athlyne*, *Snowbound*, *The Lady of the Shroud*, and *The Lair of the White Worm*. In other words, Fayter's definition of science fiction would include more than half of what Stoker wrote.

   Fayter's definition may be uncomfortably broad, however, for I can see that one might easily use his definition to characterize novels such as *Middlemarch*, *Mary Barton*, and Bronte's *Shirley* as science fiction simply because the events in them are influenced by changes in science and technology. Indeed, it would be difficult to find a Victorian work that is not somehow influenced by the changes taking place in science and technology, as a cursory reading of Tennyson or Dickens or George Eliot will attest. The mere fact that a particular work alludes to scientific or technological change is not enough for it to be classified as science fiction. Indeed, for me to classify a work as science fiction, the science and technology must be more than part of the historical apparatus. For a work to be classified as science fiction, science and technology must be brought to the forefront as part of the issues in question. Furthermore, the science in science fiction must be somewhat speculative rather than an articulation of current science. I would thus eliminate *A Glimpse of America*, *Personal Reminiscences*, and *Famous Imposters* from consideration. *Glimpse* is simply NOT fiction even though Stoker certainly celebrates American scientific and technological expertise in it and provides one reason that Stoker expects the United States to become a world leader. *Personal Reminiscences* and *Famous Imposters* occasionally treat science and technology also, but neither of them is fiction either.

Of course, the question that initially led me to this study was what seemed to me to be a strange interplay of Gothic mystery and scientific assurance in several of Stoker's novels. Other scholars who have pursued the direct connection between science fiction and the Gothic suggest that the interplay may be less peculiar than I originally thought. Sutherland, for example, notes that certain early science fiction (he mentions specifically Wells's *The Invisible Man* [1897], and *The Island of Dr Moreau* [1896], "re-established a link with the gothic tale of terror, also exploited by R. L. Stevenson, Oscar Wilde and Arthur Machen" (560). As is evident in Chapter 3, *The Jewel of Seven Stars*, because of the questions that it asks about the power of science, is very close in spirit to *Invisible Man*, *Moreau*, *Jekyll and Hyde*, and "The Great God Pan." It is important to remember that *Jewel* is anomalous for Stoker, though, as he is much more likely to side with science and its practitioners. Even when his novels and short stories reveal that scientists are flawed or ineffectual, he rarely suggests that they are evil or that their pursuit of scientific answers is a move in the wrong direction.

Judith Wilt, who is interested in "the mutation of gothic into science fiction" at the end of the nineteenth century (618), looks specifically at Stoker's novels in terms of this transformation:

But as the end of the nineteenth century approaches, anxieties about the future consequences of present actions grow even more powerful, and science or 'future' fiction emerges as a gothic form. Bram Stoker's novels ride the borders of this change. . . . Fears connected with the demands of progress, the perceived direction of evolution forward, have their important outlets in Victorian essays and in mainstream literature, but suppressed fears of regression, the secretly-perceived inevitable running-backwards of things, grow more powerful as science displaces, and at the same time partakes of, magic. (620)

Wilt thus emphasizes atavism, a tendency for species to revert to an earlier and more primitive form. Most definitely Stoker's Gothic novels and even his other fiction frequently presents more primitive characters who might even be considered members of entirely different species. Clearly thinking along the lines of evolutionary biology, Stoker presents Dracula and his fellow vampires as members of another species, one that is physically more evolved but also one that is morally trapped at an earlier stage. Both the vampires in *Dracula* and Lady Arabella in her guise of white worm are formidable foes, and so is Queen Tera whose strength comes both from her physical power and from her knowledge of science. Even Oolonga and Edgar Caswell, who are presented only as evil humans, share in this tendency to revert to the primitive. Because these primitives are unfamiliar with the science of Stoker's own day, all are revealed as anachronisms. Rooted in the knowledge of the distant past, they can be destroyed by people wielding the knowledge of modern science.

Whereas Wilt is more interested in the biological and social sciences and their influence on science fiction and the Gothic, Veronica Hollinger zeroes in on the hard sciences in "The Vampire and the Alien: Gothic Horror and Science Fiction" [6] and focuses on plausible science. In fact, she opens her discussion by quoting from H.G. Wells's 1933 "Preface to the *Scientific Romances*" in which he stresses the issue of plausibility:

"Nothing," he writes, "remains interesting where anything may happen." For this reason, the sf writer should provide the reader with orderly ground rules for his or her fictional universes. Wells concludes that "[the writer] must help [the reader] in every possible unobtrusive way to *domesticate* the impossible hypothesis." (214)

Lynn Hamilton, who wrote the entry on "Science Fiction" for *Victorian Britain: An Encyclopedia*, [7] agrees with Wells and Hollinger that the science must be plausible for a work to be classified as science fiction:

Science fiction, speculative fiction with a basis in plausible, if untested, scientific theory, emerged alongside the tremendous advances made in science and industry in the nineteenth century. Victorian science fiction . . . shows the writers' fascination with the possibilities inherent in new scientific discoveries while simultaneously reflecting a certain despair concerning the potentially destructive results of such investigation. This despair is evident in three concerns of early science fiction: travel in time and outer space; world cataclysm; and scientific breakthroughs resulting in transformations or adaptations of the human physique and psyche. (696)

If science fiction must have a basis in plausible scientific theory and if science fiction also encourages the reader to consider the place of science in its fictional world, then the following works by Stoker can arguably be classified as science fiction: *The Snake's Pass, Dracula, The Jewel of Seven Stars, The Lady of the Shroud*, and *The Lair of the White Worm*. I would omit *The Shoulder of Shasta, The Mystery of the Sea*, most of the stories in *Snowbound, The Man*, and *Lady Athlyne* from the category of science fiction both because the science depicted in them is simply not speculative enough and because the science contained in them is used only to provide a plausible background. Rather like *Middlemarch, Mary Barton*, and *Shirley*, the Stoker works in the second category simply describe an existing science and technology such as train travel in *Shasta* and *Snowbound*, explosives in *Mystery*, and the automobile in *Lady Athlyne*.

Therefore, although the current study of Bram Stoker has examined the scientific underpinnings of many of his works, his connection to the science fiction tradition can rest on only a handful of his books. The remainder of this chapter looks at *The Snake's Pass, Dracula, The Jewel of Seven Stars, The Lady of the Shroud*, and *The Lair of the White Worm* within the broad context of science fiction. It also makes sense to divide these five works into two separate categories: (1) works in which the science is entirely plausible though Stoker's use of science often goes beyond usual practice to produce an apocalyptic or utopian conclusion—*The Snake's Pass* and *The Lady of the Shroud*; and (2) works in which systematic scientific knowledge is used to counterpose the mysterious effects of supernatural forces—*Dracula, The Jewel of Seven Stars*, and *The Lair of the White Worm*. However, because the question of whether science fiction can include the supernatural remains a major issue among science fiction theorists, this question will be answered last.

The *Snake's Pass* and *The Lady of the Shroud* are far less controversial. Indeed, both of them fall logically under the heading of Utopian Fiction, one of the categories listed by Michael Burgess in *Reference Guide to Science Fiction, Fantasy, and Horror* [8] and recognized ordinarily as a legitimate subcategory within the genre of science fiction. At the time Stoker was writing, numerous other writers were also producing utopian fiction, much of it also based on scientific and technological developments. Although many of these utopias have been lost to all but scholars, Edward Bellamy's *Looking Backward* (1888) remains in print; [9] and, like *Lady*, it includes a vision of the future that is possible primarily because of the judicious use of new machinery. As a result, it is a technological utopia rather than a scientific utopia. Indeed, although I promised in the Introduction to attempt to keep science and technological advancements separate whenever possible, I find that Stoker is rarely interested in pure science. Instead, he examines the manner in which technological developments in medicine, transportation, civil engineering, geology, and electronics can be used to make the world better.

Before Rupert St. Leger, the protagonist in *The Lady of the Shroud*, can go about creating a technological Utopia, however, it is necessary for him to effect a military victory. Here too, Stoker's military equipment falls within the boundaries of what is entirely plausible even though much of it was untested at the time that Stoker wrote. A similar enthusiasm for armaments is also evident in a number of other fictional works that feature recent scientific developments. Clareson, for example, describes *The Great War Syndicate* (1889) by Frank Stockton in "The Emergence of Science Fiction," and reveals that Stockton has a similar enthusiasm for the technological aspects of warfare. As in *Lady*, the result here is finally peace as well after a group of American businessmen develop "an armored vessel and an electrically powered 'instantaneous motor,' seemingly a cross between a jet-propelled shell and an atomic bomb" (55). After declaring victory, an Anglo-American alliance declares war to be illegal. Clareson examines the military aspects of science fiction in ways that may be useful to our understanding of *Lady*. Indeed he looks at a number of works written in the years before *Lady*. He explains that one idea seemed to dominate early science fiction, the idea of future war. One early example, published anonymously in the May 1871 edition of *Blackwood's* is *The Battle of Dorking: Reminiscences of a Volunteer*. Written during a period of growing nationalism and imperialism, *The Battle of Dorking*, as Clareson notes, caught the British "in a mood of foreboding and uncertainty regarding the future of the empire" (14).

There is certainly no evidence that Stoker ever read *The Battle of Dorking* even though *Blackwood's* was a respected periodical at the time that Stoker was submitting short stories to various periodicals and attempting to establish his reputation as a writer. Moreover, as Clareson demonstrates, *The Battle of*

*Dorking* was only one example of works that depicted future wars. Clareson also observes that books by British writers, as one might expect, often featured naval wars. A few of the better known include *The Great Naval War of 1887* (1887) and *Trafalgar Refought* (1905) by William Laird Clowes and A.H. Burgoyne; *The Captain of the 'Mary Rose'* (1892) by Clowes; *Blake of the 'Rattlesnake'* (1895) by Frederick T. Jane. According to Clareson, these authors were fascinated "with the new 'ironclads,' those 'dreadnaughts' that became the battleships of the line by the turn of the century." However, they "also gave much attention to the tiny 'torpedo boats,' like Jane's *Rattlesnake*, whose speed and mobility made them the despair of the ponderous, seemingly invincible ironclads" (14). [10]

It is difficult to imagine that the well-read Stoker would have been totally unaware of the genre.[11] However, none of these titles shows up in Shepard's account of Stoker's library. On the other hand, Stoker's interest in the sea and in shipping is evident in so much of what he wrote.[12] *The Watter's Mou'*, *The Man*, *Lady Athylene*, and *Personal Reminiscences* all have scenes on board ship; and *Lady* and *The Mystery of the Sea* incorporate actual sea battles. Although *Lady* demonstrates the successful uses of technological advances in warfare, one would do well to remember that H.G. Wells wrote *War of the Worlds* in 1898. Unlike *Lady* and many of the works that Clareson discusses, however, Wells demonstrates that British technological expertise is ineffectual against the Martian invaders. Wells, however, provides an additional cautionary note to all those believers in science and technology at the novel's conclusion. Not only are the British unsuccessful in using technology to repel the invaders, but the Martians ultimately succumb to bacterial infection rather than to potent and directed science and technology.

Wells seems to be the odd man out, however, in this group of writers of military science fiction; and Stoker's enthusiasm for technological gadgetry seems to be in line with most of the other books that feature science. In addition to the books that include sea battles, many of the books that explore future wars and future Utopias also include aviation as had Verne's *Five Weeks in a Balloon* (1863), *From the Earth to the Moon* (1865), and *Around the World in Eighty Days* (1873). Among the books that Clareson discusses is a book of short stories by Rudyard Kipling, *With the Night Mail: A Story of 2000 A.D.* (1909), which he describes as follows and which seems remarkably similar to the end of *Lady*. In the title story, published in 1905, dirigible balloons, such as Postal Packet 162 from London to Quebec, fly all over the world. In fact, the story demonstrates that aviation has changed the world so completely that it is "governed by the Aerial Board of Control (A.B.C.), whose laws permit anything—including war—that does not obstruct 'traffic and all it implies'" (46). Published the same year as *The Lady of the Shroud* and before World War I demonstrated the practical use of aircraft, Kipling's book of stories also features the way that flight can be used to economic and political advantage.

*Lady* and "Night Mail" ultimately explore the effective peacetime use of technology, both of them as well as *The Great War Syndicate* concluding with the idea of a world federation brought about by technology. Thus, they implicitly celebrate the ability of technology to bring about progress. Definitely Utopian, occasionally apocalyptic, all three works also use science that was entirely plausible to bring about this progress; all three also establish "orderly ground rules" for their use of science and technology as Wells argued was necessary; and all three seem to suggest that science and technology are sufficiently advanced to solve some of the problems that they and their contemporaries faced.

Although Utopian in its own way, *The Snake's Pass* is written on a more modest scale with technological solutions applied to Ireland that had already been tried successfully elsewhere. The fairyland that Arthur Severn describes as the home to which he will bring his future bride is a frankly technological product, the result of engineer Dick Sutherland's ability to reclaim the land from the shifting bog. Although Stoker's native Ireland had been relatively slow to take advantage of recent technology, such efforts had already made a tremendous impact on Britain, as T.S. Ashton describes in his classic study of industrialism:

There was an increase in the acreage of land under cultivation. Much attention was given to the draining of fens and marshes, to the breaking up and turning to arable of the old, rough, common pastures ( . . . usually spoken of as the waste), and to the hedging of land, so as to make it more productive of both crops and livestock. . . . It is sufficient there to make the point that land previously outside the system of economic activities was being drawn in, and put to better use.[13]

Ashton's study goes on to describe the better standard of living available to most people in Britain but also refers to various famines in Ireland (1782–1784, 1821–1823, 1840s) that would have been well within the memory of Stoker's ancestors. Even though he himself was born after the most serious of the famines, Stoker was certainly aware of these famines, referring to them in his article on industrialism in Ireland: [14] "For, after all, Ireland is poor, and its population . . . has dwindled in the last sixty years to a little over one-half of its former number" (573). Furthermore, Stoker traveled the Irish countryside as a civil servant from 1868 to 1878, and *The Snake's Pass*, which is the most Irish of his works,  reveals his profound sympathy for the Irish peasantry, his awareness of their debilitating poverty, and his belief that only greater scientific and technological sophistication would enable them to improve their lots in life. Indeed, *The Snake's Pass* suggests that it is the absence of capital more than anything else that handicapped the Irish. Commenting on *The Snake's Pass*, Hughes observes that English capital and English technological expertise will make the difference:

'Limestone' becomes a metonym for the changes that will take place consequent to Arthur's possession of the land and draining of the bog. In part this implies the replacement of irregular Irish methods, subsistence farming almost, by the regularities of English capitalism, and a division of the productive from the commercial. Arthur notes that Dick 'had devised a plan for building houses for them—good solid stone houses, with proper offices and farmyards.' . . . The rhetoric suggests that previous methods have been 'improper', irregular, as opposed to 'proper.' (63)

By 1907, Stoker indicates that the Irish had begun to catch up, his article on Irish technology noting that "wonderful things are being done to start the island upon a new career of industrial progress" (571).

Because Chapter 4 covers the technological progress that Stoker conveys in *The Snake's Pass* and *The Lady of the Shroud* in greater detail, it is sufficient to conclude the discussion here by reiterating that both novels meet Gunn's stipulation that science fiction must include plausible science that the writers pick up "from scientists, particularly from those who are willing to speculate." Gunn adds moreover in an introduction to *Chemistry and Science Fiction* that research into science is essential for science fiction writers:[15]

And every author of serious SF does the research necessary to provide a plausible scientific background for his narrative, and in so doing passes along to readers information about science, a belief in the importance of science, and the possibilities for drama and excitement in a scientific environment. (xx)

As is evident from previous chapters, Stoker clearly did the research necessary to provide a plausible scientific background for most of his novels. He also demonstrates his belief that science (or more accurately, technology) can help people to solve the problems that he witnessed in his own day. These problems include political oppression, poverty, disease, and ignorance.

Because Stoker is so identified with the Gothic, however, the real issue for many readers is whether Stoker's overtly Gothic novels can also be classified as science fiction. It is true that in *Dracula*, *The Jewel of Seven Stars*, and *The Lair of the White Worm* Stoker weaves plausible science into otherwise Gothic plots. *Dracula*, for example, refers to mesmerism, criminology, and the science of blood transfusions among other scientific subjects; *Jewel* weaves together knowledge of Egyptian culture as well as information on archeology, astronomy, and physics; and *Lair* includes references to the evolution of dinosaurs as well as knowledge of mineralogy. Moreover, all three works demonstrate the advantages of science and technology, betraying no nostalgia for the primitive worlds depicted in them.

It is also true that these novels include a number of implausible elements that cannot be explained by the science of Stoker's own day or even by the science of our own. Indeed, if one of the goals of science is to understand the natural world (a point made by historian of science Thomas S. Kuhn[16]), then much that is contained in these three works is entirely supernatural. As this study has already observed, a number of critics of science fiction argue that science fiction and the supernatural are not compatible. However, in "A Science Fiction Primer for the Uninitiated," Jack H. Stocker [17] clearly and precisely addresses the issue of Gothic elements in science fiction and explains that the two can exist together:

The apparent distinction between "supernatural" and "scientific" has become a challenge for many writers. When one "explains" an apparently "supernatural" phenomenon in "scientific" terms, does the story then become science fiction? Various authors have had their protagonist challenge (and defeat) "supernatural" forces by their intellectual skills and scientific knowledge. (9)

The characters in *Dracula* and *The Lair of the White Worm* certainly use their intellectual skills and scientific knowledge to challenge supernatural forces and, according to many commentators, ultimately defeat those forces because of them. It is true, however, that their ultimate victory over Dracula and over the White Worm is due as much to luck as to science. It is also true that nature intrudes on the great experiment in *The Jewel of Seven Stars* and may ultimately determine the conclusion to that endeavor. On the other hand, both Adam Salton and *Dracula*'s Crew of Light approach their battle in a thoroughly systematic manner and use the best scientific and technological knowledge of their day. Thus these novels would seem to meet Stoker's definition of science fiction as "fiction based on logical projections from currently established scientific principles" (5).

Continuing to explore various genre distinctions, Stoker asks an obvious question of science fiction aficionados, especially of those who tend to insist on the scientific rigor of science fiction:

Is there a clear borderline between science fiction and fantasy? . . . Arthur C. Clarke . . . is credited with the saying that "sufficiently advanced technology is indistinguishable from magic." Often the distinction is merely a matter of whether the phenomena are "explained" regardless of the degree of double-talk involved. (5)

This study should be proof that no such clear borderlines exist between science fiction, fantasy, adventure, romance, and the Gothic at least during the period when those genres were in their infancy. A man thoroughly familiar with all kinds of stage magic, Stoker was more aware than most of his generation of the similarities in technology and magic.[18] Stoker, of course, seems to take a slightly different approach than Clarke, for his novels reveal that the science of his day was not quite magical. Thus, it is luck that Adam Salton's explosives manage to destroy the White Worm in its lair; and it is a combination of factors (including Van Helsing's knowledge of folklore and myth, Mina Harker's problem-solving ability, and the Crew of Light's access to modern forms of communication and transportation) that enables them to track Dracula to his lair and destroy him before he reaches safety. One wonders what might have happened to Lucy Westenra had Van Helsing's knowledge of blood transfusion been slightly better. There are lots of "what ifs" involved in these novels, and they all combine to make Stoker's exploration of science more interesting, if ultimately more problematic.

Clareson's essay does touch on several issues that Stoker's novels address, including the borderline between science fiction and fantasy. He notes, for example, that science fiction writers "make use of the discoveries, theories, and speculations in the fields of science that appeal to the imagination at the time the story is written" and adds that readers should not discard anything that "is thought to be scientific at the time the story is written" or treat it as "mere fantasy" (4–5). Even today, people want to believe in the existence of dinosaurs (such as the Loch Ness Monster), and every discovery of a supposedly extinct species makes that belief more probable. No one really expects those creatures to transform into beautiful women, however. And the possibility of extending life expectancy far beyond the usual three score years and ten is now much closer to reality than anything that Stoker's audience might have imagined. That

Dracula and his fellow vampires had managed to extend their lives for centuries by drinking the blood of people on whom they preyed is certainly more exploitative than cloning individuals for body parts; it just might not be qualitatively different from the clone's perspective.

Clareson's essay is a useful reminder of what is important about science fiction as a genre, a reminder that eventually takes us back to consider the relationship in Stoker's fiction of science fiction elements and the Gothic. For example, Clareson is quick to remind us that, unconcerned with either science or technology per se, science fiction has instead focused on the impact those developments have had on individuals and on the larger society. Recent developments in criticism, which have attempted to "distinguish sharply and completely between science fiction and fantasy instead of seeing them as intermingling in a complex literary tradition borrowing from and equal in importance to the tradition of social realism and literary naturalism" (4) continue to perplex readers and ignore the strong element of social awareness at the center of both genres. In fact, Clareson suggests that the best examples of works that reveal their authors' social awareness come from fiction that deals "with horror—from the gothic novel, at least, to the contemporary best-seller; from Mary Shelley and Edgar Allan Poe to the film *Aliens*" (4). In other words, literature of all kinds is really about the world of the authors who create it. Stoker, despite his scrupulous research into science, is far less concerned with science per se than he is with its impact on the lives of individual human beings. Indeed, Stoker's fiction often focuses on the obstacles that young couples have to overcome before they can marry and begin a family; and the two characteristics of his fiction that most annoy readers at the beginning of the twenty-first century are his sentimentality about these romantic relationships and his frequent racism. These beliefs in the superiority of one sex and one race were validated by the best science of his day. Furthermore, his belief that technology could be used to transform the landscape of his own day had not yet been called into question by the horrors of World War I, the first great war to use technology in a systematic way to destroy a generation of young men, or by the awareness of the present day that such technology may have an enormous impact on the environment. Thinking of the benefits of science and technology that Stoker weaves into most of what he wrote, one would do well to remember that Stoker lived during a period when engineers and scientists were working to improve the lives of ordinary human beings and during a period when the standard of living for almost all residents of the United Kingdom improved dramatically and quickly. In fact, Stoker died only five days after the sinking of the *Titanic*. That supposedly unsinkable ship had been built at the very shipyards whose praises Stoker sang in "The World's Greatest Ship-Building Yard." Belford concludes her biography of Stoker by noting that the weakened Stoker was nonetheless aware of the tragedy and even participated in the discussions of what had caused it. There was no time for him to write about what caused the tragedy, and scholars still debate whether the disaster was primarily due to management errors or technological failure. Stoker, who believed in both technology and in masculine heroism, would undoubtedly have been unwilling to believe in either explanation.

Surrounded by mysteries that the science of his day could not begin to address yet hopeful that science and technology would ultimately advance to the point that they would improve the lives of individual human beings, Bram Stoker wove together plausible science with both Gothic horror and an interest in the workings of the human heart. That almost everything he wrote expresses the belief that science will eventually reach the point that people can use it and its practical applications qualifies him as a writer of science fiction. That his works also reveal the mysteries that science has yet to explain reveals the Gothic underpinnings of that science fiction. Stoker continued to work in a number of different genres, often combining elements of several of them into one, and that flexibility is one of the major reasons I find his works interesting. Although his characters often place their trust in the science and technology of their own day, Stoker nonetheless presents the world his characters inhabit as infinitely complex and ambiguous. It is a world with which we at the beginning of the twenty-first century continue to grapple. More scientifically astute than Stoker and his contemporaries, we continue to face mysteries that we cannot begin to solve.

## NOTES

1. *Merriam Webster's Encyclopedia of Literature.* Springfield, MA: Merriam-Webster, Inc., 1995.
2. Brian W. Aldiss. *Trillion Year Spree: The History of Science Fiction.* New York: Atheneum, 1986.
3. James Gunn, "Introduction: The Strange Journey," in *Anatomy of Wonder 4: A Critical Guide to Science Fiction,* edited by Neil Barron, pp. xix–xxiv. New Providence, NJ: R.R. Bowker, 1995. The citation occurs on page xix.
4. John Sutherland, *The Stanford Companion to Victorian Fiction.* Stanford, CA: Stanford University Press, 1989, 559–60.
5. Paul Fayter, "Strange New Worlds of Space and Time: Late Victorian Science and Science Fiction," in *Victorian Science in Context,* edited by Bernard Lightman, pp. 256–280. Chicago: University of Chicago Press, 1997.
6. Veronica Hollinger, "The Vampire and the Alien: Gothic Horror and Science Fiction," in *Bram Stoker's Dracula: Sucking through the Century, 1897–1997,* edited by Carol Margaret Davison, pp. 213–30. Toronto: Dundurn Press, 1997.
7. Lynn Hamilton, "Science Fiction," in *Victorian Britain: An Encyclopedia,* pp. 696–97. Scientific plausibility is also stressed in the definition provided in *Merriam Webster's Encyclopedia of Literature* (Springfield, MA: Merriam-Webster, Inc., 1995). In fact, this definition suggests the wide range of words that may fall into the category of science fiction:

Fiction dealing principally with the impact of actual or imagined science upon society or individuals, or more generally, literary fantasy including a scientific factor as an essential orienting component. (1004)

These definitions are remarkably different from that presented by Margaret Drabble in *The Oxford Companion to English Literature,* 5th ed. (Oxford: Oxford University Press, 1985), a definition that emphasizes the implausibility and fanciful nature of science fiction:

Science Fiction is the current name for a class of prose narrative which assumes an imaginary technological or scientific advance, or depends upon an imaginary and spectacular change in the human environment. (876)

8. Michael Burgess in *Reference Guide to Science Fiction, Fantasy, and Horror*. Englewood, CO: Libraries Unlimited, Inc., 1992.

9. A search of the Amazon site reveals the following editions—Bedford, Applewood, Buccaneer, Signet, Dover Thrift, and Penguin.

10. Darko Suvin presents even more examples of future technological warfare in *Victorian Science Fiction in the UK: The Discourses of Knowledge and of Power* (Boston: G.K. Hall & Co., 1983). Several of these works are particularly interesting to our discussion of Stoker bcause they suggest ways that Ireland might gain independence from England. One, *The Battle of the Moy: or, How Ireland Gained Her Independence, 1892–1894*, was published in 1883. Even more interesting is Thomas Greer's *A Modern Daedalus*, which was published in 1885 and which Suvin summarizes as follows:

Hero invents winged flight, English government tries to appropriate it but he escapes to Ireland and trains squad who bomb English armed forces with dynamite. Ireland gains independence, flying will be used for the original peaceful purposes. In story, and in introduction set in 1887, narrator proclaims preference for equal Anglo-Irish union by peaceful means. (27)

A number of other works feature technological warfare, including *The Battle of Worthing: Why the Invaders Never Got to Dorking: A Prophecy*. (1887) by A Captain of the Royal Navy (pseud.).

11. Stephen Arata in *Fictions of Loss in the Victorian Fin de Siècle* (Cambridge University Press, 1996) notes how frequently Stoker's fiction explores the threat of invasion:

A concern with questions of empire and colonization can in fact be found in nearly all of Stoker's tales. In works such as "Under the Sunset" (1882), *The Snake's Pass* (1890), *The Mystery of the Sea* (1902), and *The Man* (1905), narratives of invasion, while not central to the plot, intrude continually upon the main action of the story. Legends of French invasions of Ireland in *The Snake's Pass*, attacks by the Children of Death on the Land Under the Sunset in the fairy tales; accounts of the Spanish Armada, Sir Francis Drake, and, in a more contemporary vein, the Spanish-American War of 1898 in *The Mystery of the Sea*; allusions to the Norman invasion of Saxon England in *The Man*—in each work, seemingly unrelated narratives of imperial expansion and disruption themselves disrupt the primary story, as if Stoker were grappling with issues he could not wholly articulate through his main plot. (213)

12. Indeed Clive Leatherdale looks at the research Stoker did on the sea in *The Origins of Dracula* (Westcliff-on-Sea, Essex: Desert Island Books, 1987).

Stoker's enthusiasm for naval folklore is reflected in his source notes. During his visits to Whitby he recorded conversations with fishermen and coastguards and took note of several shipwrecks, including that of the Russian schooner *Dimetry* in 1885. He records the Beaufort windscale and other meteorological information taken from Robert Scott's *Fishery Barometer Manual*. (160)

13. T.S. Ashton, *The Industrial Revolution, 1760-1830*. New York: Oxford University Press, 1968, 5–6; introduction to the 1997 edition by Pat Hudson. Hughes also looks at the allegorical significance of the bog in *The Snake's Pass* in *Beyond Dracula: Bram Stoker's Fiction and Its Cultural Context* (New York: St. Martin's, 2000):

The bog in general is, in English prejudice, an overt signifier of Irish topography, and the source of derogatory racial stereotypes—the bog dweller, the 'bog trotter'. In *The Snake's Pass* it is an especially rich symbol, one which encodes a reading of Irish problems and British solutions. (60)

Even though Stoker is less prejudiced than the typical Englishman of his day, it is true that the bog is identified with the lack of technological advances in Ireland.

14. "The Great White Fair in Dublin." *The World's Work* (Special Irish edition), May 1907, 570–76.

15. James Gunn, "Introduction," in *Chemistry and Science Fiction*, Edited by Jack H. Stocker, pp. xix–xxii. Washington, DC: American Chemical Society, 1998.

16. Kuhn notes, "The scientist must . . . be concerned to solve problems about the behavior of nature" (168). He also observes that science continues to build on previous beliefs and theories and that the developmental stage of most sciences is "characterized by . . . competition between . . . distinct views of nature, each partially derived from, and all roughly compatible with, the dictates of scientific observation and method" (4).

17. Jack H. Stocker, "A Science Fiction Primer for the Uninitiated," in *Chemistry and Science Fiction*, edited by Jack H. Stocker, pp. 3–19. Washington, DC: American Chemical Society, 1998.

18. For a discussion of Stoker's familiarity with stage magic, see Stephanie Moss, "Bram Stoker and the London Stage," *Journal of the Fantastic in the Arts* 10 (1999), 124–32.

# Appendix

## CHRONOLOGY OF STOKER'S BOOKS

*The Duties of Clerks of Petty Sessions in Ireland,* 1879.
*Under the Sunset,* 1882.
*A Glimpse of America,* 1886.
*The Snake's Pass,* 1890.
*The Watter's Mou',* 1894.
*The Shoulder of Shasta,* 1895.
*Dracula,* 1897.
*Miss Betty,* 1898.
*The Mystery of the Sea,* 1902.
*The Jewel of Seven Stars,* 1903.
*The Man,* 1905.
*Personal Reminiscences of Henry Irving,* 1906.
*Lady Athlyne,* 1908.
*Snowbound: The Record of a Theatrical Touring Party,* 1908.
*The Lady of the Shroud,* 1909.
*Famous Impostors,* 1910.
*The Lair of the White Worm,* 1911.

## SUMMARIES OF STOKER'S MAJOR WORKS

Because so much of what Stoker wrote is not readily available outside research libraries, the following summaries may prove useful to people who want to get a better idea of everything that he wrote. Readers interested in a particular work can also track down some of them either through interlibrary loan or through modern reprints. Even though some reprints abbreviate Stoker's originals, these modern editions can nonetheless serve as useful introductions to Stoker's works.

### *Under the Sunset,* 1882

This collection of short stories, which was dedicated to his two-year-old son Noel, includes the following short stories: "Under the Sunset," "The Rose Prince," "The Invisible Giant," "The Shadow Builder," "How 7 Went Mad," "Lies and Lilies," "The Castle of the King," and "The Wondrous Child." According to family stories, "The Invisible Giant" is probably modeled on one of Charlotte Stoker's experiences as a girl during the cholera outbreak in Sligo in 1832. "How 7 Went Mad" weaves in some of Stoker's mathematical background.

All the stories take place in a beautiful country under the sunset that people see only in dreams. Although Stoker and his contemporaries regarded the stories as appropriate for children, Gothic undertones pervade many of the stories. For example, in "The Invisible Giant," the plague that visits the country under the sunset appears as a giant that is visible to only a few of the characters.

### *A Glimpse of America,* 1886

This slender volume of factual information is based on Stoker's early visits to the United States as he set up the tours for the Lyceum Theatre and also toured with the company. Originally delivered as a lecture at the London Institution on December 28, 1885, it was later printed. Although quirky and sometimes eccentric, it provides insights into what Stoker found important about Americans and American culture as well as material about life in the United States during the last quarter of the nineteenth century. Because *A Glimpse of America* is slated to be released by the Desert Island Dracula Library, it will eventually be available to both English and American audiences.

### *The Snake's Pass,* 1890

A romantic adventure story, *The Snake's Pass* is narrated by Arthur Severn, a wealthy Englishman who visits Ireland and decides to stay when he falls in love with the Irish people. Hearing of a treasure that French soldiers had buried in the Snake's Pass, an opening in the mountain, Arthur decides to seek it. He also falls in love with Norah Joyce, the daughter of an Irish farmer. He finally rescues her from the book's villain, the usurious money lender Black Murdock, from whom her father has borrowed money.

Arthur renews an acquaintance with an old school friend, Dick Sutherland. An engineer and geologist, Dick has been hired by Murdock to survey the bog on his land in hope of discovering the treasure. However, Murdock drowns because he fails to listen to Sutherland's warning about the shifting bog. Once Murdock is out of the way, Arthur is free to marry Norah, and he and Dick proceed to use their technological knowledge to bring greater prosperity to Ireland. Thus the novel, which begins with romance and adventure, concludes with a vision of a Utopian future.

*The Snake's Pass* is also interesting for its presentation of local color, for Stoker had traveled throughout Ireland as a member of the Irish civil service and had both a good eye for natural scenery and a good ear for dialect. The carter

Andy Sullivan reveals a comic side that is rare in Stoker's works, and Black Murdock is a naturalistic forerunner for Stoker's more Gothic villains.

### The Watter's Mou', 1894

Another story of love and heroism, *The Watter's Mou'* also combines local color, evocative descriptions of the landscape, romance, and tragedy. The realistic novella tells of the coast guard, William Barrow, and his lover Maggie MacWhirter, the daughter of a fisherman, and what happens when her father and brothers become involved in smuggling to protect their boat from being seized by a money lender.

When Maggie sails out to warn her family that Willy will arrest them if they are discovered with contraband goods, she is drowned in a sudden storm. Willy then drowns attempting to rescue her body. In addition to the sentimental love story, *The Watter's Mou'* also includes a tribute to Cruden Bay, the Scottish seaport town where Stoker and his family often went on vacations and where he wrote many of his books and short stories.

### The Shoulder of Shasta, 1895

Stoker's only novel set in the United States, *The Shoulder of Shasta* ends happily and is also interesting for its American setting and American characters. Its protagonist, Esse Elstree, is a young English woman whose physician has prescribed mountain air and other natural tonics to cure her anemic condition. Her mother has purchased a cabin in the California mountains and has taken her daughter and an entire entourage of retainers and servants there.

In the mountains, Esse regains her health and saves the life of their guide, a mountain man named Grizzly Dick when he is attacked by a grizzly bear. Nursing him back to health, Esse believes she has fallen in love with him, so she invites him to visit them in San Francisco.

By the time Dick visits Esse in San Francisco, she has already fallen in love with a more suitable young man of her own class. Moreover, she realizes that Dick's behavior, which had seemed so romantic in the mountains, is less acceptable in sophisticated San Francisco. Momentarily embarrassed by Dick's unpolished behavior, she ultimately accepts him as a primitive, and the story concludes with renewed friendship.

Although the conflict in cultures is real in this novel, all the conflicts are resolved amicably. It is thus a very different novel from *Dracula*, Stoker's next fictional work. Unavailable for almost a century in the United States, an annotated edition was recently published by The Desert Island Dracula Library.

### Dracula, 1897

In *Dracula*, a work that defines fin de siècle Gothic more effectively than any other work, the conflict of cultures is not as easily resolved as it was in *The Shoulder of Shasta*. Beginning with the visit of young solicitor Jonathan Harker to Transylvania, *Dracula* constantly reminds readers of the contrast between

England and Eastern Europe and of the horror that results when these cultures clash.

Dracula, the villain of the piece, is presented as a bloodthirsty warlord intent on leaving Transylvania for London where there will be more people for him to prey on. Once there, he chooses Lucy Westenra as his first victim. Unfortunately for him, Lucy is loved by three wealthy young men, and one of them, Dr. Seward, is the pupil of Dr. Van Helsing, an expert in both folklore and medicine. Van Helsing informs the rest of the group about vampiric behavior and about this particular historical figure. He also uses an entire arsenal of weaponry from both folklore and modern medicine to attempt to save Lucy, though he is ultimately unsuccessful in that attempt. Although it is difficult for these modern characters to believe in the existence of a supernatural bloodsucker, they eventually join forces and, after Lucy's death, collaborate with Harker and his wife Mina to track Dracula to his castle, where they ultimately destroy him.

A work that combines elements of the adventure story, the detective novel, and the erotic thriller with the Gothic, *Dracula* also provides a number of insights into the popular culture of Stoker's day and reveals a fascination with its technological gadgetry.

### Miss Betty, 1898

Stoker's only attempt at writing historical romance, *Miss Betty* is set in the first years of the eighteenth century and relates the love of Rafe Otwell, a poor gentleman, for Betty Pole, as well as the obstacles they must face and overcome before they can marry.

Although the two fall in love shortly after Rafe saves Betty from drowning, Rafe is imprisoned for debt. Instead of marrying another wealthy heiress or accepting an offer of money from Betty, Rafe turns highwayman.

Suspecting that he had gotten money on the highway, Betty sets herself up as a victim and confronts him. Ashamed of himself and also aware that a less scrupulous man might have killed the woman he loves, Rafe leaves. In the published version, he proves his bravery in battle, returns to England five years later, and marries Betty.

In an unpublished manuscript version, however, Rafe dies before returning to England, and Betty is an old woman before she learns of his heroic behavior from a man whose life he had saved.

### The Mystery of the Sea, 1902

Currently available in an inexpensive paperback edition published by Sutton, *The Mystery of the Sea* is another of Stoker's romantic adventures. The two central characters are Archibald Hunter, the narrator, and Marjory Anita Drake, an American heiress and patriot. The two fall in love after Archie saves Marjory and her companion from drowning, use a variety of technological devices in their search for buried treasure, and battle villains who attempt to steal the treasure from them. The novel is interesting both because it takes place during the Spanish-American War and includes Stoker's news on that conflict and because of its technological gadgetry. Both Archie and Marjory are techno-nerds who ride bicycles, enjoy a variety of armaments, and use cipher to communicate when Marjory is kidnapped.

In addition, the novel includes a variety of primitive characters including Don Bernardino, a Spaniard whose ancestor buried the treasure, and an old witch woman Gormala MacNiel, who is gifted with Second Sight (a preternatural ability that Stoker explores again in *The Lady of the Shroud*).

### The Jewel of Seven Stars, 1903

This novel combines Gothic horror with romance and detection. It is narrated by the lawyer Malcolm Ross, who receives a midnight summons to the home of a young woman he had just met, Margaret Trelawney, when her father, an amateur Egyptologist, is attacked by something that puts him into a trance.

Trelawney ultimately recovers, though not before Malcolm and a number of other characters experience the same power that had affected Trelawney. In addition, as Ross realizes that he is falling in love with Margaret, he is also troubled by the strange connection between Margaret and the mummy of the Egyptian queen Tera that Trelawney has brought back to England and that he plans to resurrect.

The novel allows Stoker to explore differences between the ancient past and the scientific present. What is probably most interesting about the novel is the fact that subsequent editions drastically changed the catastrophic conclusion to the first edition. In the first edition, the Great Experiment to resurrect Tera ends with the deaths of all the modern characters except for Ross. In subsequent editions, the experiment fails, and Ross and Margaret marry. Several recent editions of the novel, including a paperback edition by Oxford University Press and an annotated edition by The Desert Island Dracula Library, allow readers to compare the two different versions of the novel.

### The Man, 1905

This romantic adventure tale, which was also published in 1908 in the United States as *The Gates of Life*, is currently not available except in research libraries.

The story of an heiress with the unlikely name of Stephen Norman, the novel explores what happens when a young woman tries to be her father's son. Attempting to control her life, Stephen proposes marriage to a totally unsuitable young man, Leonard Everard, and rejects a loyal suitor, Harold An Wolf.

Rejected by the woman he loves, Harold leaves England for the gold fields of Alaska, and the novel goes to great lengths to illustrate his heroic behavior and demonstrate that he is "the man" of the novel's title. He rescues a child from drowning, acquires a fortune in the gold fields, builds a city in Alaska, and prevents the ship on which he is returning to England from being destroyed on the rocky coast. During his absence, Stephen recognizes his worth and inherits both a fortune and a title from a distant relative.

When the ship on which Harold is sailing is wrecked on the shore near Stephen's new home, she is initially unaware that the heroic individual who risks his life to save the ship is her childhood friend. She does offer him a place to rest and recuperate from his ordeal, and the two are reunited. The novel concludes happily with Harold and Stephen declaring their love for one another.

### Personal Reminiscences of Henry Irving, 1906

The year after Irving's death, Stoker published a two-volume biography of his employer that covered the thirty-year period from the day he met Irving to the day the actor died. It also provides information about theatrical practices as well as interesting gossip about various public figures.

Stoker's obituary in the *Times* [1] commented that *Personal Reminiscences* would be Stoker's chief literary memorial, a conclusion not shared by most readers a century later. On the other hand, *Personal Reminiscences* provides numerous insights into Stoker's own life and suggests that many of the adventures that he relates in his novels stemmed from firsthand experience.

### Lady Athlyne, 1908

Another romantic adventure novel, *Lady Athylene* also features American characters as well as several scenes that take place in the United States. In fact, the novel opens with the Ogilvie family, which includes a Kentucky colonel, his wife and her sister Judy, and daughter Joy, getting ready to take a European grand tour.

The story is complicated, however, because Aunt Judy and Joy refer to Joy as Lady Athylene because they have heard of this English nobleman from a former nurse. Hearing that someone is using his name, Athlyne travels to New York under the name of Richard Hardy. In New York, when he rescues Joy when her horse runs away with her, the two plan to meet in England when the Ogilvies arrive.

In England the two renew their acquaintance. During an unchaperoned automobile trip to Scotland, Athlyne is arrested for speeding. To enable Joy to return home without damaging her reputation, he lets her drive his car. Unfortunately, because she gets lost, the two of them wind up staying at the same inn, a situation they discover only moments before Colonel Ogilvie arrives to accuse Hardy of destroying Joy's honor.

When Colonel Ogilvie threatens to challenge Athlyne to a duel, a wise Scotch magistrate reveals that Athlyne and Joy are married according to Scotch law. As a result, the novel concludes with the promise of marriage.

This novel, which is almost impossible to find, is especially interesting because Stoker is one of the first writers to use the automobile as a plot device.

### Snowbound: The Record of a Theatrical Touring Party, 1908

This collection of short stories includes a frame tale about a theatrical touring company whose train is snowbound between Aberdeen and Perth. The fourteen stories in the collection are told by members of the company and reveal the range of his literary abilities. The collection is also useful for the insights it provides into a theatrical touring company.

Because this collection was recently reissued by The Desert Island Dracula Library, it is now available to English and American readers.

### The Lady of the Shroud, 1909

Because many editions of this novel are abridged, readers may miss many of the political aspects of this novel, which takes place in a mythical Balkan country called the Land of the Blue Mountains.

No matter which edition a reader locates, however, he or she will encounter a very unusual work that seems to begin as a Gothic novel but concludes with a technological Utopia. Moreover, the novel is interesting because, like *Dracula*, it experiments with narration. The story is told through a variety of perspectives which includes an excerpt from *The Journal of Occultism*, letters and diaries written by the principle characters, letters and diaries of supporting characters, news clippings, and other sources of pertinent information.

The novel begins with a will that sends the protagonist Rupert St. Leger to the Land of the Blue Mountains, where he encounters a supposed vampire and, against his better judgment, falls totally in love with her. Fortunately for him, the suspected vampire is really the Princess Teuta, who has been merely pretending to be a vampire to avoid being kidnapped by the Turks.

Written shortly after the Wright brothers' first successful flight, the novel includes an air battle in which Rupert rescues Teuta's father from the Turks. Having proved his bravery, he is permitted to marry Teuta and is crowned king. Moreover, being given total control over his new country, he trains the residents in the use of technology and turns the rather primitive Land of the Blue Mountains into a modern technological Utopia.

### Famous Impostors, 1910

This nonfiction book compiles the stories of various impostors, including impersonators, pretenders, swindlers, and humbugs. Among the ones that were well known to Stoker's contemporaries were Perkin Warbeck, Cagliostro, Hannah Snell, Arthur Orton, and the Chevalier D'Eon. However, one of the most interesting is the Bisley Boy, a child supposedly substituted for Henry VIII's daughter Elizabeth by her frightened governess when the young princess died unexpectedly. According to *Famous Impostors*, this boy later grew up to be Queen Elizabeth I.

### Lair of the White Worm, 1911

Stoker's final novel, *The Lair of the White Worm* combines Gothic materials with adventure and romance. The villain here is perhaps Stoker's most inscrutable, a dinosaur that can transform itself at will into the beautiful Lady Arabella March. Other human villains include Edgar Caswell and his African servant Oolanga. They pale in comparison with the white worm, who, even in her human form, is almost entirely diabolical. In fact, Stoker has her tear a mongoose in two with her bare hands and drag Oolanga to his death in her lair.

Like so many of Stoker's novels, *Lair* illustrates the conflict in cultures by having representatives of pre-Roman Britain encounter representatives of the modern world. Adam Salton, the hero, uses modern explosives to destroy the primeval monster and wins the hand of Mimi Watford as well as wealth in the form of valuable clay deposits. Thus the novel is interesting for its presentation of archeology and natural history as well as for its depiction of a whole range of Gothic characters.

**NOTE**

1. "Obituary: Mr. Bram Stoker," *Times*, April 22, 1912, 15d.

# Works Cited

Aldiss, Brian W. *Trillion Year Spree: The History of Science Fiction.* New York: Atheneum, 1986.

Arata, Stephen D. *Fictions of Loss in the Victorian Fin de Siècle.* Cambridge University Press, 1996.

———. "The Occidental Tourist: *Dracula* and the Anxiety of Reverse Colonization." *Victorian Studies* 33 (Summer 1990): 621–45.

Ashton, T.S. *The Industrial Revolution, 1760–1830.* New York: Oxford University Press, 1968.

Belford, Barbara. *Bram Stoker: A Biography of the Author of Dracula.* New York: Alfred A. Knopf, 1996.

Bierman, Joseph S. "*Dracula*: Prolonged Childhood Illness and the Oral Triad," *American Imago* 29 (1972), 186–98.

Boone, Troy. "'He Is English and Therefore Adventurous': Politics, Decadence, and *Dracula*." *Studies in the Novel* 25 (Spring 1993): 76–91.

Botting, Fred. *Gothic.* New York: Routledge, 1996.

Brantlinger, Patrick. *Rule of Darkness: British Literature and Imperialism, 1830–1914.* Ithaca: Cornell University Press, 1988.

Bristow, Joseph. *Empire Boys: Adventures in a Man's World.* London: Harper Collins Academic, 1991.

Burgess, Michael. *Reference Guide to Science Fiction, Fantasy, and Horror.* Englewood, CO: Libraries Unlimited, Inc., 1992.

Chapman, William. "Toward an Institutional History of Archaeology: British Archaeologists and Allied Interests in the 1860s." In *Tracing Archaeology's Past: The Historiography of Archaeology*, pp. 151–62. Ed. Andrew L. Christenson. Carbondale: Southern Illinois University Press, 1989.

Chippindale, Christopher. "'Social Archaeology' in the Nineteenth Century: Is It Right to Look for Modern Ideas in Old Places?" In *Tracing Archaeology's Past: The Historiography of Archaeology*, pp. 21–33. Ed. Andrew L. Christenson. Carbondale: Southern Illinois University Press, 1989.

Clareson, Thomas D. "The Emergence of Science Fiction: The Beginnings Through 1915." In *Anatomy of Wonder 4: A Critical Guide to Science Fiction*, pp. 3–61. Ed. Neil Barron. New Providence, NJ: R.R. Bowker, 1995.

Coe, W. E. *The Engineering Industry of the North of Ireland.* Newton Abbot, Devon: David & Charles, 1969.

*A Companion to Victorian Literature and Culture.* Ed. Herbert F. Tucker. Malden, MA: Blackwell Publishers, 1999.

Coundouriotis, Eleni. "*Dracula* and the Idea of Europe." *Connotations* 9 (1999/2000): 143–159.

Craft, Christopher. "Gender and Inversion in *Dracula*." In *Dracula: The Vampire and the Critics*, pp. 167–194. Ed. Margaret L. Carter. Ann Arbor, MI: UMI Research Press, 1988.

*The Critical Response to Bram Stoker.* Ed. Carol A. Senf. Westport, CT: Greenwood, 1993.

Daly, Nick. "Irish Roots: The Romance of History in Bram Stoker's *The Snake's Pass.*" *Literature and History* 4 (1992), 42–70.

*Degeneration: The Dark Side of Progress.* Ed. J. Edward Chamberlin and Sander L. Gilman. New York: Columbia University Press, 1985.

Desmond, Adrian. *Archetypes and Ancestors: Paleontology in Victorian London 1850–1875.* Chicago: University of Chicago Press, 1982.

Edwards, Robert. "The Alien and the Familiar in *The Jewel of Seven Stars* and *Dracula*." In *Bram Stoker: History, Psychoanalysis and the Gothic*, pp. 96–115. Ed. William Hughes and Andrew Smith. London: Macmillan Press Ltd.: 1998.

Fair, Kenneth W. "About Bram." *The Romantist* 4-5 (1980–1981): 39-40.

Farson, Daniel. *The Man Who Wrote Dracula: A Biography of Bram Stoker.* New York: St. Martin's, 1975.

Fayter, Paul. "Strange New Worlds of Space and Time: Late Victorian Science and Science Fiction." In *Victorian Science in Context*, pp. 256–80. Ed. Bernard Lightman. Chicago: University of Chicago Press, 1997.

Fleming, A.P.M. and H.J. Brocklehurst. *A History of Engineering.* London: A. & C. Black, Ltd, 1925.

Fontana, Ernest. "Lombroso's Criminal Man and Stoker's *Dracula*." *Victorian Newsletter* 42 (1972): 20–22.

Fry, David. "Danger Ahead: Historic Railway Disasters." December 12, 1999. May 19, 2000. <http://danger-ahead.railfan.net/search.html>

Frye, Northrop, Sheridan Baker, George Perkins, and Barbara M. Perkins. *The Harper Handbook to Literature*, 2nd ed. New York: Longman, 1997.

Gagnier, Regenia. "Evolution and Information, or Eroticism and Everyday Life, in *Dracula* and Late Victorian Aestheticism." In *Sex and Death in Victorian Literature*, pp. 140–157. Ed. Regina Barreca. Bloomington: Indiana University Press, 1990.

Glenny, Misha. *The Balkans: Nationalism, War and the Great Powers, 1804–1999.* New York: Viking, 2000.

Glover, David. *Vampires, Mummies, and Liberals: Bram Stoker and the Politics of Popular Fiction.* London and Durham: Duke University Press, 1996.

Greenway, John. "Seward's Folly: *Dracula* as a Critique of 'Normal Science.'" *Stanford Literature Review* 3 (1986): 213–30.

Gunn, James. "Introduction." In *Chemistry and Science Fiction*, pp. xix–xxii. Ed. Jack H. Stocker. Washington, DC: American Chemical Society, 1998.

———. "Introduction: The Strange Journey." In *Anatomy of Wonder 4: A Critical Guide to Science Fiction*, pp. xix–xxiv. Ed. Neil Barron. New Providence, NJ: R.R. Bowker, 1995.

Guy, Josephine M. *The Victorian Age: An Anthology of Sources and Documents.* London: Routledge, 1998.

Haining, Peter, and Peter Tremayne. *The UnDead: The Legend of Bram Stoker and Dracula*. London: Constable, 1997.

Hamilton, Lynn. "Science Fiction." In *Victorian Britain: An Encyclopedia.* pp. 696–97. Ed. Sally Mitchell. New York: Garland, 1988.

*The Harper Handbook to Literature.* Ed. Northrop Frye, Sheridan Baker, George Perkins, and Barbara Perkins. New York: Longman, 1997.

Hollinger, Veronica. "The Vampire and the Alien: Gothic Horror and Science Fiction." In *Bram Stoker's Dracula: Sucking Through the Century, 1897-1997*, pp. 213–230. Ed. Carol Margaret Davison. Toronto: Dundurn Press, 1997.

Holman, C. Hugh, and William Harmon. *A Handbook to Literature*, 6th Ed. New York: Macmillan, 1992.

Horner, Avril and Sue Zlosnik. "Comic Gothic." In *A Companion to the Gothic*, pp. 242–54. Ed. David Punter. Malden, MA: Blackwell Publishers Inc., 2000.

Hughes, William. *Beyond Dracula: Bram Stoker's Fiction and Its Cultural Context.* New York: St. Martin's, 2000.

———. "'Militant Instinct': The Perverse Eugenics of Bram Stoker's Fiction." *Bram Stoker Society Journal* (1994): 11–19.

Irlam, Michael J. Mike's Railway History. Manhick Engineering Ltd. May 19, 2000. <http://mikes.railhistory.railfan.net/r051.html>.

Jann, Rosemary. "Saved by Science? The Mixed Messages of Stoker's *Dracula*." *Texas Studies in Literature and Language* 31 (Summer 1989): 273–87.

Kuhn, Thomas S. *The Structure of Scientific Revolutions*, 3rd ed. Chicago: University of Chicago Press, 1996.

Kumar, Krishan. *Utopia and Anti-Utopia in Modern Times*. Oxford: Basil Blackwell, 1987.

Leatherdale, Clive, Ed. *Bram Stoker's Dracula Unearthed*. Westcliff-on-Sea, Essex: Desert Island Books, 1998.

———. *Dracula: The Novel and the Legend*. Wellingborough, Northamptonshire: The Aquarian Press, 1985.

———. *The Origins of Dracula: The Background to Bram Stoker's Gothic Masterpiece*. Westcliff-on-Sea, Essex: Desert Island Books, 1987.

Lombroso, Cesare. "Criminal Anthropology: Its Origin and Application." *The Forum* 20 (1895), 35.

Luce, J.V. *Trinity College Dublin: The First 400 Years*. Dublin: Trinity College Dublin Press, 1992.

Ludlam, Harry. *A Biography of Dracula: The Life Story of Bram Stoker*. London: Foulsham, 1962.

McDowell, R.B., and D.A. Webb. *Trinity College Dublin 1592–1952: An Academic History*. Cambridge: Cambridge University Press, 1982.

*Merriam Webster's Encyclopedia of Literature*. Springfield, MA: Merriam-Webster, Inc., 1995.

Milbank, Alison "'Powers Old and New': Stoker's Alliances with Anglo-Irish Gothic." In *Bram Stoker: History, Psychoanalysis and the Gothic*, pp. 12–28. Ed. William Hughes and Andrew Smith. New York: St. Martin's, 1998.

Miller, Elizabeth. *Dracula: Sense and Nonsense*. Westcliff-on-Sea, Essex: Desert Island Books, 2000.

Moretti, Franco. *Signs Taken for Wonders: Essays in the Sociology of Literary Forms*. London: New Left Books/Verso, 1983.

Moss, Stephanie. "Bram Stoker and the London Stage." *Journal of the Fantastic in the Arts* 10 (1999): 124–32.

———. "Bram Stoker and the Society for Psychical Research." In *The Shade and the Shadow: Papers Presented at "Dracula 97," a Centenary Celebration at*

   *Los Angeles, August 1997*, pp. 82–92. Ed. Elizabeth Miller. Westcliff-on-Sea, Essex: Desert Island Books, 1998.

Nayder, Lillian. "Virgin Territory and the Iron Virgin: Engendering the Empire in Bram Stoker's 'The Squaw'." In *Maternal Instincts: Visions of Motherhood and Sexuality in Britain, 1875–1925*, pp. 75–98. Ed. Claudia Nelson and Ann Sumner Holme. London: MacMillan, 1997.

*Oxford Companion to English Literature*, 5th ed. Ed. Margaret Drabble. Oxford: Oxford University Press, 1985.

Pick, Daniel. *Faces of Degeneration: A European Disorder, c. 1848–c.1918*. Cambridge: Cambridge University Press, 1989.

Rolt, L.T.C. *Victorian Engineering*. London: Penguin, 1970.

Sagan, Carl. *The Demon-Haunted World: Science as a Candle in the Dark*. New York: Random House, 1996.

Sage, Victor. "Exchanging Fantasies: Sex and the Serbian Crisis: The *Lady of the Shroud*." In *Bram Stoker: History, Psychoanalysis and the Gothic*, pp. 116–33. Ed. William Hughes and Andrew Smith. London: Macmillan Press Ltd.: 1998.

Seed, David. "Eruptions of the Primitive into the Present: *The Jewel of Seven Stars* and *The Lair of the White Worm*," In *Bram Stoker: History, Psychoanalysis and the Gothic*, pp. 188–204. Ed. William Hughes and Andrew Smith. London: Macmillan Press Ltd.: 1998.

Senf, Carol A. "*The Lady of the Shroud*: Stoker's Successor to *Dracula*." *Essays in Arts and Sciences* (1990): 82–96.

*Shades of Dracula: Bram Stoker's Uncollected Stories*. Ed. Peter Haining. London: William Kimber, 1982.

Shepard, Leslie. "The Library of Bram Stoker/ A Note on the Death Certificate of Bram Stoker." In *Bram Stoker's Dracula: Sucking through the Century, 1897–1997*, pp. 411–415. Ed. Carol Margaret Davison. Toronto: Dundurn Press, 1997.

Showalter, Elaine. *Daughters of Decadence: Women Writers of the Fin-de-Siècle*. New Brunswick, NJ: Rutgers University Press, 1993.

Sowards, Steven W. *Twenty-Five Lectures on Modern Balkan History*. Mississippi State University. <http://www.lib.msu.edu/sowards/balkan/lect10.htm> August 28, 2000.

State, Ray. Archivist for "Danger Ahead—Historic Railway Disasters" (http://danger-ahead.railfan.net/search.html), a site maintained by David Fry. Stepan, Nancy. "Biological Degeneration: Races and Proper Places." In *Degeneration: The Dark Side of Progress*, pp. 97–120. Ed. J. Edward Chamberlin and Sander L. Gilman. New York: Columbia University Press, 1985.

Stocker, Jack H. "A Science Fiction Primer for the Uninitiated." In *Chemistry and Science Fiction*, pp. 3–19. Ed. Jack H. Stocker. Washington, DC: American Chemical Society, 1998.

Stoker, Bram. "The American 'Tramp' Question and the Old English Vagrancy Laws," *North American Review* 190 (1909): 605–14.

——. *Famous Impostors*, printed in the United States 1911.

——. *A Glimpse of America: A Lecture Given at the London Institution, 29th December, 1885*. London: Sampson Low, Marston & Co., 1886.

——. "The Great White Fair in Dublin." *The World's Work* (Special Irish edition), May 1907, 570–76.

——. *The Jewel of Seven Stars*. Ed. Clive Leatherdale. Westcliff-on-Sea, Essex: Desert Island Books, 1996.

——. *Lady Athlyne*. New York: Paul R. Reynolds, 1908.

————. *The Lady of the Shroud*. 1909. Reprint Dover, NH: Alan Sutton Publishing, Inc., 1994.

————. *The Lair of the White Worm*. London: Rider and Son, 1911.

————.*The Mystery of the Sea*. Gloucestershire: Sutton, 1997.

———— .*Personal Reminiscences of Henry Irving*. New York: Macmillan, 1906.

————.*The Primrose Path*. Ed. Richard Dalby. Westcliff-on-Sea, Essex: Desert Island Books, 1999.

————. *The Shoulder of Shasta*. Westcliff-on-Sea, Essex: Desert Island Books, 2000.

————. *The Snake's Pass*, 1890; Reprint. Dingle, Co., Kerry, Ireland: Brandon, 1990.

————. *Snowbound: The Record of a Theatrical Touring Party*. Westcliff-on-Sea, Essex: Desert Island Books, 2000.

————. "The Squaw." In *Midnight Tales*, Ed. Peter Haining. London: Peter Owen, 1995.

————. *The Watter's Mou'*. In *The Bram Stoker Bedside Companion: 10 Stories by the author of Dracula*. pp. 166–224. Ed. Charles Osborne. New York: Taplinger Publishing Company, 1973.

————. "The World's Greatest Ship-Building Yard," *The World's Work* 9 (special Irish edition, May 1907), 647–50.

Sutherland, John. *The Stanford Companion to Victorian Fiction*. Stanford, CA: Stanford University Press, 1989.

Suvin, Darko. *Victorian Science Fiction in the UK: The Discourses of Knowledge and of Power*. Boston: G.K. Hall & Co., 1983.

Tracy, Robert. "Loving You All Ways:   Vamps, Vampires, Necrophiles and Necrofilles in Nineteenth-Century Fiction." In *Sex and Death in Victorian Literature*, pp. 32-59.  Ed. Regina Barreca.  Bloomington:   Indiana University Press, 1990.

Turner, Frank M. "Practicing Science: An Introduction." In *Victorian Science in Context*, pp.   283–89. Ed. Bernard Lightman. Chicago: University of Chicago Press, 1997.

van Keuren, David K. "Museums and Ideology: Augustus Pitt-Rivers, Anthropological Museums, and Social Change in Later Victorian Britain." In *Energy and Entropy:  Science and Culture in Victorian Britain,  Essays from Victorian Studies*,  pp. 270–88. Ed. Patrick Brantlinger. Bloomington: Indiana University Press, 1989.

Van Riper, A. Bowdoin. *Men among the Mammoths:  Victorian Science and the Discovery of Human Prehistory*.  Chicago:  University of Chicago Press, 1993.

*Victorian Britain: An Encyclopedia*. Ed. Sally Mitchell. New York: Garland, 1988.

Walkowitz, Judith. *City of Dreadful Delight: Narratives of Sexual Danger in Late Victorian London*. Chicago: University of Chicago Press, 1992.

Wicke, Jennifer. "Vampiric Typewriting: *Dracula* and Its Media," *ELH* 59 (1992): 467–93.

Willis, Connie. "Science in Science Fiction: A Writer's Perspective." In *Chemistry and Science Fiction*, pp.  21–32. Ed. Jack H. Stocker. Washington, DC: American Chemical Society, 1998.

Wilt, Judith. "The Imperial Mouth: Imperialism, the Gothic and Science Fiction" *Journal of Popular Culture* 14 (1981): 618–28.

Winthrop-Young, Geoffrey. "Undead Networks: Information Processing and Media Boundary Conflicts in *Dracula*," In *Literature and Science*, pp. 107–129. Ed. Donald Bruce and Anthony Purdy. Atlanta, GA: Rodopi, 1994.

Wolf, Leonard. *A Dream of Dracula*. Boston: Little, Brown, 1972.

Worthham, John David. *The Genesis of British Egyptology 1549–1906*. Norman: University of Oklahoma Press, 1971.

# Index

## About the Author

CAROL A. SENF is Associate Professor of English at Georgia Institute of Technology. Her previous books include *The Critical Response to Bram Stoker* (Greenwood, 1993).